THE S. MARK 7

IMPRINT IN

D0617913

BY THIS ENDOWMENT

THE S. MARK TAPER FOUNDATION SUPPORTS

THE APPRECIATION AND UNDERSTANDING

OF THE RICHNESS AND DIVERSITY OF

JEWISH LIFE AND CULTURE

The publisher gratefully acknowledges the generous contribution to this book provided by the S. Mark Taper Foundation.

The Life of Judaism

The Life of Religion
Mark Juergensmeyer, editor; Richard Carp, photo editor

1. *The Life of Buddhism,* edited by Frank E. Reynolds and Jason A. Carbine
2. *The Life of Judaism,* edited by Harvey E. Goldberg

The Life of Judaism

Edited by
Harvey E. Goldberg

UNIVERSITY OF CALIFORNIA PRESS

Berkeley / Los Angeles / London

Figures 3, 5, 6, and 14 courtesy Novelty Ltd., Israel, tel. 972-9-741-7304.

University of California Press
Berkeley and Los Angeles, California

University of California Press, Ltd.
London, England

© 2001 by the Regents of the University of California

Library of Congress Cataloging-in-Publication Data

The life of Judaism / edited by Harvey E. Goldberg.
    p.   cm. — (The life of religion ; 2)
   Includes bibliographical references and index.
    ISBN 0-520-21267-3 (cloth : alk. paper) — ISBN 0-520-22753-0
(pbk. : alk. paper)
    1. Judaism—20th century.   2. Jewish way of life.   3. Judaism—
Customs and practices.   I. Goldberg, Harvey E.   II. Series.

BM42 .L54   2001
296—dc21   2001027669

Manufactured in the United States of America

10 09 08 07 06 05 04 03 02 01
10 9 8 7 6 5 4 3 2 1

The paper used in this publication meets the minimum requirements
of ANSI/NISO Z39.48-1992(R 1997) (*Permanence of Paper*). ⊗

To Rosalie Braverman
for the hours of sharing her life

Contents

Acknowledgments

The help and experience of many people went into creating this collection. Warm thanks are due to Doug Abrams Arava, Richard Hecht, Jack Kugelmass, Hagar Salamon, and Rebecca Schorsch. I completed my work for this volume during a fellowship at the Center for Advanced Judaic Studies, the University of Pennsylvania. There, Etty Lassman was unstinting in her willingness to assist in its final phases. The book is dedicated to Rosalie Braverman, of Iowa City, for welcoming my family and me into one experience of Jewish life, which we will always cherish.

Introduction

Jewish life has diverse faces. The six-pointed star of David appears in synagogue design, on the flag of the State of Israel, and as a pendant on a necklace. Some aspects of Judaism seem closed to the outside world, such as the practices of ultraorthodox Jews garbed in black. Others may receive extensive exposure; in recent years the president of the United States has participated in lighting Hanukkah candles. Judaism has its own calendar—its New Year is in the fall—and its own life-cycle markers—the circumcision of boys at eight days after birth and the celebration of bat and bar mitzvah for girls and boys at ages twelve and thirteen, respectively. Within those frameworks, contemporary Jews from different parts of the world express their religion in many forms.

Today's diversity must be viewed against the background of major demographic shifts that took place in recent centuries. At around 1700, there were about two million Jews in the world. Half of them were Ashkenazim in Western, Central, and Eastern Europe, and the other half were Sephardim, in Southeastern Europe, North Africa, and the Middle East and, in small numbers, in Northwest Europe and the Americas. By the end of the nineteenth century, the total number of Jews had increased dramatically, to about twelve million. Much of the increase was in the Ashkenazi world, particularly in Eastern Europe. The number of Sephardim was still around one million.

Transformations that shaped today's portrait of the Jewish people were already taking place. Most dramatic was the mass migration of Eastern European Jews to the West—notably to the United States. At the same period, Zionists, seeking to create a new kind of Jewish society, began immigrating to Palestine. Half a century later, Nazi atrocities reduced world Jewry from about sixteen million to ten million. In 1948, three years after the end of World War II, the State of Israel was founded, and its Jewish population grew from about six hundred thousand to about five million.

Israel's emergence as a sovereign state made it a lodestone of immigration in the second half of the twentieth century as well as a stimulant to Jewish migration elsewhere. Within three and a half years of its establishment, Israel took in over three hundred thousand survivors of Nazi Europe and a roughly similar number of Jews from Arab countries, Turkey, and Iran. In the next three decades, the Jewish communities in the Middle East dwindled to very small numbers, with Israel being the main, but not the only, destination of migration. From the late 1960s on, migration from the Soviet Union was selectively allowed, and after 1989 it continued in larger numbers from the states of the former Soviet Union. Now in Israel, there is a rough fifty-fifty demographic division of Sephardim and Ashkenazim. The only other country with similar demographics is France, where North African Jews are in the majority. Today Sephardim constitute less then 20 percent of world Jewry (and intermarriage between Sephardim and Ashkenazim is frequent), but the cultural importance of Sephardic communities outweighs their numerical value.

Along with these demographic changes were far-reaching social, political, and cultural developments. Until just slightly more than two hundred years ago, in Europe and the Middle East, Jews were institutionally separate from the rest of society. They interacted with Christians and Muslims in the work world, but their social and religious lives were distinct from those of the majority. Jews were often distinguishable by the clothes they wore and by their language or dialect and typically were concentrated in certain areas of a city or town. There they were usually free to follow their laws and customs, as long as their practices did not impinge on the sensibilities of the dominant religion. Although important variations existed within and among Jewish communities, all saw their lives as based on the Torah: the Hebrew Bible, the Talmud, and subsequent rabbinic interpretations. These books provided guidance in ritual, communal, and even commercial matters. Communal leaders had the power to enforce social and religious norms and could proclaim a ban against a recalcitrant individual who continually challenged accepted norms. Such a person had nowhere to go, short of converting to Christianity or Islam. This control over the lives of

Jews stemmed from the autonomy granted communal leaders by the ruling power, whether Christian or Muslim. This situation changed radically with emancipation.

Emancipation was the legal and political shift in European countries that allowed Jews, in principle, to be members of civil society. Emancipation took place for the first time in France in 1791, thereafter spreading unevenly to other parts of Europe. Jews could fully become French citizens, for example, while keeping their religion as a matter of personal conscience. When Jews later became members of German society, they sometimes referred to themselves as Germans "of the Mosaic persuasion."

Jews began to integrate themselves into their surroundings. They learned the national languages of their countries and gained the education necessary to enter the growing middle class, which was built on industrializing economies. This integration, however, seemed to demand that they abandon practices associated with segregated Jewish living. In addition, in late-eighteenth-century Europe, ideological changes within Jewish society undermined traditional attachments to a religious way of life. Jews were encouraged to be active participants in the wider non-Jewish culture. They began to make their way in society as individuals rather than as members of a group. Yet these changes did not result in a full disestablishment of organized Jewish life. France, and other countries that emancipated the Jews in the course of the nineteenth century, created various forms of state-supported Jewish communal structures. The power that these organizations had over Jews, however, was restricted to matters of religion and was no longer all encompassing. At the same time, Jews who wished to hold on to religious and communal forms began to do so voluntarily.

This new situation, in which Jews saw themselves as members of different national communities, had a far-reaching impact both on their sense of identity and on their approach to religion. Jews sought ways in which they could maintain religious values, anchored in ancient texts and in practice over the centuries, while at the same time identifying with the societies of which they were now a part. This dilemma gave rise to various directions of religious change. The Reform movement altered the prayer service, declared that many ritual rules were no longer binding, and stressed the universal values of Judaism. Advocates of Reform Judaism also based their beliefs and practices on new intellectual understandings. Viewing Judaism historically, they claimed that it had always evolved and that the current changes were justified by social and ideological circumstances.

Later, in reaction to this trend, some Reform leaders claimed that change was happening too quickly. They wanted to retain Hebrew in the synagogue liturgy, for example, while the more radical reformers felt that Jews should pray in the languages they now spoke. In addition, there were conservative reactions on the part of many ordinary Jews. A small group of reformers in the mid-nineteenth century sought to abolish circumcision, citing both health reasons and the desire to move beyond outdated rituals, but most Jews would not relinquish a practice that since antiquity had been an intimate sign of belonging to the Jewish people. Eventually an approach called Positive Historical Judaism emerged, whose supporters accepted the basic notion that religious change was necessary but believed it should take place more gradually and with continued respect for rabbinic tradition. Both these approaches became important in the United States, in the shape of Reform Judaism early in the mid-nineteenth century and of Conservative Judaism around the turn of the twentieth.

The original growth of these movements should be understood in sociopolitical terms as well as religious ones. They were most prominent in Germany, which was not a unified nation-state in the first part of the nineteenth century and therefore provided an open field for competing religious ideologies and their organizational expressions. In that setting, Jews who opposed the various trends of the Reform movement, identifying themselves as Orthodox Jews, were also able to organize and promote their own ideology, claiming that Judaism never changed. Orthodox groups pressed to be allowed to leave the general Jewish community and to set up autonomous organizations following their own norms. This meant that Orthodox ideology was not connected to a full local community but was followed by some Jews, in any locale, who wished to voluntarily base their practices on its precepts. From this point of view, orthodoxy must be seen as a religious trend growing out of the modern situation. As in the case of Reform Judaism, it entailed a new vision of the relationship between Judaism and Jews' new social identities.

Eastern European Jews' experience with modernity was different from that of Jews in Central Europe or America. The ideas of emancipation had only begun to affect these regions toward the end of the nineteenth century. Most Jews did not see themselves, for example, as "Russians of the Mosaic persuasion." Rather, their identity was based on belonging to the Jewish people. The Jews compared themselves to the peoples around them such as the Slavs or Greeks. As a nation, they strove to become part of the emerging economic and intellectual world. In response to poverty and oppression, many were attracted to socialist ideologies—either combined with Zionism or with Yiddish-oriented Jewish nationalism. As their economic and social positions improved, Jews in Western Europe also concerned themselves with bettering the situation of their less fortunate brethren. They did this in the form of humanitarian assistance, not as acts of national self-help and renewal.

In turning to new political ideologies, Eastern European Jews often rebelled against religion, which they saw as a force fostering ignorance and economic backwardness. They wished to be free from rabbinic authority and from communal control. To them, the main cultural task was to forge a new type of Jew. They reworked ancient symbols to take on secular meanings. Most of these Jews knew only one type of religion—that represented by traditional rabbis; they had little interest in new formulations of Judaism that had arisen in Central Europe. This left the realms of religious creativity and organizational initiative in Eastern Europe open to various trends within orthodoxy. Because Jews from that region were the numerically dominant group in the small but growing Jewish society in Palestine, the tension between Jews defining themselves as "free" and secular and those who were "religious" later became a basic feature of Israel's culture.

Neither the liberalizing religious trends of West-Central Europe nor the growth of orthodoxy had much of an immediate impact on Jews in the Middle East. In some countries, like Yemen, Jews were minimally touched by the forces of European modernity, while in others, such as Algeria, the influence was more direct. In the latter country, French citizenship was bestowed on the Jews in 1870. This initiative was led by French Jews and did not grow out of the desire of North African Jews themselves to become French citizens. These Jews felt no need to adopt new religious perspectives. They were content to maintain traditional patterns that had long existed or to slowly drop some ritual practices without ideological justification or a shift in their basic identity. In the mid-twentieth century, most Jews in the Middle East eventually migrated to Europe and Israel, where they came into more direct contact with new religious ideologies that had emerged and been established there.

If we link the demographic trends discussed earlier to these religious developments, we begin to grasp the social and political frameworks of the present diversity of religious life among Jews. Roughly thirteen million people define themselves as Jews today. About three-fourths of them reside in two countries, Israel and the United States, and more than two million elsewhere, with Europe having the largest concentration. That so many people today are counted as Jews is complex in itself. For example, many people with Jewish parents choose not to define themselves as Jewish. And although intermarriage brings about a decrease in the number of Jews, it also is capable of attaching individuals, through conversion, to Jewish communities. In addition, a small but growing number of people see themselves as Jews in some contexts and connected to a different religion in other settings. For example, it is not unusual for Jews to practice meditation, with some seeing themselves as Buddhist as well as Jewish.

Most basically, being Jewish usually entails a sense of ethnic or communal belonging. In the case of Israel, and some Diaspora Jews, this sense takes the form of a national identity. Many Jews also see themselves in religious terms. Before emancipation, belonging to the Jewish people and following the Jewish religion were two sides of the same coin that reinforced each other; but this connection has become seriously loosened. As discussed, the liberal forms of Judaism that arose in Europe had their greatest impact in North America, where, in the context of democratic regimes, competing versions of Judaism developed voluntarily. In contrast, various kinds of orthodoxy arising in Europe became dominant in Palestine and were given the official position as the only legitimate expressions of Judaism within the State of Israel. There, only Orthodox rabbis may carry out the rituals of marriage and divorce or convert people to Judaism, rites that determine the religious status of individuals or of their children. In the background of all these trends is an increasing complexity and tension between the ethnic and religious sides of Judaism.

Orthodoxy, of course, exists in North America as well; it began to establish its own institutions there at the end of the nineteenth century and was reinforced, demographically, by surviving Jews who reached the United States after World War II. It is sustained in the United States within a wider democratic culture. Orthodox Jews are free to choose to live within Orthodox frameworks and to select from a range of options, all falling under the Orthodox rubric. Some of them, often deemed ultraorthodox Jews, have religious commitments that accord minimum value to the wider American society in which they are found or to the State of Israel. These politics are seen only as useful frameworks enabling observant Jews to cultivate their own lives according to strict religious standards.

In Israel, despite the monopoly that the state has given to Orthodox expressions of religion, there in fact exists a great variety of religious sensibilities. The immigrants from Middle Eastern societies brought a style now called "traditional," which values religious practice in the home and synagogue but doesn't follow orthodoxy in its strictness or worldview. Among European Israelis, there has been a decline in the secularist ideology that animated some of the early builders of Zionist society. Many of them are still critical of the entrenched authority of Orthodox rabbis but express an interest in some attachment to traditional religious symbols. In addition, there are small groups of organized Conservative and Reform Jews in Israel. They take on significance because of the support they receive from American Jewry, within which they are the dominant religious streams.

Viewed broadly, it is precisely the demographic success of Israeli society, its ability to take in Jews from all over the world with diverse religious histories, that accounts for the varieties of, and tension over, religion in Israel today. An obvious example is found in the recent debate, which seeks to enshrine in law the monopoly of Orthodox rabbis over conversion to Judaism. Large numbers of women from the former Soviet Union who are married to Jewish men but who are not themselves Jewish have migrated to Israel and given birth to children who will not be considered Jews religiously. Life in the Soviet Union, where Jews were barred from cultivating their traditions, is the background to this widespread intermarriage. The children of such couples now grow up speaking Hebrew, living side-by-side with fully recognized Israeli Jews and serving in the army. The rabbinate has been reluctant to convert such people unless they pledge to follow a fully Orthodox life, which most immigrants refuse to do. This situation raises the possibility, of course, that conversion by Conservative or Reform rabbis, who have a greater openness to general cultural currents, might be appropriate. Such a possibility, or course, threatens the monopoly of orthodoxy. There have been serious attempts to find a compromise solution to this particular dilemma, but Israeli society remains a hotbed of contestation in which Jewish issues, reflecting postemancipation developments in various parts of the world, are debated and fought out.

This latter example also points to the growing interlinking of religious issues in Israel and the United States, even though in many ways the histories and milieus of the two countries have encouraged very different religious formations. In both societies, during the past two generations, a variety of new religious groups and ideologies have emerged.

These new expressions of, or emphases within, Jewish life are very much a product of wider trends in America and of political developments within Israel. A quick look at the decade of the 1960s will put these trends into context.

One development within the United States was the demand for greater political power by American blacks and a growing awareness of their heritage and history. This movement evoked an emphasis on ethnicity among many groups in America, including Jews. Jewish reactions ranged from the founding of the Jewish Defense League (JDL), which advocated "Jewish power" through the turn to orthodoxy by those with no involvement in it previously to the cultivation of Jewish studies in universities, open to any student. Some issues mobilized Jews of diverse backgrounds, such as opposition to the policies of the Soviet Union, which suppressed religious life and prohibited emigration to Israel or elsewhere. The plight of Soviet Jewry was a rallying cry of the JDL in America, but its leader later moved to Israel and was elected to the Knesset on an ultranationalist platform based on religion. These developments are one example of the intermeshing of perceived Jewish existence in different parts of the world, even as the way such perceptions were translated into action varied in each country and locale.

Another example of interwoven Jewish concerns is provided by the 1967 war in Israel in relation to the involvement of the United States in Vietnam. Opposition to the latter war grew throughout the 1960s, and college campuses were a major site for the expression of such opposition. The high percentage of Jews attending college meant that Jews were heavily exposed to ideas critical of imperialism, but they were also faced with a situation in which Israel suddenly and unpredictably came to dominate large territories of neighboring Arab states and to rule over many Palestinians. Young Jews often faced the dilemma of sympathizing with anticolonialist critiques and at the same time identifying with Israel even as it was being cast in the role of an oppressor. They therefore had to find their own way and identities in the emerging counterculture, which both criticized American foreign policy and supported ethnic expression at home, which to them meant pro-Jewishness.

Yet another prominent force in the 1960s was, and continues to be, feminism. In mid-twentieth-century America, Conservative and Reform congregations, in Hebrew schools and Sunday schools, gave basically the same education to boys and girls. Yet the religious roles available to women, after the age of bat mitzvah, were not the same as those that could be assumed by men. In tune with the feminist critique of American society in general, women began demanding the right to lead prayers, read from the Torah in public worship, and eventually be ordained as rabbis. The feminist search dovetailed with a rebellion against the formality and passivity of synagogue life in post–World War II American suburbia. Various ideological positions, ideas about how change should take place, and actual practices gave rise to a range of experimental groups from the 1960s onward, which are sometimes collectively referred to as the *havura* (a group that prays or studies together) movement. These developments also implied questions about the locus of religious authority in contemporary society. Although they first were formulated most poignantly within American Jewry, they also are relevant to Israeli society.

The 1967 war turned out to be a religious as well as a political watershed in Israeli history, raising profound questions about the meaning of Israeli society and its relationship to the Jewish past. The events of the war constituted an existential paradox. During the weeks before its outbreak, there was widespread anxiety that the Jewish state, and therefore Jews everywhere, might be facing a major catastrophe. Within six days, however, Israel emerged with the strongest armed forces in the Middle East. This drama, and the subsequent war in 1973, helped cement the Holocaust in Israel's national consciousness. In the decade after Israeli statehood was declared, Jews born in Palestine or Israel found it hard to understand the passivity of Europe's Jews in the face of Nazi aggression, while after 1967, collective memory of the Holocaust came to figure prominently in Israelis' perception of their own situation. It was expressed in a foreign policy, which was reluctant to cede territory because of the society's seemingly eternal vulnerability in the face of implacable enemies.

The 1967 victory thus seemed to some to bring relief—even salvation—of near cosmic dimensions to Israel. Though the results of the war created new configurations of realpolitik, many Israelis saw the emerging situation mainly through religious eyes. Some of the territories conquered (the West Bank, for example) were precisely those that appear prominently in biblical history, and the new Gush Emunim religious movement insisted that it was a religious duty to live in this region and never relinquish it to Gentile hands. Their creation of new settlements was a pious act of far-reaching political consequence, the outcome of which remains a matter of international maneuvering today. This relatively small movement undertook politically significant acts, believing that it represented and spearheaded the direction of divine will with regard to Israel as a whole.

In spite of such rhetoric, which depicted the people of Israel as a single entity, Israeli society was becoming more diversified both socially and religiously. Some symbols of unity emerged right after the war, such as the plaza constructed adjacent to the ancient Western Wall of Second Temple Jerusalem, where all Jews could come to visit, pray, or meditate regardless of their specific identities. It is precisely under this umbrella of unity, however, that the diversity of Judaism became apparent, to say nothing of the outright conflict between its various segments. One example is the group called Women of the Wall, including Israelis and women from abroad, which seeks to carry out public worship in the women's section of the Western Wall plaza in a manner not acceptable to the official rabbinate. Another is the regular attack, in recent years, by ultraorthodox Jews on Conservative Jews who come on the festival of Shavuot and pray at the periphery of the plaza. This struggle has required police intervention and highlights the divisive place of Judaism in Israeli life.

In the 1960s, furthermore, the religious heterogeneity introduced to Israel by Jews from the Middle East began to be expressed more clearly. Contrary to the expectations of authorities, who guided immigration in the 1940s and 1950s, immigrants were not rapidly absorbed into the host society. Their overall numbers, and their concentration in certain settlements and urban enclaves, meant that they preserved many aspects of their previous religious practice. Their approach to religion came to be known as "traditional," because it was not backed up by an ideology. The preservation was a dynamic one, however, and patterns from abroad were modified to fit the new challenges of Israeli life. One such pattern, prominent among North African Jews, entailed pilgrimages to the graves of sainted rabbis. These pilgrimages, known as *hillulot,* have a basis in Jewish mystical writings but reflect popular social and religious sentiments as well. While mothers in North Africa prayed to sainted rabbis for the health of their children, in Israel such supplications were expanded to include the well-being of sons serving in the army and indeed of all Israeli soldiers. Since the 1960s pilgrimage shrines have spread throughout Israel, and *hillulot* have become an established feature on the map of religious life, often reflecting a combination of local and ethnic identities merged with broader Israeli ones.

Links between religiosity rooted in Europe and those originating in the Middle East have also emerged. An example is the SHAS (The Torah-Observant Sephardim) political party, now the third largest in Israel. Activists in SHAS are young men whose parents migrated to Israel from Middle Eastern countries but who received education in ultraorthodox institutions, even to the extent of learning some Yiddish used in the study of Torah. When those youngsters felt that their mobility within the Ashkenazi ultraorthodox world was blocked, they turned to Sephardi rabbis and formed their own party in the 1980s. The party has mobilized a cadre of yeshiva (academy of advanced Torah study) students but has also appealed broadly to families that are traditional in orientation but sympathize with the recently regained sense of Sephardi pride. SHAS, which now cultivates its own school system and religious worldview, reflects a new kind of identity born of a previous intense involvement with several disparate religious arenas.

The case of SHAS also highlights the dynamic quality of religious life in Israel. New identities are formed, challenged, and further reshaped, always with an ability to call on ancient texts and traditions to give backing to religious creativity and innovation. At times, social and political change presents the religious imagination with situations that require more daring than usual. In addition to the many families of mixed marriages from the former Soviet Union, the 1980s and 1990s saw the immigration of tens of thousands of Jews from Ethiopia to Israel, whose religious status was also a topic of much debate. Among the variety of ways that people have related to Judaism in postemancipation times—in terms of religion, culture, peoplehood, or nationality—this immigration unexpectedly inserted the question of race into the field, demanding a religious response.

The selections that follow provide the background to, and exemplify, many of the trends during the past two decades to which I have alluded. The first three illustrate aspects of traditional Jewish life, with one taken from Europe and two from Middle Eastern settings. The last of these focuses on the religious activities and understandings of women, a topic that has been neglected until recently. The following two chapters present pictures of what were fairly typical religious patterns among American Jews at mid-century, one portraying a Reform synagogue and the other an Orthodox congregation. The remaining ten selections attempt to capture the diversity and specificity of some of the religious developments since the 1960s, both in America and Israel. The introductions to the chapters locate each expression of Judaism on this background and point out links among them.

With all the variety in content and in the range of contexts, a number of themes emerge in the selections. One is the continued expression of Judaism in the details of daily activity, whether this activity is preparing food at home, celebrating a bar mitzvah, solemnizing a wedding, worshiping, or studying. Another is the attachment of Jews to the cultures of specific communities, whether they be the Soviet Union or Morocco, even as they seek to make their way in a new country. At the same time, all Jews, whatever their provenance, are forced to ponder the impact of the Holocaust, although the lessons they have derived from it may vary dramatically. The State of Israel, too, has created a new reality about which most Jews explicitly or implicitly take a stand. The link between politics and religion characterizing that society sometimes threatens to estrange it from Diaspora communities, but other topics, like feminism—which includes concrete issues such as the rights of women in marriage and divorce situations—has created a community of concern for Jewish women wherever they are. In general, the ease of communication and travel in the late twentieth century has made possible frequent contact, and at times conflict, between Jews of both similar and diverging backgrounds. Visiting distinctive Jewish spaces has become a major mode of cultivating specific identities and senses of a Jewish past. Finally, Judaism continues to be a religion that demands study. As ritual, prayers, and attitudes toward authority undergo new constructions and personal interpretations, Judaism of "the book" also takes on new forms. The multiple forms of living Judaism entail different ways of understanding its history and reading its texts.

All the selections show how various themes are intertwined in practice and are not easily divided into separate "topics." Both worldview and a sense of history are embodied in rituals that use ritually correct food. Details of synagogue worship create identification with some coreligionists around the world, while separating individuals and groups from other Jews. And the study of texts and of the Jewish past may become relevant to married life or to attempts to grasp the Holocaust. The selections that follow, which have been slightly edited for the purposes of this volume, all illustrate the interconnectedness composed of threads of the Jewish past that give color, texture, and meaning to the immediacies of the present.

Additional Reading

Gideon Aran. "Jewish Zionist Fundamentalism: The Bloc of the Faithful in Israel." In *Fundamentalisms Observed,* ed. M. Marty and S. Appleby. Chicago: University of Chicago Press, 1991, pp. 265–345.

Joëlle Bahloul. *The Architecture of Memory: A Jewish-Muslim Household in Co-lonial Algeria, 1937–1962*. Cambridge: Cambridge University Press, 1996.

Sergio DellaPergola. "Arthur Ruppin Revisited: The Jews of Today, 1904–1994." In *National Variations in Jewish Identity: Implications for Jewish Education*, ed. Steven M. Cohen and Gabriel Horencyzk. Albany: State University of New York Press, 1999, pp. 53–84.

Shlomo Deshen and Moshe Shokeid. *The Predicament of Homecoming: Cultural and Social Life of North African Immigrants in Israel*. Ithaca: Cornell University Press, 1974.

Janet Dolgin. *Jewish Identity and the JDL*. Princeton: Princeton University Press, 1977.

Harvey E. Goldberg, ed. *Sephardi and Middle Eastern Jewries: History and Culture in the Modern Era*. Bloomington: Indiana University Press, 1996.

Sam Heilman and Menachem Friedman. "Religious Fundamentalisms: The Case of the Haredim." In *Fundamentalisms Observed*, ed. M. Marty and S. Appleby. Chicago: University of Chicago Press, 1991, pp. 197–264.

Jack Kugelmass. *The Miracle of Intervale Avenue: The Story of a Jewish Congregation in the South Bronx*. New York: Columbia University Press, 1996.

Jack Kugelmass and Jonathan Boyarin, ed. and trans. *From a Ruined Garden: The Memorial Books of Polish Jewry*, 2d. ed. Bloomington: Indiana University Press, 1998.

Samuel C. Leslie. *The Rift in Israel: Religious Authority and Secular Democracy*. London: Routledge and Kegan Paul, 1971.

Charles S. Liebman and Steven M. Cohen. *The Two Worlds of Judaism: the Israeli and American Experiences*. New Haven: Yale University Press, 1990.

Steven M. Lowenstein. *Frankfurt on the Hudson: The German-Jewish Community of Washington Heights, 1933–1983, Its Structure and Culture*. Detroit: Wayne State University Press, 1989.

Michael A. Meyer. *Response to Modernity: A History of the Reform Movement in Judaism*. New York: Oxford University Press, 1988.

Barbara Myerhoff. *Number Our Days*. New York: Simon & Schuster, 1978.

Riv-Ellen Prell. *Prayer and Community: The Havurah in American Judaism*. Detroit: Wayne State University Press, 1989.

Marshall Sklare. *Conservative Judaism: An American Religious Movement*. New York: Schocken, 1972.

Haym Soloveitchik. "Rupture and Reconstruction: The Transformation of Contemporary Orthodoxy," *Tradition* 28 (1994):64–130.

Alex Weingrod. *The Saint of Beersheba*. Albany: State University of New York Press, 1990.

Jack Wertheimer. *A People Divided: Judaism in Contemporary America*. New York: Basic Books, 1993.

Jack Wertheimer, ed. *The Uses of Tradition: Jewish Continuity in the Modern Era*. New York: The Jewish Theological Seminary of America, 1992.

Walter P. Zenner, ed. *Persistence and Flexibility: Anthropological Perspectives on the American Jewish Experience*. Albany: State University of New York Press, 1988.

Figure 1. A traditional wedding procession in a shtetl in Eastern Europe. (A. Tranowsky, nineteenth-century Russia, oil on canvas. Courtesy Judah L. Magnes Museum.)

CHAPTER 1

The Ethos of an Eastern European Community

Ghitta Sternberg

In the nineteenth century, the largest concentration of Jews in the world was in Eastern Europe. It was a time of extensive social change and of migration from rural towns to large cities. Still, many Jews continued to live in small communities, known by the Yiddish term "shtetl." The shtetl, by no means isolated from change, was a place where many traditional patterns of religious and social behavior were preserved or modified gradually. In the late nineteenth century, the shtetl became the subject of satirical portrayal in the writings of Yiddish authors such as Sholom Aleichem. After much of Eastern European Jewry was destroyed during World War II, there developed a more nostalgic view of the shtetl, which in reality no longer existed. One expression of that nostalgia is found in the play and film *Fiddler on the Roof,* which is based on Sholom Aleichem's stories but takes the satirical bite out of them. The following selection pictures life in a Romanian shtetl with the aid of anthropological concepts. Moving beyond the details of the earlier chapters of her book, Ghitta Sternberg portrays the overall ethos, or worldview, of the shtetl. She describes how Jews in small towns in Romania viewed themselves in relation to the changing, non-Jewish world around them.

Morality

The term "ethos" has been referred to as the conscience of a people. It is the manner in which a particular society views the world (*Weltanschauung*), the way it perceives itself, including the moral ideals it upholds. It is expressed in the norms by which the individuals of the society live. Ethos, not to be confused with "ethics" (though both derive from the Greek word meaning "custom"), is much more inclusive, focusing on ideals rather than on the actual implementation of these ideals. Both deal with the intangibles of human values viewed from different angles. There is an inevitable overlapping between the two constructs, the difference being one of perspective.

In discussing the ethos of the Romanian shtetl, the emphasis will be primarily on the ways in which it differed from the larger Eastern European cultural complex of which it was a part. An attempt will be made to indicate where the Romanian shtetl may be situated on the continuum between the ultratraditional shtetl of the Pale at one extreme and the larger urban Jewish communities at the other. A brief summary will be given on how the Romanian shtetl regarded the various Western cultures, encompassed by the term *strainatatea* ("abroad" or "foreign lands"), since this, too, is an aspect of the shtetl's worldview.

How did the Romanian shtetl view itself? Jewish communities everywhere learned to incorporate elements that reflected the neighboring non-Jewish cultures. This process was more pervasive in the Romanian shtetl. Inhabitants often used the term *assimilirt* ("assimilated"). This term implied a betrayal of ancestral heritage and was spoken with reproof and condemnation. But while the shtetl regarded the Hasidim as fanatics and outmoded, it clung to its faith and traditions and would not have admitted that it was *assimilirt*. This was a term reserved for the city Jews, and especially for the Jews in Western countries.

From a historical perspective, the two great movements of the past, the enlightenment of the *Haskala* and the religious revival of Hasidism, both left their imprint on the Romanian shtetl. The upsurge of Zionism brought about a series of conflicting views and values. In place of the traditional inward-looking view, a new openness appeared. The shtetl found itself somewhat precariously balanced between the two currents: on the one hand, the tradition-oriented but constraining Jewish world, which offered a confined form of security and, on the other, the wish to gain acceptance, to become part of the broader world, to escape. The latter was prompted more than anything else by the hope of assuring for their children a security they had been denied and that they continued to crave.

In accepting the replacement of Yiddish with Romanian as the spoken language, the shtetl had taken a decisive and irreversible step on the road to acculturation. The attitude toward religion and the entire social structure may have changed gears, but it did not change direction. Linguistic behavior patterns express correspondingly different values. The individual's position on the cultural continuum in the shtetl was predictable by his position on the linguistic continuum. His skill in using the language of a second culture symbolized his status in society. It was therefore possible to place individuals on a scale in terms of the language they spoke and the level at which they functioned.

Each successive generation spoke a better, purer Romanian. An intensive and deliberate effort was made to speak Romanian without any telltale Yiddish accent. This was no doubt a common phenomenon wherever Jews willingly adopted the language of the host country. To speak Romanian without a Jewish accent was a sign of good breeding, whereas the Jewish inflections were esteemed vulgar and were apt to elicit derision. The kinship terms used distinguished the social classes. In most middle-class families, the parents conversed in Yiddish with each other but always spoke Romanian to the children. Children learned Yiddish only through speaking to the grandparents or listening to adult conversations. *Mamme-lushn* ("mother tongue") Yiddish was replaced with Romanian in one generation.

Self-improvement was an intrinsic aspect of shtetl ethos, and speaking a pure Romanian was seen as self-improvement, as was learning in general. But whereas traditionally it was the men who were entrusted with study, the new current involved women as well. Men were still supposed to study the sacred writings but increasingly channeled all efforts into entering the professions. *Litéré* ("arts and letters"), literature, and modern languages became the woman's domain.

Contact with cities, whose inhabitants tended to look down on the shtetl, made shtetl residents fully aware of their own disadvantages regarding possibilities for improvement. Luxury items, such as better-quality furniture, silverware, and china were sought after though still looked on as extravagances. The strict necessities of life having been taken care of, efforts were made to improve the immediate surroundings.

Prohibited by Judaic tenets, painting and sculpture did not have any place in shtetl life. Church icons seen during religious processions were not regarded as works of art but instead were associated with religious symbolism and, when not ridiculed as pagan idolatry, were ignored. Even a furtive glance at an icon or a religious statue was considered sinful. Aesthetic needs were fulfilled at a different level by embellishing utilitarian objects and by needlework and embroidery.

Evil was envisaged as punishment for sins. "I must have committed some grave sin to be so punished" was fervently believed, inferring that the fault was entirely one's own. The inevitable result was self-blame and guilt. Guilt was enshrined at every level in the shtetl ethos. Parents did not hesitate to point out to their children what sacrifices they had made or to spell out their expectations. "You will regret this when I am gone" was one of those self-fulfilling, guilt-provoking prophecies. One felt guilty for breaking any of the 613 mitzvot. Two concepts permeating the entire social fabric were the ideas of self-discipline and self-restraint. From observance of strict hygienic rules to adherence to dietary laws, the underlying principle was mastery of oneself and, as a corollary, of personal responsibility. The postponement of momentary pleasures for increased future good was stressed explicitly and by subtle implications. Temperance and self-control were basic virtues. Comparisons with animals were often brought as arguments to instill self-restraint. Self-control in itself was regarded as a form of personal growth. By setting limitations for oneself, one created the feeling of mastery over any given situation. One acquired the decision-making power of choice in limited areas, and, by implication (or illusion), this power extended to other areas of life. Immediate gratification was goyish ("not Jewish"); delaying gratification was Jewish and, by definition, right.

Hospitality, enshrined through biblical writings, was institutionalized in the traditional *oyrech for Sabbath*. The *oyrech* ("guest") was selected from among the poor mendicants at the synagogue and invited home for the Sabbath meals by the prosperous members of the congregation. This practice was considered a charitable act. In daily comportment, too, hospitality was a virtue. It was, however, extended only to one's equals. The Romanian expression when someone dropped in during mealtime was "Poftim la masa" ("Please join us at the table"). This phrase was not to be taken literally, however, as the rhyming retort shows: "But bring your own food." Yet there was always room in any home for an out-of-town relative who was visiting for several weeks. This practice was concomitant with the degree of kinship or friendship. "When there is room in the heart, you find room in the house."

In *Dynamics of Benefice,* the author states that gift giving in the shtetl went only downward, from the well-to-do to the needy.[1] This was not the case in the Romanian shtetl. The Romanian saying, "To the rich, even the devil brings cakes" would suggest that the rich were rewarded with gifts by their social inferiors. The added dimension in this case was the tacit possibility of a form of bribery—in which favors were expected in return, as the saying "put an egg to obtain two" suggests. Gifts were generally exchanged among equals and only on special occasions, such as when leaving or returning from trips, at births, and at weddings. Children received gifts from their elders on their birthdays, on holy days, or simply as a show of love.

Downward giving was regarded as charity and was institutionalized. It was considered worthier to give to those in need without waiting to be asked and to give as discreetly as possible. Charity was not devoid of a whiff of self-interest, since by giving charity one stored up merits in heaven and would be rewarded tenfold. On the other hand, the professional beggar, the *shnorer* ("beggar") was a contemptible figure in the shtetl. These beggars developed a veritable talent for asking, which most people found humiliating to stoop to and detestable in others.

Generosity was a virtue—in theory. The concept of "limited good" and the belief that all desired things in life existed in limited quantities hampered free sharing or giving without some personal gain.[2] The shtetl accepted the proposition that there was not enough to go around, and consequently one's good fortune was considered to be at the expense of another's loss. Envy, though fervently denied by all, was not unknown, especially toward one's equals, as the wish, "May we not envy one another" suggests.

Giving to the needy was charity, institutionalized through synagogue donations such as the Passover *moschitten* ("charity") and the charity for the departed, *yisker gelt,* given to ensure repose for the soul. These acts illustrate the interdependence of cultural patterns in which social needs are fulfilled by tending to the emotional needs of the individual. The institution of *gimeles chessed* ("friendly loan") was established to avoid asking for favors, which was humiliating and put one in an inferior position. The relationship between borrower and lender was thus one of reciprocity and interdependence, and the one in need was not regarded as incompetent, since he, too, might have the opportunity to reciprocate in the future.

Egalitarian principles were not part of shtetl values; children owed deference to their parents, youth respected old people, students respected teachers, and the wife owed obedience to her husband. All people had their roles, and the expectation was that their turn would come to elicit respect from their inferiors. The entire social structure of the shtetl was based on the accepted reality that people were different and had their own roles to play. The fallacy of the principle of equality was taken for granted. It was summed up in one favorite Romanian fable, in which dogs seeking equality within the animal kingdom conclude that what they really wanted was equality with the lions, not with the insignificant lapdog.

The hierarchical view of the world was acknowledged, since there did not seem to be any evidence to the contrary. This was an authoritarian society where social stratification was undisputed, where ranking was part of every aspect of life, and where each member of society was aware of his or her standing. The question of ascribed versus achieved status may have been debatable, but no one denied the reality that some were more equal than others. It was on this vulnerable point that Marxism was able to attack tradition-oriented shtetl values.

Imported through neighboring Bessarabia, where Jews still spoke Russian and were therefore more amenable to the propaganda, Russian-style Communism began to influence young idealists. Where religious beliefs were the raison d'être of the shtetl, "Communist godlessness" was a dangerous menace; "free love" was seen as a direct threat to marriage and the family. Economic determinism, a meaningless phrase for the self-employed individualists, appealed to the naive young. The older generation as well as Romanian officials viewed these simmerings of unrest with alarm. Midnight arrests of ringleaders and their converts stemmed the tide for a time; the war and subsequent contact with reality did the rest.

In a small community where daily, face-to-face encounters make posing artificiality impossible, people are judged, weighed, and measured by their peers. Reputations, based on past experience, once established, were difficult to forget. Labels stuck. Nicknames, often painfully cruel, testified to this fact. By the same token, self-praise was shunned, as was any form of hypocrisy, which was easily detected. No one is able to wear a mask at all times.

A *bekuveder Yid* ("a dignified Jew") dressed properly (meaning "neatly and in somber tones") and showed moderation in every respect. The "seven years from home," that is, background and the home environment were credited for dignified behavior in adults.

Derech eretz may be translated as "respect for one's elders." The term is more suggestive however; the mot-à-mot translation is "the way of the land" and implies a respect for the accepted manner of doing things and for tradition. It sums up the concept of accepted and expected behavior. One showed *derech eretz* by standing up before an older person, by using the respectful pronoun, and by observing the Sabbath. Any breach of conformity was attributed to ill manners, befitting only a *grobyon* or a *grobber yingh* ("redneck").

Arrogance and aloofness were not appreciated, while modesty was highly prized. Posing or behaving above one's standing was ridiculed and scoffed at. Should anyone behave in a manner considered by others as above his assigned standing, he was greeted with "Nu Graff Pototsky!" (roughly, "Do you think you're a Polish count?") and immediately cut down to size. Ridicule was a potent, frequently used weapon. There was acceptance of and pride in the "local boy making good," but one had to win recognition from the outside world before being accepted by the shtetl. This dynamic may be interpreted as a feeling of low self-esteem in which shtetl inhabitants held themselves, reflected in their reluctance to admit that one of them was worthy.

In theory, truthfulness, honesty, and sincerity were virtues upheld in the shtetl. In practice, expediency and realism prevailed. Not surprisingly, society protected itself by underscoring honesty and proving that dishonesty did not pay in the end. As in any small community, public opinion and social sanctions were potent deterrents for any antisocial behavior. Many proverbs buttress this. Trust was important in the functioning of society, and any breach was easily discernible.

Interpersonal relationships were of two distinct types. With those one considered social equals, shtetl residents were close, warm, and outgoing. Across social class or age barriers, relations were reserved and polite. The respectful pronoun *yir* ("thou") was used for older persons or those of a higher social standing. A *per-tu* or *per-dyi* (for which there is no equivalent in English) relationship was reserved only for close friends and immediate family of the same age group. Parents, aunts, and uncles were addressed with the respectful plural pronoun *yir*.

Calling people by first name was not customary. A man was addressed by his family name prefixed by *Domnu* ("mister") or the Yiddish *Arb* or *Reb* ("sir"), using the first name or the family name, depending on the person's social standing. Working-class people were usually addressed by their first names, whereas they addressed a merchant or shopkeeper by his family name. A woman was called *Doamna* (or "madam"). A single woman was addressed with the prefix *Domnisoara* ("miss"). Servants addressed their employers simply with *Domnu* and *Doamna*.

Friendships were established along age lines, often within the extended-family circles and always among social equals. Parents discouraged any close relationships with children of families they estimated to be of a lower social level and, conversely, encouraged relations with equals or those one notch above. Friendships were based on compatibility, common interests, and affection. To be *afurisit* (literally, "cursed") was a term applied to those individuals who held themselves aloof from the community. They were regarded with suspicion. Once established, friendships were maintained throughout the years and were based on reciprocal loyalty and a strict code of ethics, with mutual moral support and expectations of genuine understanding. Men formed lasting friendships during their years of military service. The generation of the First World War maintained friendships, even when circumstances disrupted normal expectations. Among the young, personal confidences were exchanged, especially concerning the opposite sex.

Physical proximity was not stigmatized; walking *bratz la bratz* ("arm in arm") with a friend of the same sex was commonplace. Conversely, no such permissiveness was allowed between members of the opposite sex. Only engaged couples were granted such intimacies as holding hands or walking arm in arm in public. In general, showing affection in public was not acceptable.

Babies and young children were hugged, kissed, and caressed in public by parents and relatives or friends. It was not uncommon for well-meaning strangers to kiss babies. One way of showing affection for young children was a pinch on the plump cheek.

Kissing a lady's hand was a genteel gesture practiced by gentlemen, who bowed, doffed their hats, and touched the lady's hand with their lips. This custom, practiced by upper-class Romanians, was borrowed from the West, as the accompanying greeting *sarut mana* ("I kiss your hand") or the German equivalent *Küss die haende* would suggest. It is interesting to note that the Romanian peasantry practiced this custom in quite a different context. The peasants, both men and women, kissed the hands of their social superiors but not those of their equals. This was no doubt a relic of feudal times, in the not-too-distant past, when the landless peasants were indeed subservient to their masters and had to kneel and kiss the hand of the *boyer* ("landowner" or "nobleman"). Jews, who did not kneel even to their God, considered any kneeling a form of self-abasement; kissing a lady's hand, however, was regarded as good manners.

The emotional bond between parents and children was one of those values deeply embedded in the shtetl ethos, to the point where it was taken for granted. Parental love and concern for children was as natural as breathing. Parents achieved personal fulfillment through the success of their children; no effort was insurmountable, no sacrifice too great to achieve this end. This was a child-oriented culture and proud of it. This little song, taught in nursery school, sums up parental attitudes:

Iské l'irot baniim, baniim ou banot
Oskiim ba Torah, ou be avodah.

Let us be worthy to see our sons and daughters
Successful in Torah and in work.

Many parents deliberately accepted assimilation with the sole intent of sparing their children the hurt they had known. Nazi Germany proved that they were misguided in this belief. When parents in Israel were asked why they had uprooted themselves and left comparatively successful lives, the unanimous reply was: "For the sake of our children's future; we didn't want for them the hardships we had experienced."

Children, in turn, owed respect and felt indebted to their parents. This attitude was not a burden but rather a responsibility that they, in turn, would expect of their children. To disobey a parent was a guilt-laden act. No son or daughter, for instance, would have placed a parent in an institution to be cared for by strangers under any circumstances.

The image of the shtetl has often been one of overcrowded, dilapidated, or slovenly surroundings. Yet one of the prime virtues in the Romanian shtetl was being a *gospodar or gospodina* ("good manager"). This term referred to the manner in which the home was maintained. Keeping the house neat and orderly at all times was the wife's domain. The term *shlimezolnitze* ("bad housekeeper") was an insulting epithet. The *gospodar* was supposed to provide the wherewithal, look after household repairs, and ensure plentiful food supplies. Though interchangeable, the responsibilities were specified for husband and wife. Being a *gospodar* had little to do with financial means, since there were both good and bad housekeepers at all class levels.

Thrift was a virtue of necessity. Clothing and household articles were expected to last, often for a lifetime, and waste was considered downright sinful. One did not throw out anything that could still be used. This applied to food as well. A piece of bread was picked up off the floor, wiped, and kissed. (The same was true of any book or sacred writing). Clothing was handed down from parents to children and so on, down the line to the youngest. A popular anecdote has it that when the father or oldest son chose the cloth for a suit or an overcoat, the youngest child examined the reverse side, convinced that by the time it reached him, it would be the right side. Women remodeled dresses, combined and transformed to be *la moda* ("in style").

Frugality ended with food. The Romanian shtetl appreciated and enjoyed a hearty meal and a *shpritz* ("wine with soda water"). The Sabbath meal was never skimped on. One saved on many other items but not on the quality or quantity of food. The line between thrift and stinginess was often difficult to tread. As in other respects, individuals were spotted and judged accordingly. Neither the spendthrift *mana sparta* ("cracked hand") nor the avaricious fared too well; moderation, as in other matters, was the ideal to strive for.

Privacy was one value conspicuous by its complete absence in the shtetl. There is no equivalent term in either Yiddish or Romanian for our concept of—and consequently the need for—privacy. The term *privata* in Romanian refers to the toilet and carries connotations appropriate to such circumstances. Not only among the poor, who were of necessity living in overcrowded conditions, but among the relatively affluent, privacy was unknown. There was no awareness of any duress in this respect. The feeling of togetherness compensated for any possible physical discomforts. It was rather the feeling of loneliness that was dreaded and avoided. On the other hand, judging by the number of expressions meaning "bother" (*dilln, hack nisht*), one may surmise that there were circumstances when one would have appreciated some privacy.

The shtetl held the undisputed view that intellectual work was superior to manual labor. Businessmen were held as superior to other men by virtue of their using their head. Brain versus brawn was the basic cleavage within the social structure. Intellectual activity received the higher prestige, and the shtetl rewarded men of thought rather than men of action. In the shtetl of old, this fact was reinforced by many other structural elements, such as the husband's spending his time in study while the wife (or her father) carried the burden of the family. This was not the case in the Romanian shtetl, where the husband was the breadwinner. Nevertheless, the prestige of learning remained; it was directed into more contemporary channels, where the rewards of economic success accrued.

Jews have often been accused of cowardice. The shtetl was aware of this, if somewhat perplexed at the accusation, since the concept of cowardice, as of bravery, depended on interpretation. In the shtetl, courage, the sense of fearlessness in battle, was academic, since Jews were treated as foreigners in the land of their birth and were not given the opportunity to prove themselves. Bravery was extolled in biblical heroes, but for the shtetl, it was a moot concept.

Jews also had a reputation for shrewdness and were believed to fall short of the mark regarding honesty. The shtetl itself, however, did not hold this self-image; it attributed these undesirable characteristics to individuals. As is so often the case, it was the outsiders, in this case the Bessarabians, who were referred to as "horse thieves," although individuals were recognized as upright and dignified.

Fighting, in the sense of fisticuffs, was goyish: "Jews don't fight" was the frequent admonition. Parents did not encourage children to settle disagreements by fighting. The Romanians themselves did not place courage on the top of the list of virtues, as may be surmised from the phrase "flight may be shameful, but it is healthful!" Bullies were considered hooligans. Bravery in battle, though extolled in poetry, was not one of the outstanding qualities of the Romanian peasant. On the other hand, the indomitable clinging to ancestral traditions, in spite of life-threatening dangers, would certainly merit the term "courageous."

Attitudes toward sex may be summed up as Victorian, with some qualifications. The shtetl did not regard itself as deprived or oppressed in this respect. As with everything else, the Bible was the fundamental source for moral guidance, from bringing up children to every subsequent stage of life. Self-restraint was the essential principle; postponement of immediate pleasure for the more lasting future satisfactions was constantly reiterated. Temperance and moderation were virtues, while excesses of any sort were considered goyish and hence outside the confines of shtetl values.

Sex was taboo as a topic of conversation in polite society and doubly so in the presence of children. It was considered vulgar. Children were not given any instructions on the subject and learned haphazardly from peers. Sexuality, however, was recognized as a basic need. Judaism does not subscribe to asceticism or abstinence for its own sake. The community regarded celibacy as calamitous to the individual and a danger to the community, which is one reason why early marriages were advocated. No stigma was attached to the sex act, and no concept of original sin. Legitimate relations and enjoyment within the bounds of marriage were not only approved, but marital sex was seen as a positive *mitzva* ("good deed"). It was only outside the confines of marriage that sex became sinful and a danger to the community as a disrupting factor. Looked at from this point of view, the interdependence of structural elements instituted for the effective functioning of the community and for the benefit of the majority of its members becomes evident.

As admonished in the Bible, masturbation was declared a sin. It was taboo. The Romanian term *onanie,* derived from the biblical character Onan, who "spilled the seed on the ground" and was condemned to perish, was used as a supporting argument. The guilt instilled was intensified by warnings of the irreparable harm resulting from this vice. Children lived in fear of becoming blind or losing their potency as a consequence of masturbation.

Double standards were accepted without question. Men were different; they had different needs and, *vive la différence* was the prevailing sentiment. Abstinence was believed to be more trying to men than to women. Ideally, it was preferable for both boys and girls to marry young and abstain till marriage. But whereas a girl's virginity was an unconditional must, for the boy it was an *ought*. Depending on his age at marriage, a man was permitted certain indiscretions, as long as he showed prudence. The fear of venereal diseases was one of the major deterrents. It was tacitly accepted that at the age of twenty-one, when men were called for compulsory military service, it would have been unreasonable to expect them to remain abstinent. Young men were often incited by their peers to prove their virility. The prevailing attitude was that sexual activity in men was an expression of manliness, while in women it was unforgivable. Women who indulged were tainted, they were damaged goods to be disposed of at bargain-basement prices. Hanging up the bloodstained bed sheet of the bridal bed for all to see, though no longer done, was accepted since the proof of the bride's virginity at marriage was needed.

One woman told me: "There were girls who did and girls who did not play around, the boys played with those who did but married those who did not; why should he have secondhand goods? And how could he know that she won't cheat on him afterward, too? She did it before! That's the way it was."

There were no unwed mothers or children for adoption. (Adoption was only practiced within the family circle, in case of misfortunes, or—the sole case of an unwed mother in the shtetl—brought up by the mother's parents). A *mamzer* ("bastard") was an insulting epithet that popular wisdom nevertheless transformed into a compliment, in the sense of "sharp" or "canny."

The attitude of the shtetl toward the host culture was both anomalous and ambiguous. It was anomalous because although a tolerated minority, it considered itself superior. Yet it wished to be accepted. This feeling of superiority was engendered by their unswerving faith, their conviction of their own intellectual superiority reinforced by their reverence for the Bible. The Romanian peasant, in turn, regarded the Jews with some awe and respected them for what they considered their intellectual superiority. It was well known that the Jews formed the middle class in Romania, where 85 percent of the population was made up of peasants.

The shtetl attitude toward the peasants differed from that held toward upper-class Romanians. Though individual peasants were recognized as shrewd; upstanding, and hard working, the culture as a whole was regarded as rude, primitive, and illiterate by comparison to their own. The shtetl considered its religious rituals as right and just, whereas the observances of the gentiles were viewed as primitive and ridiculed as childish.

Vi ba die goyim ("like the gentiles") expressed anything not befitting a Jew. Bright colors and excessive adornments, such as glass beads, were goyish. Shtetl values were the antithesis of the values of non-Jews. Whistling was not Jewish; *a sheigetz faift* ("a gentile boy whistles"). Brawling was goyish. Walking around barefoot, like the *shikses* ("gentile girls") was demeaning for a Jewish person. These sentiments were summed up by the phrase *a goy blabt a goy* ("a gentile remains a gentile"). Where Jews extolled temperance and self-restraint, gentiles were prone to excess. *Shiker is a goy* ("Drunk is a gentile").

Notes

1. Natalie Joffe, "The Dynamics of Benefice Among East European Jews," *Social Forces* 27 (1949): 238–39.

2. Jack M. Potter, May N. Diaz, George M. Foster, eds. *Peasant Society: A Reader* (Boston: Little Brown, 1967), p. 303.

6502   SCÈNES ET TYPES. — La Cérémonie de la Circoncision. — LL.

Figure 2. A Jewish circumcision in the town of Nabeul, Tunisia, after World War I. (From a postcard provided by Bernard Allali.)

CHAPTER 2

Preparing for Passover
in North Africa

Irene Awret

Traditional Jewish life took many forms. This excerpt portrays the life
of Jews in Nabeul, a small town on the Tunisian coast. It is based on
the memories of Rafael Uzan (Fallu), who moved to Safed, Israel, in
the 1950s, as he looks back at his boyhood with amusement and affection. While describing the preparations for celebrating Passover, the
chapter also gives us a glimpse into the family, a focus of that festival.
Jewish family life reflected, but was not identical to, the surrounding
North African culture. Uzan points out the active relationships between the Jewish and Muslim families in relation to the holiday food
and customs. At the same time, the details regarding Passover preparations—the great effort to eliminate *hametz* from the house and the
overall cleaning—would be recognized by Jews everywhere. So too
would the child's question: "if *matza* is the 'bread of affliction' re-
minding us of slavery in Egypt, why do we enjoy it so?" Passover provides a prototype of many Jewish celebrations in which domestic customs, and in particular special foods, are linked to the grand themes
of the ritual calendar and awareness of sacred history.

Passover Is Coming!

Passover preparations got under way the very moment
Purim flickered out. As only four weeks separate Passover from Purim
there was much to be done if we wanted to celebrate our feast of free-

dom properly and even children had to pitch in. School was closed so that our classrooms could be taken over by a crowd of matzoh [matza] bakers, men working in shifts day and night, preparing the mountains of matzohs needed to feed the Jews of Nabeul for a week. Small portions of unleavened dough were flattened out with sticks; patterns were punched through the thin discs with the help of ten fingers, miraculously transforming lifeless lumps of dough into large flowers and crisp wagon wheels. The oven did the rest. Boys employed alongside the men would be running all over the place carrying flour and firewood, while women and grown-up girls, unclean for reasons that are obvious, had to stay away. As those hand-fashioned matzohs were naturally expensive, our *comité* would distribute them to the needy free of charge; my father, however, always made a point of paying for our rations. It was not the price of the matzohs, though, that was his greatest worry. The house had to be whitewashed inside and out; new shoes and clothes bought for the entire family; plenty of eggs and vegetables for the traditional dishes. What is more, without the slaughter of a sheep Passover was unthinkable.

For months my father had saved every franc he could possibly spare, hiding his hoard in a spot whose secret was unknown even to my mother. He had become doubly cautious because of the misfortune which had befallen us the year before. Then, as now, our door had been pushed open by a big ladder followed by the Arab house painter. Then also, as now, he had shouted a cheerful "Aslama!" and proceeded to daub everything in view with sky-blue lime, the first step on the arduous road to a clean, kosher Passover. Then, just as now, my father had wanted to pay the painter with some bills taken from his hard-earned savings, the only difference being that last year he could not find them. The treasure had been hidden away in the half-broken chest which was our only piece of furniture, my grandfather's wedding present to my parents. Safely knotted into an old handkerchief with yellow dots resembling gold coins, it had wintered in a corner of the upper drawer. After some pushing and shoving, the drawer opened with a shriek that set my teeth on edge. In place of the handkerchief my father's hand came up with a pair of socks in need of mending.

"Where is the money, Meesha?" Slow and deep, the question seemed to come out of a hole in the ground. My mother's eyes grew black and round the way they always would at an approaching tempest.

"May the Almighty strike me dead if I ever touched it; I did not even look at it," she said in a choked voice. My father had yanked all three drawers out of the rickety skeleton. Crumpled books, chipped wooden spoons, candle stumps and broken buttons tumbled to the floor. Trying not to attract his attention I had stood stock-still, riveting my eyes on some bits of paper that had settled on my feet, my father's accounts written in strange Aramaic scribble.

"My God, why did I ever marry her?" he was now groaning. "Why did You let her round calf's eyes trick me into it? What good are they to me if she can't see? Last week she lets the cat steal half a pound of tripe from under her nose. Now she cannot see thieves on two legs either. Don't just stand there, staring like a cow! Move, woman, better find that handkerchief!" My poor mother did not say a word; tear after tear silently running down her cheeks were caught up in the chaste neckline of her blouse. Convinced that somehow she must be guilty and had mislaid the handkerchief unknowingly, she had started to turn every garment inside out, had opened the big mattress, unfolded diapers and blankets, but there was no trace of the dotted handkerchief.

Slowly though not calmly my father had realized that his loss was final.

"So that's it. For her I let the sun scorch the flesh off my bones. For her I let myself roast on the roads. . . . I have more blisters on my soles than she has bubbles in her washtub. I am breaking my back to feed her and her children! Has she ever given me anything in return but bad luck? How many of her sons are still alive?" For an answer big sobs came out with a flurry of flour. In her desperation my mother was poking through our bags of provisions, emptying the salted fish over the rush mat and searching my baby sister's crib.

"Here." My father had thrown her clothes at her. "Get out of my sight! Take your children and go back to that black star where you came from!" By now completely soaked with tears and still without a word, my mother had tied her few belongings into her own kerchief—the striped one which is the only keepsake she has left me. The bundle slung over one arm, she gathered up my sister with the other and in a valiant attempt to hide her shame before the neighbors, enfolded both in her big, white wrapper. I trudged out behind her.

"Don't ever come back here. Let your brothers feed you from now on!" my father had thundered as she turned for a last look from the threshold.

As she had always done on similar occasions, my mother's mother, bedridden and half paralyzed, would welcome us warmly with her one good arm. Also as usual, after a week or so of part exile, part vacation in my grandmother's house, my mother's brothers would negotiate our return with my father, asking for his forgiveness. Once more my mother hid the baby inside the folds of her shawls as we trotted home.

Here I must add that among Jews, temporary banishment was the most common punishment for undutiful wives. An erring Moslem woman was simply shut up in a room without food or water. An ordinary beating, a husband's bout of infidelity, would be accepted without much of a fuss. Only if he did not provide for his wife and children was the matter considered serious enough to bother the rabbi. If some woman, on the other hand, infringed religious law, having served her husband meat and cheese at the same meal for instance, then it was the rabbi's task to punish her.

Men could ask for a divorce for two reasons: if a wife had borne no children after ten years of marriage or if two reliable witnesses had found her in a flagrant act of infidelity. The latter, thank God, was an extremely rare occurrence in Nabeul, but it happened. If it did, the cheated husband would assemble his witnesses and go before the Chief Rabbi. Not to offend the saintly ear though, he would take off one of his shoes and turn it upside down to intimate the full gravity of the matter. If no fault could be found with the evidence, the man got a divorce and custody of the children. The woman was sent off to another town.

It is hard to believe how things have changed. Take my wife, Fortuna, for example. Thirty years ago in Nabeul, had I told her that the moon was falling and asked her to catch it for me in one piece, she would have murmured:

"As you say, my husband," and waited all night in the courtyard with an open basket. You should hear her now—talking back from morning till night.

"Why do you paint nothing but nonsense? Why don't you ask more money for your pictures? Why can only our neighbors have wall clocks?" (In the end I got her the ugly contraption.) I should not complain though. I know of many doves that fluttered shyly all the way from Nabeul, only to start throwing plates at their husband's head in Safed.

My mother, however, was of the old stock, thankful to be taken back in by my father, who, resigning himself to a meager Passover, had accepted that thieves also are the Will of God. My mother had done wonders with the eggs and vegetables her brothers could spare, while on my father's side it was Uncle Goliath who charged into our room like a wounded bull, shouting that slow death from starvation was much too good for careless squanderers like us, after which he disbursed twenty-five francs for a lamb and matzohs.

Here now was our family, assembled in the same room one year later, all set to strike that last Passover from the record. Once again the Arab house painter splashed away at the ceiling, painting it so blue that the sky behind the lattices looked wan and pale. I was in a cheerful mood, as always when I sniff fresh lime. My mother was out on the terrace, making coffee for Aunt Kooka. My father, huddled in a corner, sat worrying over his new hoard as if counting and recounting the bills would add to them. I remember my little sister standing beside me, blissfully slapping blue lime on her curls with the thin palm leaf strips of an abandoned paintbrush, when suddenly shreds of paper, dirt and straw rained down upon us as the painter cleaned out a rat's nest holed in between the ceiling and a wooden beam.

"Thump," the rag had landed at my feet. Of such short build that her eyes are forever close to the ground, my Aunt Kooka had already pounced on the bargain.

"What do you know, yellow polka dots. My sister must be swimming in money," she said pointedly, "throwing a perfectly good rag into the trash. Watch how I'll wash it into a towel," and picking up the mess Aunt Kooka started to shake out the dust. Her mouth fell open. "Meesha, a miracle, a miracle!" she cried as coins rolled in every direction and paper money fluttered before her nose. Over two hundred francs! My father's lost treasure in its entirety was falling out of the folds. Fondling the dotted handkerchief, now several shades darker and dirtier than it had been a year ago, my mother wept for joy.

"Thank You, thank You, dear God, for giving my poor husband's sweat money back to us," she murmured over and over as she pressed the crumpled bills to her heart, kissing them instead of my father. I never saw my parents hug or kiss in front of me, nor any other couple in Nabeul for that matter. A great deal of kissing was going on, but it was strictly limited to either one's own sex or grown-ups embracing small children.

That Passover we felt as rich people do the whole year round. Even my father, possibly bothered by the memory of my mother's unjust banishment, loosened his ordinarily tight fist and took us on a shopping spree. I became the only boy to tramp Bab Salah Street on real leather soles, while my father bought the violet-and-gold-striped skirt my mother was to wear for many years to come. After that he got hold of the fattest sheep he could find in the market. The thieving rat was never seen again. Maybe it went treasure hunting at a neighbor's or it may have fallen prey to the cat or the house snake. Its nest, in any event, remained bare of bedding and uninhabited from then on.

Whatever became of the rat, once our room had received its new coat of blue lime, Passover cleaning could begin in earnest. The short weeks still separating us from the Seder night were spent scouring, scraping and washing to make sure not the tiniest bread crumb, a speck of flour or anything else likely to ferment had been overlooked in our household. It is by refraining from contact with bread or other leavened food and drink that we try to relive the hardships our fathers suffered on their passage from slavery to freedom, from Egypt to the other side of the Red Sea over three thousand years ago. Rightly fearing that the Pharaoh would have second thoughts and pursue the builders of his towns into the desert, our people left in great haste. They had not even waited for their dough to rise, taking wafer-thin bread called matzoh with them on their flight. I have never understood why eating matzohs is considered a hardship. Those we crunched every year for eight days in honor of the Exodus were so delicious that our Moslem neighbors liked them better than any other of our holiday specialties, gratefully accepting every morsel we could spare.

For the moment, though, much remained to be done before we could recline at the Seder table eating matzohs. Anything movable in the house was taken apart for a thorough cleaning. Doors and shutters were taken off their hinges; all clothes, curtains and blankets were washed. My mother and her neighbors spent their days in the courtyard amid the soapy steam of linens boiling in copper vats, amicably chattering over the noise of water buckets rattling up and down the cistern. Patient and unruffled throughout the year, my mother became frantic during Passover cleaning.

"Fallu, fan the fire. . . . Fallu, fetch more green soap. . . . Don't run away now!" She would not give me a moment's peace. Then, early one morning, my father would harness his donkey to a rented cart, loading it with all our sheepskins and the heavy mattress. My mother added pails, brushes, soap and a basketful of food for the day, sat my little sister on top of everything and took us down to the shore. There I would help her unload everything on some mossy boulder, pull out the wool from the big mattress and drown it in the salty sea together with the bedbugs. While I was spreading out the washed wool to dry on the warm rocks, the beach was coming alive. The whole length of the shoreline was dotted with women and children rinsing wool, hides, doors and shutters. Mothers and daughters, bent side by side over the dripping sheepskins, carefully combed them out curl by curl so that no bread crumb could possibly get by, as the boys, told to watch the family belongings, would instead play the kind of games that build up an appetite. When the sea was aglitter, dancing with sparks and patches of white sun, it was decided that it must be noon and food and drink were parceled out. From that moment on, the cleaning party turned into a lively picnic. Stories were told and the singing ended only after sundown when rows of donkey carts, piled high with clean wool and sleepy children, would slowly stagger homeward in the soft evening air.

The next morning was slaughter day at my grandfather's house. Grazing on whatever there is to graze upon in a bare yard, our beautiful fat sheep had been there for some time in company of three, four others belonging to my uncles. It was a dark little yard, shadowed on all sides by a wall taller than the house itself, a thick, crumbly white wall full of holes. Goat cheese, I called it.

The old family fortress, wall and house, had been built by my grandfather's grandfather—the one they said had come from Italy. Only very old Jews would haltingly speak of those times—fearful times, when the Turks had been the masters of Nabeul. The strongest house had not been strong enough to protect our people from robbery, rape and murder then, they would murmur, pointing to a brown spot and rust-eaten iron ring beside the entrance to Rahamim's house. There the one knife the Turks had allowed for the use of Bab Salah Street's inhabitants had been chained to the wall, they said. The walls of my grandfather's house, walls wider than the space in between were the stony inheritance that had come down to us from our distant Italian ancestor. He must have brought some wealth from the other side of the sea to build this maze of narrow passages, uneven steps, and doorways with rooms so low a man must stoop to avoid hitting the ceiling. The fortunes of our family had long since dwindled and my grandparents, seeing their children stare at the naked walls with hunger in their eyes, had often wished the stones would turn to bread.

I loved the old house. Having known no true hunger in my childhood I liked the walls just as they were, full of holes and crevices. It was there my grandfather taught me to catch my first bird and how to recognize its eggs. There that I learned which snakes were harmless and which were poisonous and had to be treated with respect. Under the grapevine I would tame my pet mice; over by the well play yo-yo with big brown spiders dangling from their threads. Overgrown with moss, the well shaft was teeming with pretty, black, redheaded worms; its depths were alive with green frogs and, sometimes when I was in luck, a pair of golden eyes would stare at me from the bottom of the pail my grandmother was bringing up with water. Once in a while during a night at the old house I would wake up to deep croaks and low humming, while light from an oil lamp filtered through my closed eyelids. Opening them with effort, I would look up at an immense, shaggy shadow tottering all over the vaulted ceiling—my grandfather's bearded profile bending and straightening, as he read the Bible to the song of the frogs.

It was bright morning and in one more day it would be Passover eve. Rabbi Shushan, the slaughterer, was standing in my grandfather's yard, sharpening his knife. He did so for a long time, drawing the blade back and forth, back and forth over his stone until the blade was sharp enough to kill a sheep with one single, swift stroke through the throat. There are things of which an animal has more knowledge than man. The sheep were getting nervous, bleating frightfully. I had never quite forgiven Rabbi Shushan for what he had done to my rooster years ago, although I had with time accepted that his work was sacred and important, the more so since without his intervention I would not be able to eat meat. I had, however, learned my lesson, keeping a distance from those sheep, chickens and pigeons destined for slaughter, afraid that otherwise we might become too friendly. Rabbi Shushan was ready. My grandmother, praying for a happy Passover, was kissing the mezuzah as he gave the blade a last test on his fingernail. One slit—the blood gushed out and everybody tensed, breathlessly looking at the rabbi as he pulled the bowels out of the carcass. One blemish on the stomach, a blue spot on the liver, a tear in the intestine and our beautiful sheep would be declared unclean, barely good enough to be sold to a Moslem at half price. Only after Rabbi Shushan had blown up the lungs through the windpipe and had found them whole would he at last smack his bloody hand on the sheep's hind legs—his way of saying that the meat was fit for Passover.

With broad smiles, men's blessings, women's ululations, one sheep after the other passed the test. Proud that I could stand the sight of blood without crying, I plunged my hand into the red stream, then, held up by my grandfather, planted it over the gate, beside his own broad, furrowed print. Everybody was singing and joking, the men busily stripping skins, the women cutting meat and scraping the bowels that would be made into spicy sausages and other stuffed delicacies. My mother drove a red-hot nail into the severed head of our sheep, right in between the horns. Well-cooked with the help of this simple expedient, the animal's brains were a treat reserved for the family's firstborn, which is to say myself; they were supposed to make me clever. I have yet to meet a quick-witted sheep, but I certainly enjoyed the taste of this delicacy. Apart from teeth and hooves, not a morsel of the animal was thrown away. The meat, of course, was cooked or roasted, including the skin covering the head. The bones went into soups and stews. And if the sheep had been a ram, its horns were destined to become a shofar, to sound in the new year in the fall. The hide, smeared with salt and lime, was nailed to the door where it was left to dry skin side up until after the holiday when, well rinsed in the sea, it would make me a soft and springy new bed.

Around noon on that busy day before the eve of Passover my mother and I went back to our own house where Nisria, the mother of my three little Moslem friends, was already waiting to buy our *hametz*.

"God bless you, Nisria, what would we do without you?" My mother kissed our neighbor on both cheeks, then helped her carry over to her cave whatever was still left of our winter provisions: dried couscous, beans, flour—in short any food forbidden to us on Passover. Nisria was well versed in the game; making believe this was a true transaction, she paid us two sous for the whole bargain and left. But my mother did not have to worry: once the holiday was over Nisria would return everything untouched. Not a bean, a lentil or grain of couscous would be missing. On the contrary, Nisria would always add freshly baked bread for the whole family, a sudden taste of heaven when you have gone without it for a week. How avidly we always fell upon her bread and how thankful she was for our matzohs.

For the rest of the day and far into the night my mother was completely absorbed in her cooking. She and her four neighbors squatting on low stools behind the charcoal burning in their tripods were cutting vegetables, chopping meat, swapping recipes and spices to the sound of bubbling stews and brass pestles, lustily pounding sesame seeds and cinnamon. Munching lettuce leaves and carrot chunks, I flitted about among the pots, pestles and women, fanning fires to burn brighter and faces to cool off.

"Fallu, dear, a drink of water . . ." or "Fallu, pass me the spoon over there . . ." Unable to hoist herself off her stool, fat Lajla came up with one request after another. Her face, which looked ready to blow up any minute, was glowing hotter than the coals. Her formidable bosom was heaving and falling at the same pace as the lid of her equally formidable cooking pot, the biggest of them all. Full to the brim with giant pads of stuffed intestine, a thick sauce loaded with artichoke hearts, garlic and tomatoes was noisily sputtering over the sides. The only one among our neighbors to use a cow's bowels instead of the traditional, daintier sheep's intestines, fat Lajla's *otsbana* resembled overstuffed cushions rather than human nourishment. Always a little envious of her children, I could not for the life of me understand why they were so skinny, especially her daughter whom I loathed. Already at the age of four she was making eyes at me, but I steadfastly ignored her then, and for many years to come when she was not so skinny anymore. Even so, she loved to see me cringe in embarrassment at her advances. Although nobody could possibly see me blush in the heat of all that cooking, I ran off anyway, to help my mother find hiding places for the bread, I said. Custom requires that we conceal ten small pieces of bread in our home on the night before Passover.

Getting up in the morning our first thought was again for the bread. Carefully counting, we collected the ten pieces from under the bed, the drawer, and from behind the water jug to burn them in the yard. Our neighbors were doing likewise and after we had all checked and rechecked the premises, convincing ourselves nothing leavened had been overlooked, we broke into loud congratulations.

"Happy holiday, happy holiday—next year in Jerusalem!" The women embraced as the *sahruta,* their high-pitched, warbling howl of joy echoed from one yard to the other. Surprising us with some last-minute shopping and the astonishing announcement, coming from him, that "You can't eat money, can you? Passover comes but once a year . . ." my father put a big bag of almonds in my mother's hands. Then shops bolted their doors though it was still early in the day, and while the Jews got into their new clothes Bab Salah Street lay empty in the sun, lazily stretching out in her own festive dress of freshly painted lime. Nothing more for me to do than wait, I thought, as I sat in the shelter of three big red hands that had barely had the time to dry, one just on top of me over the gate, and one on each side of the doorpost. Not even Mahmood, Kasham and Abdel Kader, my three Arab friends, were out in the street; nobody to play with but the mewing cats. Driven half crazy by the vapors of stewing lamb floating from every window, the cats came at me with trembling, upturned tails, furiously rubbing their heads against my legs.

"Patience, patience," I told them, waiting more ardently for the first stars to show up and Passover to begin than I have ever yearned for the arrival of the anointed one on his white donkey. Instead of stars, prophets or messiahs, it was my cousin Gaga who appeared on the horizon. As he hurried toward me on his short bowlegs, his broad body swung from side to side on its stunted foundation. His naked heels riding atop a pair of old black shoes made him look as if he were shuffling along in slippers. He was coming from the direction of the railway station lugging two big baskets.

"Goo, goo, goo!" he crowed excitedly as he caught sight of me. Smiling back at the warm berry eyes so eagerly striving to unite at the root of his nose, I noted with satisfaction that Cousin Gaga was unchanged. Tucked-up crumpled trousers, sleeves stopping short below, shirttails flapping in the breeze—there was still the same old orphan look about him, the same French beret dangling precariously over one useless ear. Deaf and dumb, my father's cousin was indeed an orphan, fortyish, and the friendliest, most outgoing soul I have ever met. Once a year the broom that helped Gaga sweep a living together in the shops of Tunis would be put to rest as its owner took the train to spend Passover with his family.

"Goo, gee, gack . . ." Overjoyed to see me he planted kisses where they fell, on my nose, my chin, my shoulder, while I was wriggling to get a look at the treats sticking out of the baskets. Faded skullcaps, ill-matched socks, cheap perfume, underwear that had sprung a run and toys missing either a wheel, a tail or a few fingers—from one Passover to the next Cousin Gaga would collect a vast array of slightly damaged knicknacks from the shopkeepers, his employers; one present for every member of our clan.

Our cousin's week-long kissing spree had only just begun: first the mezuzah was, of course, embraced with great effusion, then it was my father's turn, wincing at the explosion of wet busses on his ear. My little sister was drowned in kisses, and my mother had a leftover smack blown at her from a respectful distance.

Figure 3. Mother and daughters preparing for the Sabbath in an Israeli home. The special role of women in domestic rituals is transmitted over the generations. (Photo by Daniel Gilburd. Courtesy Novelty Ltd.)

CHAPTER 3

Religious Roles
of Elderly Women

Susan Starr Sered

Local practices, like those distinguishing Jews in Eastern Europe from those in North Africa, may complement, and sometimes even conflict with, authoritative interpretations. One need not compare different geographical areas to discover this. Susan Starr Sered has examined the religious understandings of elderly Middle-Eastern (mostly Kurdish) women in Jerusalem, highlighting the way that their views of religious practice, such as those connected to holidays, differ from that of the men in their families and communities. Sered met with these women over the course of a year at a municipal Senior Citizen's Day Center in Jerusalem. These women had immigrated to Palestine about the time of World War I from Iraq, Persia, and Yemen, and most could not read or write. The importance of grasping the religious views of women, however, is relevant to all traditional Jewish communities. Even when girls received some textual schooling it was different from that given to boys, and it is important to understand the differences. Sered's portrayal of how women see the holiday of Passover is usefully compared to that provided by Rafael Uzan in the previous chapter. Because of the centrality of rules concerning food in that holiday, and because women were in charge of meal preparation and ridding the house of the forbidden "leavened" foodstuffs, they emerge in their own eyes as ritual experts. Sered argues that the Passover holiday gives special meaning to the work of women not only on that occasion, but throughout the year.

From the Female Perspective

Both the rabbi and the rabbanit (rabbi's wife or learned woman) who teach Judaica lessons to the audience at the Day Center present the normative Jew as male. In her lessons the rabbanit frequently says things like, "We should not have sexual contact too frequently with women." Now, her audience is entirely female, and it is unlikely that Rabbanit Zohara intends to preach against homosexuality. Rather, she chooses to identify herself with the brand of Judaism that defines maleness as normative and femaleness as "Other." On one occasion she told the women that "everyone should learn Torah every day." Her audience, being illiterate and female, could not possibly be expected to become Torah scholars. Rather, she has described the "Jewish" norm of Torah study, which in reality is a male norm.

The rabbi's lessons also exhibit a perspective that sees male behavior and concerns as normative. The subject of one of his lessons was the holiday of Tu Bi-Shvat (New Year for the Trees), when he told the women that at the festive meal for this holiday, "You should be careful to see only one type of fruit at a time so that it will be permissible to repeat the blessing over fruit. The way to do this is to have *your wife* keep the fruit in the kitchen and only bring *you* one type of fruit at a time (my emphases)."

The women of this study consider themselves part of the larger great tradition of male-oriented, literate Judaism. They consider themselves obligated by Jewish law—a legal framework that in many ways limits women's religious opportunities and places constraints upon women's social behavior. However, these elderly women subtly reinterpret aspects of the great tradition in ways that they, as women, find fulfilling and perhaps even empowering. This chapter looks at several areas that the women consistently reinterpret: literacy, modesty, miracle stories, *halakha,* and Jewish holidays.

THE HOLIDAYS

Jewish sacred texts primarily describe male modes of sacralizing time and space, male spiritual concerns, and male religious rituals. According to the *Babylonian Talmud* (Kiddushin 29a), only men are obligated in the active observance of rituals that are connected to specific times. Official Judaism makes holy the male day, the male week, the male year.

When we think about the acts that make each holiday special, we tend to think in terms of rituals that are performed by and for men. Men come to synagogue on Rosh Ha-Shana to listen to a man blowing the *shofar*, the ram's horn. Men eat and sleep in the outdoor booth for the week of Sukkot. Men light the Hanukka candles. Men read the Scroll of Esther at synagogue on Purim. Men conduct the Passover *seder*, celebrating the Exodus from Egypt. Men stay awake all night studying sacred texts on Shavuot, the holiday commemorating the giving of the Torah to Moses at Mount Sinai. Although according to Jewish law women must participate in some (not all) of these rituals, female participation is passive, secondary, often from a distance.

The women of this study do not share that androcentric perspective. They are part of a highly sexually segregated culture in which women have traditionally had the autonomy to develop their own, usually complementary, sometimes parallel, occasionally conflicting religious world. While the women are aware of the official reasons, laws, and customs for the various holidays, they stress aspects that are not considered important when thinking about the holidays from a male perspective.

PASSOVER

The Day Center women are part of the Jewish people, and as such know about and identify with the official, male-oriented meanings and customs of each holiday. However, when they are asked, "What do you do on Passover/Purim/and so forth?" or "What is done by you (or by your ethnic group) on Hanukka/Tu Bi-Shvat/and so forth?" the answer almost always pertains to food and food preparation. I am not arguing that the women reduce the complex observances, meanings, and symbolism of each holiday to food. They certainly participate in other aspects of holiday observance. Yet, it does seem that for the women of the Day Center food is the central symbol of each holiday, and food preparation is the most important ritual activity that they as women perform.

Passover commemorates the Exodus of the Jews from Egypt. During Passover it is forbidden, according to the Pentateuch, to eat leavened bread (Exodus 12:15). In later Jewish sources, this is interpreted to include use of any of the five recognized types of grain, except the use of wheat to make *matza* (unleavened bread). Ashkenazi Jews also do not eat legumes or any other grains (such as corn or rice). Food products containing any of those substances that are not specially permitted on Passover are also forbidden. Observant Jews use special cooking and eating utensils during Passover and scrupulously clean their kitchens before the holiday in order to ensure that not one crumb of forbidden grain remains in the house.

The Day Center women view Passover as the most important, as indeed, the ultimate holiday. The women begin their Passover preparations months in advance. Despite the hard work involved in Passover cleaning, most women claim to like doing it—they like seeing everything clean and shiny. For several weeks before Passover, normal life comes to a halt. Female time and energy are directed toward but one goal—getting the house ready in time for Passover. For the month or so preceding Passover many of the women stop coming to the Day Center, and few women have the leisure time to talk to visiting anthropologists.

Jewish women have made a cult of Passover cleaning. Investing weeks creating an immaculate house is one of the most important measures of a pious woman. Not only do they sweep and wash away any crumbs of forbidden grain, but they also do a thorough spring-cleaning. Many women whitewash their kitchens before Passover; most clean their carpets, their curtains, the closets, and windows; all clean the floors, sinks, counters, kitchen cabinets, stove, and oven. Two weeks before Passover a woman walked into the Day Center saying that she had been doing Passover cleaning and "the work will kill us." When I asked the rabbi why he does not teach the women which work is really necessary (according to Jewish law it is only necessary to remove the forbidden grains, not to scrub toilets and polish windows) and which is not, he answered that even his own wife ignores what he says and performs superfluous cleaning. The women claim that they never need to ask a rabbi's advice about Passover cleaning; they already know how to do everything. Even when the women moan and groan about the work, there is a strong element of pride in their ability and willingness to carry out a divine command in what they perceive to be the correct, female manner.

Simha B. tells about Passover preparations as a young girl: "I was used to it. I grew up like that. Why shouldn't I like the work? We cleaned the pots from morning to night. Everything was copper, not like today. Each family did its own cleaning. Single girls would help pregnant women and women with many small children. When you were done, everything was clean and shiny and white. When you walked into the house, your eyes would pop open."

One of the most difficult ritual tasks that the women perform is cleaning rice for Passover. Although many Middle Eastern Jews (unlike Ashkenazi Jews) do eat rice during Passover, it must first be thoroughly checked to ensure that no forbidden grains were accidentally mixed in during harvesting or storage. To this end, the women sort the rice grain by grain, going through it seven times or more in order to clean it properly. Many of these women cook for large extended families and so sort through ten or fifteen or even more kilograms of rice in this painstaking manner. Those women whose vision is weak call on daughters and granddaughters to help them sort, but the sorting has always been and remains today a women's job.

As an outsider observing this task, I found it difficult to understand why the women felt it necessary to examine each individual grain of rice seven separate times. Did they have so little trust in their own ability to recognize different species of grains? Had some sadistic male rabbi told them that they are obligated to do this exacting and dizzying task? Further discussion with the women proved to me how difficult the shift in consciousness from an androcentric to an androgynous understanding of religion really is. These women sorted through the rice seven times because they believe that this is a form of worship. They believe that sorting the rice pleases God in much the same way that it pleases God to hear prayers and Psalms of praise. Why seven times? This is simpler. Seven is a "good" (magical, auspicious) number and the women all want "that everything should be good, for our families and for all of Israel."

The food that is eaten at the Passover *seder* takes days to prepare. In the Old Country the women baked their own *matza,* an arduous and time-consuming task. In Israel today, most buy *matza,* but continue to prepare other such traditional dishes as the head of a cow. Before all holidays, the women prepare several kinds of meat and vegetables and numerous salads. Passover cooking makes great use of nuts, which must be cracked and chopped (by hand). Some aspects of the preparation are very social; several women may gather to make a huge quantity of *haroset* (a fruit and nut dish traditionally eaten at the Passover *seder* or festive meal), which is then given out to their relatives.

Many of the women report that in the Old Country they were stricter concerning Passover food laws. For example, according to Simha, in Persia her parents did not eat coffee, oil, any milk products, or rice on Passover. If they wanted to fry they used some of the fat from the meat. She herself does not know why they did not eat these things, and when she married began eating rice because her husband's family did.

Simha relates that when she was young, her family did not eat rice or oil during Passover. (She began eating rice in Israel during the severe food shortages of World War I. At that time, the rabbi of her husband's synagogue gave permission to use rice.) Her family would make grease from the fat of the sheep, which was then prepared in a kosher manner and salted and suspended from a string into a hole and resalted every two weeks. This is how they made their own *matza:* After Passover the wheat harvest was brought in and threshed by the men. They put it in a bin and covered it with a rag. One month before the next Passover, the women cleaned it (sorted it grain by grain) one time. Then they sorted it another seven times to make sure that it was clean. They would take turns doing this in order to help each other. Then, carefully, they took the grain to the mill to grind it. Afterward, the women sifted it three times through cloth. On the day before Passover they would roll it out by hand and bake the *matza.*

The women sense God's presence helping them as they carry out their Passover preparations. One very old woman had invited all of her many children and grandchildren to her house for the Passover *seder.* When I commented that this must entail a great deal of work for her, she answered, while looking up at the ceiling, "Blessed God will help." Later, this same informant noticed that it was raining outside and declared, "This is how God cleans the streets for Passover. We can clean the insides of our houses but all the *hametz* (forbidden food) stays outside. So, God cleans the outside for us with rain."

The women do not work during Hol Ha-Moed (the five days of Passover following the *seder*). In this instance, work means laundry, sewing, and household repairs. However, they do clean and cook. Some of the women reminisce about the old days when they would go on trips during Passover, to springs and on picnics, but especially to holy tombs. "Every day of Hol Ha-Moed we went off on a trip. The girl cousins would go off alone and play and sing and dance. Life was better then." The women tell that when they were younger, they would go on picnics on the day after the last day of Passover. To the picnic they would bring meat and salads, but no baked goods. Arab friends would bring them *pitot* (flat bread), oil, olives, and other foods that Jews would not have time to prepare immediately after Passover.

Several days after Passover most women still do not come to the Day Center, and those who do come continue wishing each other "Happy Holiday." One woman even wished her friends "Shana Tova ve Hatima Tova" ("A Good Year and a Good Fate")—the traditional blessing or greeting given at Rosh Ha-Shana (the New Year), and no one looked surprised. On the folk level there seems to be an elaboration of the Talmudic parallel between Rosh Ha-Shana and Passover; customs and beliefs are relatively easily moved from one to the other.

Renewal is a major theme of Passover. Passover is a spring holiday; it comes at the end of the winter and brings with it budding trees and blossoming flowers. While at Rosh Ha-Shana Jews metaphorically begin anew, at Passover the new beginning is more tangible. The kitchen (or entire house) is repainted; leftover bits of food that have been lying in the refrigerator and kitchen cabinets are discarded; new utensils are purchased. Just as the Jewish people started over again as a nation after the Exodus from Egypt, so does the Jewish house renew itself each Passover. It seems that for the women of the Day Center, Passover, more than any other holiday, represents the possibility of another chance, of wiping the slate clean, of a fresh start.

Passover is seen by the women of the Day Center as the holy season par excellence. The first and most obvious explanation for this is the sheer amount of work involved in Passover preparation—preparations that, because they involve food and housework, fall into the female domain. And although women are in charge of the cooking and cleaning, men are obligated to live in a house that is kosher for Passover and eat food that is kosher for Passover. The men, then, are dependent upon the women for the fulfillment of the most important aspects of Passover observance. As mentioned earlier, the women of the Day Center do not go to rabbis with questions about Passover preparation—they already know what they must do. At Passover, as at no other time in the ritual year, women are ritual experts in a field that affects both men and women. In other words, men are dependent upon women's expertise for *their* correct observance of an important Jewish law.

Passover laws of cleaning and food preparation give spiritual meaning and legitimization to their everyday, female activities. Passover means that cooking and cleaning—time-consuming, repetitive, unremunerated, generally unappreciated, physically demanding activities that women do all year—become, at least temporarily, religious activities par excellence. By cooking and cleaning correctly (and let us point out that correctly means "correctly as their mothers taught them"), they enable their entire families to do what God has demanded that Jews must do.

Preparing for Passover is essentially purifying the home—removing all *hametz* or leavened food—allowing in only *matza,* the quintessentially pure food. And women are in charge of this purifying. I would suggest that the women see in Passover cleaning the translating of the most profane of activities—cleaning—into the most sacred—purification, and in Passover food the translating of the most mundane of substances—bread—into the most holy—the *matza* that God commanded the Jews to eat. In other words, Passover makes sacred women's entire profane domain: the domain of sinks, buckets, mops, and rags.

YOM KIPPUR

In contrast to Passover, the women have little to say about Yom Kippur (Day of Repentance on which Jews abstain from food) other than that it is difficult for them to fast. They remember fasting when they were pregnant, and that they often felt sick from it. Now that the women are old they do spend most of Yom Kippur in synagogue (as the men do). But when they were younger and had small children to care for, they were not able to leave the children in order to sit in synagogue.

From the perspective of women, Yom Kippur looks very different than it does from a male perspective. While men spend the whole day in prayer, repentance, and contemplation, much of women's work continues on even this holiest of days: babies still need to be cared for, changed, and fed, messes still need to be straightened up (even if only minimally), small children still need to be looked after. Whereas for men the sacred tends to be fully distinct from the profane, women, and particularly younger women, do not seem to designate certain days or times as fully or solely sacred. This may be why Yom Kippur—a holiday that is celebrated only in synagogue—is relatively unimportant for the women.

PURIM

The women of the Day Center see as the essence of the story of the Scroll of Esther (Purim) that Mordechai the Jew was raised up and evil Haman brought down. In one traditional story that they particularly like, Haman tried to persuade King Ahashueros to let him give Mordechai money instead of public honors, as the king had originally decreed. The king answered Haman, "Give him both money and honor!" Then Haman needed a haircut and a bath, but Jewish Queen Esther had ordered all the barbershops and bathhouses to shut down for the day, so that Haman had to lower himself to bathe and cut his own hair. Finally, Haman's daughter, by mistake, poured human excrement all over him, and then killed herself. While these are stories that appear in traditional Jewish sources, they would certainly be viewed as secondary to the central messages of Purim—human piety and the hidden divine machinations in the world. For the Day Center women, these "rich today, poor tomorrow" anecdotes *are* Purim. Rosa explains that one cannot depend upon anything; everything is from God. The rich person should not count on always having his wealth, nor the mighty his might. "As they say, the world turns. All one can do is have a clean heart."

Figure 4. The Passover *seder* in an American family. Women participate in the rituals and in reading the text of the haggada. (Photo by Gary Sutton.)

CHAPTER 4

Synagogue Life among American Reform Jews

Frida Kerner Furman

Reform Judaism developed in nineteenth-century Europe as Jews there sought to prove that they could fit into the wider society that had formally accepted them as citizens. They therefore stressed aspects of Judaism that it shared with Christianity, the ethical values of mono-theism, and downplayed rituals that separated them from their non-Jewish neighbors. This trend in Jewish life came to America with immigrants arriving from Central Europe in the middle of that century. Frida Kerner Furman illustrates how these sets of values continue in a Reform synagogue, on the West Coast of the United States, which supports social action as a central component of its Jewishness. Members of the synagogue are also critical of other Jews who hold on to "old" and "rigid" rituals. But a nagging question arises: "If the old rituals are abandoned, what makes a person or a group specifically Jewish?" This question is sharpened when members of the Reform synagogue encounter people with different kinds of Jewish commitment and behavior. The question of *identity* thus emerges as a major theme in thinking about and acting on one's Jewishness. This essay shows the dynamic ways in which identity is expressed, both in relation to classic Reform ideology and in relation to the specific setting of a local synagogue.

Social Activism

Temple Shalom sees itself and is seen by others as an activist congregation, given its ideological commitment to a liberal/prophetic interpretation of Judaism. Its rabbis are known for their participation in a variety of liberal causes, not infrequently causes that are unpopular in the eyes of the larger Jewish community. The congregation has been singularly supportive and respectful of the clergy's postures, even when in disagreement with them.

Many members state that the social-activist image of the synagogue motivated them to join Temple Shalom. Others say that what they like best about the temple is its social activism. The embodiment of such activism is to be found in the synagogue's social-action committee. According to the Temple's handbook, that committee

tries to implement the Jewish ideals of moral responsibility and involvement. Seeking to inform, sensitize or provoke the congregation, this active, concerned group of temple members brings issues of social importance to our attention, encourages cooperation with Jewish and non-Jewish organizations, and sponsors community interest programs. They combine personal participation with education in their efforts to cope with injustices effectively.

During the period of this study, however, social-action committee meetings and programs were very poorly attended. During one committee meeting, the disappointed members seriously considered the possibility of eliminating the committee, given the lack of general interest in its pursuits. This suggestion was effectively undermined when one member argued that, "Temple Shalom without a social-action committee is like Judaism without God!" In the passion of the moment, she probably did not realize what an apt metaphor she had selected. For, as we have seen, the commitment to social justice, with its implied commitment to social activism, is at the heart of Temple Shalom's ideology and of its identity as a Jewish institution. The social-action image perpetuates this arrangement, giving active validation and content to the ideology. The elimination of the social-action committee, however ineffective its programs, would, in fact, threaten the very identity that has been cultivated at Temple Shalom.

A cochair of this committee complained about the lack of real involvement by members in programs of social import that she considers critical. "Why do they maintain this fiction?" she asked. "It would be more honest to do away with the committee than to pretend it is alive and well." What she missed in her evaluation is the critical symbolic role that the social-action committee plays at Temple Shalom. The rhetoric about social justice needs a reality base, however weak, to maintain itself. The myth of social activism, as a fulfillment of the liberal/prophetic ideology, is kept alive in part by maintaining the structure that is responsible for activating such ideology. In this manner, the majority of members find a vicarious expression of the ideology they embrace, which gives content to their Jewish identity.

Another way members validate their definitions of Jewishness within Temple Shalom is through the activities of their rabbis, who are publicly involved in a variety of social causes. Like the social-action committee, therefore, they represent an expression of vicarious Jewish identity for members who subscribe to the synagogue's ideology.

The Jewish Tradition

Members of Temple Shalom are, on the whole, not a learned group in regard to Judaism. Indeed, many confess to having a very weak Judaic background. Given the universalistic and modernist commitments of Temple Shalom's ideology, the attitude toward the Jewish (rabbinic) tradition is characterized by ambivalence and, occasionally, hostility.[1] This tradition is seldom explored with attention to content. Rather, it is seen in contradistinction to Temple Shalom's ideology and self-identity, associating it with the premodern Jewish experience or with the practice of Orthodox Jews.

In contrast, congregants see themselves as pluralistic, individualistic, and secularized; in short, as modern members of American society. Yet however vague, selective, or fictitious their conception of the tradition might be, the latter is an important component in the process of identity construction and identity maintenance at Temple Shalom. The following example demonstrates this point.

THE YARMULKE CONTROVERSY

I select an example from the synagogue's ritual life, since rituals and ritual symbols provide such profound expressions of personal and collective identity and continuity with the past. They therefore serve to communicate values and to establish the individual's place in the collectivity. Ritual symbols are multivocal (Turner 1967, 50), so they have a multiplicity of possible meanings. How Temple Shalom understands and responds to a particular ritual symbol therefore can tell us a great deal about the congregants' identity as modern Jews. A heated, drawn-out argument over the use of yarmulkes (skullcaps) identifies rather succinctly Temple Shalom's general view of the tradition and the use of that tradition in defining the identity of its members.[2]

Orthodox Jewish males wear yarmulkes at all times as a sign of reverence. Among them, head covering at the synagogue is therefore obligatory. As Jews entered modern society, many uncovered their heads in public as an adaptation to Western style. Mandatory head covering in the synagogue was discontinued by the early Reform movement, and in some synagogues the use of yarmulkes was actually forbidden. However, in recent decades the Reform movement has moved toward the re-appropriation of once-rejected traditional rituals, and yarmulkes have optionally returned to many Reform synagogues. These are frequently made available at the entrance of the sanctuary for those who wish to wear them.

This is not the case at Temple Shalom. The norm here is the absence of head covering. Neither clergy nor the overwhelming majority of congregants wear yarmulkes during services. At most, a handful of men may be seen with their heads covered at a Sabbath service; very frequently these are guests rather than members.

A controversy began when a congregant complained to the president of the synagogue that she felt "shocked" by his wearing a yarmulke during high-holiday services. During services, the president sits on the *bima* (the raised platform in front of the sanctuary). She was willing to allow him the freedom to do what he wished as an individual, in keeping with liberal commitments. As her representative on the *bima,* however, she felt offended by his use of the yarmulke, since she had been brought up in a classical Reform synagogue where head covering was anathema.

The president took this issue to the synagogue's ritual committee, where heated debate about this and related issues took place for many months, with intermittent discussion of the topic occurring among congregants and members of the board of trustees, as well. Three issues, in effect, became the subject of discussion: (a) the right of the president to wear a yarmulke; (b) Temple Shalom's position regarding the use of yarmulkes during services; and (c) the advisability (or lack thereof) of making yarmulkes available for those wishing to wear them.

The arguments regarding these issues by clergy and members alike represent ways in which this community defines itself as a modern entity vis-à-vis their conception of the Jewish tradition. The process, in fact, illustrates mechanisms of separation from the tradition as well as means through which their identity remains linked to the tradition. Since identity in some ways is continually being constructed, the analysis of one such protracted event provides interesting clues about the sources and direction of such identity.

As we have seen, Temple Shalom sees itself as a modern and modernizing synagogue, one committed to dynamism, change, and openness to the future. This self-image is informed by a self-conscious commitment to the Reform movement, which arose in reaction against traditional Judaism. Thus, to the extent that Temple Shalom identifies with the early Reform movement, it places itself against traditionalism. Yarmulkes are therefore associated with the tradition and all its connotations. Through these discussions, the synagogue was making a gesture of self-disclosure, for to endorse the use of yarmulkes and to have them freely accessible represents a public alignment with a traditional ritual symbol, and by extension, with the presumably rejected tradition.

An analysis of these discussions reveals a dichotomization between Temple Shalom's identity and the tradition, a disjunction that serves as a mechanism of self-definition for this community of modern Jews. For, while a profound ambivalence toward the tradition is evident in the life of the synagogue, a pervasive preoccupation with such tradition also exists. In a sense, it could be said that Temple Shalom cannot live with the tradition, but it cannot live without it either. In this dynamic, one can perhaps understand the meaning that Jewish identity holds for this community of people who are alienated from the tradition of the past but, at the same time, are groping for an identity they can nonetheless call Jewish.

The tension between modernity and tradition may be briefly observed through an examination of the principal dichotomous pairs that emerge out of the discussions regarding the yarmulke:

1. Temple Shalom sees itself as committed to personal freedom, whereas the tradition is viewed as coercive and potentially threatening to the individual's freedom. Thus, the suggestion to provide yarmulkes outside the sanctuary was finally voted down on the grounds that individuals would feel coerced to wear them. A suggestion to place them in an unobtrusive place, to be available to those persons who ask for them, was finally passed; however, a related suggestion—to make such availability known to the congregation through the Temple's bulletin—was not approved. In the last analysis, in this context freedom of choice fa-

vors those who choose modernity over those who choose tradition. The nonwearer's rights were seen as more fundamental than the potential wearer's. One member captured the general feeling when he said, "If someone wants to wear a yarmulke, let him bring his own."

2. Although the rabbis are tolerant toward those who choose to wear yarmulkes, they also refer to yarmulke wearing and other traditional expressions as "mindless traditionalism." In contrast, they see themselves and the Reform movement in which they were schooled as champions of rationalism. The tradition is seen as mindless because its embrace is construed as unconsidered, not thought through and evaluated, but done somewhat under compulsion. One rabbi suggests that the disappointment with science and reason in recent years has led to the "escape from freedom" into "cultic tribalism," an escape to traditional structure, certainty, and security. Rationalism is thus seen as the rightful modern option, one open to the challenges, changes, and diversity of the present. By contrast, the tradition is seen as static and closed off to the dynamic calls of global concerns.

3. Related to this is the perception that Temple Shalom is committed to activism in the world, that is, to a social conscience that ideally leads to universalistic endeavors. Traditional concerns are thought to symbolize inwardness and privatism, the "cultivation of one's own garden," in short, particularism and parochialism. Discussions about yarmulkes are therefore denigrated by some, since they represent concerns that do not merit time, effort, and, least of all, anguish and potential congregational schism. They are seen as ridiculous, or, in the words of one rabbi, "yarmulkes are in the realm of *meshugas,*" the realm of craziness or the absurd.

4. Finally, Temple Shalom sees itself as having a different aesthetic from that found in the tradition. One member, for instance, said that he has a negative attitude to yarmulkes because he finds them "unattractive, silly looking. A yacht cap would be better," he concluded. Several members have suggested that they can appreciate other ritual symbols, such as the Torah or the menorah (a ritual candelabrum) only if they are aesthetically pleasing or "well put up."

This kind of dichotomization is evident in many facets of congregational life and is not restricted to the yarmulke issue alone. Sermons frequently discuss how the synagogue departs from the tradition. An extended adult education series, entitled "Tradition and Freedom: Being a Jew Today," was offered. Lecture series by the rabbis have also dealt with this topic, as have ongoing educational groups, such as the weekly Torah study group.

This preoccupation with the tradition thus betrays a need to deal with it in some way, however formalistically that might be. As mentioned, the tradition is often treated unidimensionally, either out of ignorance or with selective intent. This formal characterization serves a functional end: to give shape to a modern identity with a weakened Jewish content whose form contrasts radically with that attributed to the tradition. The tradition is therefore addressed through typification and dichotomization, but addressed it is nonetheless.

On the one hand, this continual dialogue with the tradition allows the Jews of Temple Shalom to assert their uniqueness, distinctiveness, and modernity. On the other, they can simultaneously affirm a link, however complex, fragmentary, or abrasive, with the tradition, a link that allows them to remain firmly—if never fully comfortably—within the boundaries of the Jewish world. As Smith suggests, "For a given group at a given time to choose this or that mode of interpreting their tradition is to opt for a *particular* way of relating themselves to their historical past and social present" (cited in Neusner 1977, 16; emphasis added).

The Question of Jewish Content

Ambivalence toward their Judaism is not an unusual characteristic of modern American Jews, given their twin desires of becoming fully acculturated to American society and of preserving their particular heritage. A related phenomenon, and one that contributes to the problem of ambivalence, is the ambiguity frequently associated by contemporary Jews with the meaning of Judaism and Jewishness. It is difficult to resolve ambivalence when the very meaning of one's Jewishness is unclear. The compartmentalization of Jewish identity (into religion, race, culture, and nationality) was a by-product of Jewish modernization.

Various responses to this problem have been offered. From the religious camp, it is suggested that unambiguous and authentic Jewish identity can only emerge when the religious dimension is placed at the heart of Jewish identity. Among ardent Zionists, nationalism seems to occupy center stage in their Jewish identities. A variety of Jews display an ethnic Jewish identity, frequently expressed through a commitment to Jewish peoplehood (Klal Yisrael); efforts on behalf of oppressed Jews in various parts of the world are expressions of such commitment. Finally, we might mention the secularist-Yiddishist movement, which, though no longer powerful, at one time was thought to provide countless Jewish immigrants with a secure and unambiguous Jewish identity.

At Temple Shalom the absence of a wholehearted commitment to any one element of the tradition—religious, nationalistic, ethnic, or cultural—results in an ambiguous sense of Jewish identity.[3] In addition, the universalistic and modernist commitments of the members of Temple Shalom a priori set themselves against an appreciation of an ancient and frequently particularistic tradition, as has been seen in the yarmulke discussion. The stress on individual choice, in the absence of traditional grounding or knowledge, leaves the individual free to construct his or her identity but rather unclear as to what the options are.

The close identification between liberalism and Judaism brings difficulties as well as benefits. One congregant who was brought up as a member of Temple Shalom had her first encounter with a more traditional Jewish orientation when she went to a weekend retreat in her late teens, a retreat sponsored by another Jewish institution. Exposed to religious and ritualistic expressions as she had never encountered at Temple Shalom, she went through a period of confusion trying to sort out what was meaningfully Jewish for her. She cheerfully arrived at the following conclusion: "I'm Jewish, but I'm also a Temple Shalom-er!" Faced with a different set of criteria for what is Jewish, the authenticity of Temple Shalom's vision broke down. She was forced to dichotomize between her Jewishness and her commitment to Temple Shalom, as if her identity as a member of Temple Shalom were not a Jewish one. By doing so, she called into question the soundness of Temple Shalom's view of Judaism. Whether or not this member's perceptions were correct is immaterial; however, the very fact that she raised this issue is of importance in this analysis. It points to the precariousness of the definition of Jewishness—and, by extension, to the precariousness of the Jewish identity—that potentially emerges from Temple Shalom's ideology.

One rabbi's perception was that what takes place at Temple Shalom, regardless of particular content, is Jewish, inasmuch as it arises from a specific ethos, that of a synagogue. For the young member just cited, it is clear that this definition is insufficient. More content is necessary for a clear conception of Judaism to stand on its own. I have discussed the centrality of the liberal/prophetic tradition in forming Temple Shalom's ideology, and I have cited the merits of such a link found by members who either had no Jewish identity prior to joining or felt alienated from Judaism or Jewishness for a variety of reasons. The openendedness of the definition of Judaism and Jewishness at Temple Shalom, in fact, acts as a kind of port of entry, or reentry, into Judaism for those people. But its very flexibility can be distressing, when it comes to comparing its meaning with that which others assign to Jewish identity or in transmitting this meaning to one's children. The latter raises the issue of Jewish continuity, an issue of great significance in the larger Jewish community today.

Members were surprisingly optimistic when asked what they felt was the future of Judaism and, more particularly, whether they were concerned about the survival of Judaism. Many seemed to feel that since Jews had survived for millennia, there was no question but that Judaism would continue. Few members addressed the nature of this Judaism in the future, that is, the question of content. Nor did people ponder how survival would be secured. The certainty about Jewish survival was more on the level of a faith commitment. One respondent, for example, felt "confident that, left to our own devices, we'll survive."

An opposite sentiment was expressed by another member:

I feel rather pessimistic about this. A strong religious thrust is missing today. There is nothing left to knit the group together as Orthodox Judaism used to do. Reform Judaism almost invites you to drop out; there is too much freedom, no directives. A gut-level feeling is missing.

This respondent was raising the question of content when he made the allusion to religion having knit the group together, an observation reminiscent of Durkheim (1964). In the absence of a strong religious center and the recognition of Temple Shalom's secularism, a void is perceived by this congregant; what is missing for him is the substance of what constitutes Judaism, the glue that attracts one to a tradition and secures one's commitment to it. In fact, one of the rabbis felt that the issue of content needs critical attention in the life of Temple Shalom. Suggesting that the synagogue is a "sleeping giant," he argued that

we have no excuses for *not* dealing with deep questions, for avoiding the gut issues of Jewish life such as, What is the nature of our faith? What do we believe in and not believe in? Why do we believe? How do we overcome the rigidity of our agnosticism? How do we reappropriate Jewish experiences? In regard to the religious school, how do we translate our religious school into important religious learning? We need to deal with these ideological issues now. We have the luxury and the necessity to do all this. The rabbis should be able to articulate what they believe and see. I see us on the cutting edge of religious development. . . . We are emancipated Jews whose Judaism doesn't have to be totally institutional or organizational in expression but should have content. Defining and developing content is important. So "sleeping giant" refers to our unfulfilled potentials.

Despite such statements of desired change, Temple Shalom, its ideology, and its identity have remained fairly stable for years, in continuity with its own traditions.

Labeling is a process that undergirds all identity construction mechanisms. We have seen that identity is structured through an identification of Judaism with liberalism/prophetism and, by extension, with a social-activist image. Identity is also forged by pitting present self-image against a formalistic perception of the tradition, using the latter as a backdrop against which a modern Judaism can be defined.

The identification with the Reform movement is a primary and much-rehearsed association at Temple Shalom. By calling themselves Reform, the rabbis or members not only define who they are ideologically but mark their boundaries as well, separating from non-Reform and joining with other Reform Jews (see Strauss 1959, 15–30). Naming is a normal human activity, and as such its practice, in and of itself, is not particularly interesting or provocative. The great frequency with which people at Temple Shalom name themselves as Reform Jews, however, perhaps bespeaks an identity that needs frequent reaffirmation, an ongoing restatement of who one is and what are the boundaries of one's identity. As one member put it, "It is a source of great pride to some members *just how Reform* Temple Shalom is."

The repeated emphasis on social activism, discussed earlier, plays a similar function, for here, too, naming serves to give substance to an otherwise unclear identity. The preoccupation with the Jewish tradition, discussed sketchily and often negatively, is an expression of labeling and identity construction as well, since it tells congregants who they are not. Finally, an undercurrent of self-deprecating humor about who they are as Jews informs some of the members' self-images at Temple Shalom. One congregant, for example, suggested that people are very "proud of being Jewish, yet concerned with being too Jewish." One member offered that Israeli folk dancing is not done at Temple Shalom because it is "too Jewish." And a congregant was jestingly silenced by another during services when the former sang along with the cantor during a traditional liturgical passage: "Shhh!" said her friend. "You can't do that here. It's too Jewish!"

That one activity or another should be perceived as "too Jewish" certainly speaks of ambivalence, as the following words from a member suggest: "Once in a while I think I've become too Jewish! I want to be a little less obviously Jewish. I find the overdisplay of Judaism to be embarrassing." Though such a statement might be interpreted in a variety of ways, it readily reveals, along with the statements quoted above, a discomfort with particularism and specificity of Jewish meanings. This may partly explain Temple Shalom's unwillingness to provide more clear and unambiguous meanings of what constitutes Jewish identity.

Notes

1. In this section, the Jewish tradition refers to the specific religio-legal culture of premodern Jewry. "Traditional" is used as the adjectival referent for that concept.

2. Yarmulke is the Yiddish term for skullcap. The more current term in Jewish circles today is the Hebrew word *kippa*. I chose yarmulke in this context because that is the term used at Temple Shalom. The use of that term is interesting, insofar as it carries associations with the tradition of the European past and not with the living tradition to be found either in the State of Israel or among many religiously involved American Jews.

3. Though Temple Shalom expends a great deal of energy on sermons and discussions about the State of Israel and the Middle East, the synagogue's Zionism is tempered by its liberalism. This Zionism is expressed through genuine efforts to understand the complexity of the Middle East situation, including the role of the Palestinian people. Such a position does not lead to an unquestioned commitment to Israeli policies or to what one member called a "hotly Zionistic" posture.

References

Durkheim, Emile. 1964. *The Division of Labor in Society.* Translated by G. Simpson. New York: Free Press.

Neusner, Jacob. 1977. *"Being Jewish" and Studying about Judaism.* Address and response at the inauguration of the Jay and Leslie Cohen chair of Judaic Studies. Atlanta: Emory University Press.

Strauss, Anselm L. 1959. *Mirrors and Masks: The Search for Identity.* Glencoe, IL: Free Press.

Turner, Victor. 1967. *The Forest of Symbols: Aspects of Ndembu Ritual.* Ithaca: Cornell University Press.

Figure 5. A contemporary Modern Orthodox Synagogue. (Photo by Daniel
Gilburd. Courtesy Novelty Ltd.)

CHAPTER 5

Orthodoxy in
an American Synagogue

Samuel C. Heilman

Beginning in the 1880s, hundreds of thousands of Jews from Eastern Europe reached America. This immigration introduced significant variation into the forms of Judaism practiced in the New World. One of these forms was orthodoxy, and it was bolstered by ultraorthodox immigrants who reached the United States after World War II and by the Holocaust. Samuel Heilman analyzes the synagogue life of what he calls modern Orthodox Jews who live in an East Coast city. They adhere to orthodoxy while assuming that Jews have to fit into the American way of life in the sphere of work and in other realms. He depicts how members of one shul, the Yiddish word for synagogue still used by English-speaking Jews, view themselves in relation to those who are less Orthodox, that is Conservative and Reform Jews, as well as in comparison to those who are so Orthodox that their religiosity at times is labeled "crazy." Members of the shul thus define themselves with reference to the extreme forms of Jewish religiosity (or lack thereof), while also contrasting themselves with Orthodox synagogues that are close to them in outlook and behavior. As in the previous selection, worshipers create a self-definition composed of both a broad ideological affiliation and an active attachment to a local congregation.

Relations with Other Jewish Sects

Although the shul members have begun to display a greater tolerance within their own ranks, they have not done so vis-à-vis other Jewish sects. Such groups are censured as either "too modern" or "too *frum*." *Frum*, or *frumkeit* (the state of being frum), is a Yiddish expression referring both to the actual practice of halakhic Judaism and to the religious outlook associated with it. Operationally, frumkeit is quite difficult to define, since its requirements vary in accordance with whom one asks for a definition. In effect, one must conclude that, for shul members, frumkeit is synonymous with conformity to Jewish observance as publicly practiced at Kehillat Kodesh. Any other form is deviant.

There is no lack of local embodiments of both extremes. The "too modern" Jews of Temple Or Chodosh, directly across the street, whose doctrine denies, practically as well as ideologically, the legitimacy of halakha and seeks instead to "reform" it, symbolize the excesses of modernity and are often targets of derision. For example, when Or Chodosh closes its doors for the summer while its membership is on vacation, the shul members jokingly ask if Heaven has closed its doors for vacation as well.

Shul members who make some complaint about Kehillat Kodesh prayers are derisively told to "go across the street," with the implication being that nothing in Kehillat Kodesh could be as disturbing as what is found among Reform Jews. No one dares step into the Or Chodosh building, to say nothing of worshiping there, for to do so would be to step outside, in symbol and in fact, the border defining the Orthodox community. The members of each synagogue are faceless and nameless to one another, each representing a totally alien and unacceptable viewpoint rather than a real person. As such, it is possible for the shul Jews to call the members of Or Chodosh *goyim* (Gentiles)—people totally outside the Jewish cosmos. Undoubtedly, it also makes it possible for Or Chodosh people to think of their neighbors as "fanatics"—people completely beyond the pale of contemporary normalcy.

Although the members of Moriah, the Conservative synagogue two blocks away, are subject to criticism for excessive modernity, the attitude toward them is less extreme. Unlike the Reform Jews, these people have "conserved" some of the legitimacy of halakha even as they affirm the imperatives of modernity. They may, therefore, have much in common with their modern Orthodox brethren. In fact, the congregations maintain contact in various ways. Friendships are shared. Moreover, some shul members were originally Moriah congregants. Others teach in its Hebrew school, while some occasionally attend public events held within its doors.

When an Orthodox minyan or quorum is unavailable during the week, shul members may occasionally even worship at Moriah. The halakhic transgressions that distinguish it from Kehillat Kodesh are, for all intents and purposes, removed on weekdays. Primary among these is the mixed-sex seating, which Moriah permits during public prayer. Since women do not customarily come to pray on days other than Sabbath and holy days, and since, liturgically, the conservative prayers are fundamentally indistinct from those of orthodoxy, weekday communal prayer at Moriah is conceivable, if not encouraged, for shul members.

Although differences in Jewish practice divide Moriah from Kehillat Kodesh, the criticisms of Moriah's excessive modernity are associated more with ideology than with practice. While the modern Orthodox Jews in the shul, along with the Conservative Moriah people, recognize the mutual demands of Judaism and modernity, the latter, unlike the former, consider both equally important. Where the shul Jews have allowed their support of modernity to remain essentially de facto, the Moriah members have rationalized and ideologically legitimated halakhic change de jure. One might see here an analogue between the criminal and the revolutionary as Merton describes them.[1] Both engage in the same act; yet for the former the act does not challenge the legitimacy of the law, while for the latter the transgression is revolutionary, challenging the rightfulness of the law. In terms of this formula, shul Jews can accept themselves as "criminals," while they criticize the members of Moriah as "revolutionaries."

Hence, whenever a shul member joins in Moriah activities, he accompanies his actions with lengthy explanations of his motives, lest his participation be interpreted as a wavering in his doctrinal commitment to halakha. The ambivalence suggested here is most clearly expressed in the comments of two members, both of whom have attended Moriah events. One derisively explains that Moriah is peopled by a preponderance of *trefniaks* (a Yiddishism describing those whose observance of Judaism is literally not kosher; it is within the Jewish cosmos but not properly so); the other remarks:

I don't go for this whole idea of the breakdown between Orthodox and Conservative. I mean, because there are people that I know that go to Moriah, which is Conservative, that are just as much practicing Jews as people that come to an Orthodox shul.

All members, however, agree that excessive modernity is wrong, and even this relatively tolerant member went on to say:

On the other hand, I don't think you would find someone going to a Reform temple who in his own private life would be as observant as someone who would go to an Orthodox shul.

At its worst, excessive modernity arouses deep feelings of antipathy, as exemplified in one member's analysis of the consequences of becoming "too modern." He explains:

Anyone who lets things go like that gives his children a sort of antireligion. You can't get so modern like Conservative or Reform Jews—I mean, you need some guidelines.

This statement, and the vehemence with which it was spoken, expresses antipathy; yet antipathy, as Toennies explains,

can easily, as a result of close acquaintance or other motives, be transformed into real sympathy . . . the same or similar interests are sufficient to arouse sympathy to the extent that such similarities are in the consciousness of those involved, and by the same token contrary interests will evoke antipathy.[2]

A closer look reveals that the shul members feel certain sympathies for even the most modern of Jews.

To the extent that the modern Orthodox Jew of Kehillat Kodesh is conscious that his interest in modernity is not essentially different from that of other kinds of Jews, he will sympathize with their goal if not with their means. But when he sees that the means these other Jews have chosen lead to an undermining of halakhic observance, toward "a sort of antireligion," which is intrinsically different from his own, antipathy overwhelms any feelings of sympathy.

Yet even the deepest feelings of antipathy toward the "too modern" are mitigated by one very important factor. Toennies suggests this additional ground for sympathy when he writes:

We shall usually have a certain degree of sympathy, even though this may be small, for those who side with us, whether we have known them before or come to know them only as fellow fighters, comrades, countrymen, or even home folks, or as colleagues, or as persons of the same faith.[3]

At the very least, the threatening non-Jewish world makes the shul members realize that they share a common faith and ultimate destiny with members of Or Chodosh and Moriah. Thus, for example, when one weekday morning someone discovered a sticker that overnight had been placed on the door of Or Chodosh and that proclaimed, "Free Rudolf Hess," several shul members took the sign down, pointing out that, "We've got to do it, even for them and even though they probably don't know that they're Jews like us." Mingled with the general antipathy aroused by issues of frumkeit comes the inevitable sympathy for "persons of the same faith."

While those who are "too modern" are criticized for insufficient frumkeit, the "too frum" are faulted for the opposite excesses. In the Dudley Meadows area, one outstanding source of such Jews is the Sprawl City Yeshiva (often called simply "the Yeshiva"). Although primarily an academy for the advanced study of Talmud—rabbinic law and lore—it also has a chapel, which serves as a shul for students, teachers, and others who wish to pray with them. Though some Kehillat Kodesh members occasionally worship there and consider themselves as frum as the Sprawl City Yeshiva people, the Yeshiva is fundamentally a traditional Orthodox institution. Known outside Sprawl City and America as a bona fide place of Orthodox Jewish learning, the Sprawl City Yeshiva is the first stop for the traditional Orthodox Jews who come to Sprawl City and Dudley Meadows. Hence the attitude expressed toward the Yeshiva may be seen, at least in part, as a reflection of the general attitude toward the "more frum."

Perhaps the first step to take in considering the Kehillat Kodesh feelings about traditional Orthodox Jews is to define "more frum." These traditional Orthodox Jews have been described as relatively isolated from contemporary secular America and concerned almost completely with Jewish life and observance. Of course traditional Orthodox and modern Orthodox Jews must be considered as ideal types that reality approximates but with which it never fully complies. Nevertheless, the more frum the person, the more willing he is to concern himself with the demands of halakhic observance and the Jewish world which it defines and the less energy and effort he will expend on other demands. Thus, for example, for the more frum, occupation becomes completely subservient to Jewish observance. Unlike the modern Orthodox Jew, who makes certain compromises in the pursuit of both an occupational career and a halakhically ordered life, the more frum will pursue only those careers that negligibly disturb halakhic observance. They become yeshiva teachers, ritual slaughterers, kosher butchers, Hebrew book dealers, scribes, and, in general, holders of occupations directly involved in Jewish institutions. They thereby force themselves into a community that can support such institutions, one necessarily filled with other traditional Orthodox Jews.

Though the modern Orthodox Jew also looks for an area enabling him to practice Judaism, he is satisfied with a minimum of institutions: day school, *mikve* (ritual baths), kosher butcher, and shul. His more-frum counterpart demands more. He looks for a Sabbath-observant bakery whose baked goods are not only above suspicion in terms of *kashrut* (kosherness) but whose bakers make the proper ritual benedictions over the breads when baking them. He looks not only for the mandatory mikve for women but also for a separate mikve for men, whose immersion is voluntary, and one for dishes, which are to be immersed before initial use. He looks not only for a school for his children but also for a group of learned adult Jews with whom he can regularly engage in Jewish scholarship. Observing halakha means learning all about it, a full-time occupation for which the occupations of the modern Orthodox Jew scarcely leave enough time. The more-frum Jew needs a nearby source of Jewish books for purchase and perusal. In short, the more frum need more Jewish institutions than the modern Orthodox Jews. Indeed, in Dudley Meadows, the Sprawl City Yeshiva students and faculty have in large measure been responsible for bringing many such institutions into existence.

The more frum also practice more of the halakha than their counterparts at Kehillat Kodesh. To accept the notion of a necessary minimum level of observance, as the modern Orthodox Jews do, is anathema to the more frum. Thus, for example, the members of Kehillat Kodesh may miss a prayer now and then when they are busy at work, but the more frum pray three times daily, stopping any secular activity they may be engaged in when it inhibits prayer. Or the more frum regularly engage in the study of Torah, the entire corpus of Jewish law and lore, while the modern Orthodox Jews at Kehillat Kodesh do so much less regularly, putting secular pursuits first.

When queried about halakhic observance, however, the shul Jews will more often than not express many of the same doctrinal beliefs as the more frum. In fact, through interviews one might gain the impression that no differentiation at all exists between traditional and modern Orthodox Jews, for both would express essentially the same thoughts about the importance and imperative of halakha. The distinctions between them become clear only in a comparison of how halakha is implemented, acted out, and indeed lived by each group.

The comparison might best be understood by using Fichter's distinctions among complete ideology, practical ideology, and actual behavior.[4] The first of these constitutes the "unattainable positive ideal of spiritual perfection towards which all parishioners should be striving." The second is "the value system which guides them in everyday life," which "seems to be a mental working compromise" between ideal spirituality and the demands of the real world. Finally, "the actual behavior of parishioners is usually assumed to be in accord with the second ideology, although it is 'expected' to follow the first." For the more frum, practical ideology must remain relatively indistinguishable from complete Jewish ideology, with actual behavior being an effort to live up to the latter. Though the shul members subscribe to the complete ideology, their actual behavior suggests a practical ideology that differentiates them from their more-frum brethren. De jure all Orthodox Jews, traditional and modern, are in agreement; de facto they remain at odds.

One may, incidentally, use the same schema to explain the relationship between the shul Jews and their "too-modern" kin. Though modern Orthodox and Conservative Jews appear to coincide in much of their actual behavior, they differ in that the Conservatives, by replacing complete ideology with its practical counterpart, have given a greater legitimacy to their actual behavior. As for Reform Jews, shul members (qua Jews) share with them neither complete nor practical ideology nor any actual behavior.

To return to the attitude toward the more frum: if actual behavior and its associated practical ideology distinguish modern from traditional Orthodox Jews, criticism of the latter must then focus on halakhic practice. The following characterization of the more frum by a shul member suggests that such is the case:

I think there's a difference between Orthodox and orthoprax. Some of these so-called Orthodox are nothing more than orthoprax. Orthopractice is just doing what everybody else [among the Orthodox] does, without understanding it or meaning it. People who are orthoprax may call themselves Orthodox, but they really are not so frum.

Though admitting that some Jews practice halakha more strictly than others, the speaker points out that such practice is subject to evaluation

of its genuineness and does not always indicate frumkeit. Being frum requires, additionally, comprehension and religious intent. Of course, religious intent, as well as understanding the point, purpose, and reason-
ing behind observance, is insufficient if one does not actually practice.
The same member went on to say:

People who are Conservative and who observe and understand everything
they believe—they call themselves religious, but they're not really frum.

One must practice even if one does not comprehend or believe everything. Clearly, being a frum Jew, as one ought to be, is an ideal to be
strived for but not easily reached.

Some Jews are unquestionably more frum than others. These are
the halakhic virtuosi who both understand and practice Jewish law and
tradition. Usually these people are officially ordained rabbis (although
they need not pursue a rabbinic occupation); but sometimes virtuosity
is recognized when individuals take the role of teacher in various study
groups or exhibit expertise in halakhic questions of everyday life. Of
such people it may be said, "He could have gotten *smikha* [rabbinic or-
dination] if he wanted to; he just never bothered." Such people cannot
be criticized on the grounds of orthopractice. Other ways to censure are
found. Thus one such Orthodox man, a recognized halakhic virtuoso
by virtue of his leadership in various study groups, is described as "crazy
frum" (senseless and totally unsound in his Jewish observance) by members of Kehillat Kodesh because, among other practices, he recites
psalms as he works or invites people whom he is with at prayer time to
join him in worship. At the same time that this man is thought "crazy,"
he is respected for his scholarship; he is crazy not because he believes
in the halakhic doctrine that calls for such behavior—after all, he is a
scholar and knows what the law actually calls for—but because he follows through in his actual behavior. Again, one must remember that, if
pressed to explain the label "crazy frum," members of Kehillat Kodesh
will ultimately explain that this man is probably right in his observance
and that they were just kidding. Like a slip of the tongue, the label becomes denied on closer scrutiny and when the labeler is asked to defend
the "slip."

As stated before, the Sprawl City Yeshiva is the local embodiment of
the traditional Orthodox milieu. In talking about strict ritual observance, one member says of Kehillat Kodesh, "We probably don't come
up to specs. The Yeshiva probably comes closest to it." While shul mem-

bers admit, when questioned, their collective deviance from the Orthodox standard, their behavior and unsolicited comments belie the sincerity of this admission. For example, although all Kehillat Kodesh boys of
high-school age attend a yeshiva (girls, not ritually required to study
Torah, go to day schools, which, although completely Orthodox, do
not emphasize intense and advanced Jewish scholarship), most do not
attend the local one. Members readily explain why they have sent their
sons to more modern out-of-town yeshivas. One characterizes the local
school as "pretty good in Jewish stuff, but it's not so hot in English
[that is, secular studies]." Another points out the one-sidedness of the
Sprawl City Yeshiva in the fact that students who want to study Jewish
mystical texts or anything else not in the curriculum have had to sneak
away to a midnight class at his home, given by a teacher imported from
New York. A third member remarks in anger, "The kids there aren't
even allowed to read the *New York Times*—too modern, especially the
movie page." A fourth criticizes the preparation for life which the
Sprawl City Yeshiva provides: "They make 'em study all day and never
tell 'em they have to go out and get a job." Still another parent explains
why he sent his son to a school in Baltimore:

I went with my son, Amitai, to check out the place, and I decided against
sending him there. I didn't like the types there. [Why?] Well, they're more
isolated and also they have the attitude of "I'm the best, and everything I
do is right"—that there's only one way to be a Jew. I understand why they
need such an attitude, as a defense; but still, I don't like it.

Here, then, in action—through the avoidance of sending their sons
to the local yeshiva—as well as through words, members of Kehillat Kodesh make it clear that they are not one and the same as the Orthodox
Jews which that local institution has come to represent and that they do
not want their sons to become Orthodox Jews of that "type." Although
shul members "understand" and perhaps even sympathize with the
more Orthodox way of life, they still do not "like" it and wish, therefore, to distinguish themselves from it.

This mixture of sympathy and antipathy that the members of Kehillat
Kodesh feel toward the traditional Orthodox Jews of Dudley Meadows
suggests, in Merton and Barber's terms, "an ambivalence [that] comes
to be built into the very structure of social relations." The two social
structures—one, whose associated roles and behaviors define a people
dually committed to the contemporary and Jewish worlds; the other,

whose roles and behaviors stress a cosmos totally controlled and defined by Jewish law and observance—in mutual opposition *and* apposition "generate the circumstances in which ambivalence is embedded."[5]

Although their attitudes toward both the more and the less frum help to delineate the identity of "the modern Orthodox Jews of Kehillat Kodesh," reactions to other groups who would define themselves equally as modern Orthodox Jews complete the identification of the subjects of this study. If a group may refer its behavior to, and define itself in terms of, those it is not, it must also be prepared to characterize itself in terms of those similar to itself. In other words, for Kehillat Kodesh Jews, not only the more and less but also the equally frum serve as a reference group.[6]

Since evaluation is implicit in any such comparisons, two groups likely to be defined as identical scrupulously scrutinize each other. Each realizes that on the basis of the *other* group's action, *it* may be judged. Indeed, two groups that are alike frequently threaten each other's identity the most; for, once adjudged identical, not only by others but by themselves, any discrepant activity on the part of one group calls the other's activity into question as well. When such activities are closely related to identity, discrepancy becomes an even more crucial problem. The two cannot be alike and yet also different. If they do not change together, one must be evaluated as deviant and the other as normative.[7]

Displaying concern with such issues, shul members frequently compare their institution with other modern Orthodox congregations, especially those nearby, to see if a genuine similarity exists. Liturgical form and style, frumkeit versus modernity, and the extent of active participation in shul life and other matters of Jewish or institutional behavior become the crucial criteria of comparison. While there may be other similarities, for example, political-party affiliations or economic status, these are not part of the group's concern with its Jewish or institutional self-identification.

For Kehillat Kodesh, three other shuls serve as possible comparisons: (1) the Happiton shul, from which Kehillat Kodesh sprang, (2) a recently formed shul in the nearby suburb of Drumlin, an area to which several Dudley Meadows émigrés have moved, and (3) a *shtibble* (a Yiddish term meaning "little house" and referring to a small shul, used primarily for prayer and commonly under the complete authority of one man) called Ram Sholom. Ultimately, each of these other institutions is distinguished from Kehillat Kodesh and criticized.

Thus, one member compares the size of the Happiton minyan with the Kehillat Kodesh quorum and finds the former wanting:

I've gone to Happiton, but you can't always count on a minyan there. Every time you go, you're really taking a gamble. All right, here we have problems too, but there even on a Friday night [Sabbath] you're taking a gamble.

Another member criticizes Happiton for using, as part of the weekday quorum, the beggars who daily solicit funds from the Dudley Meadows synagogues:

Even if we're one man short, we're not gonna have to ask one of them [the beggars] to make the minyan [to be the tenth man] like they do at Happiton. They'll take anyone in off the street, because they can't count on their own people to come to the minyan.

A third explains his absence on a recent Sabbath morning by saying he attended Happiton services, but he laughingly adds that only fourteen were present at this most important service of the Jewish week; that is to say, symbolically there was no minyan even if halakhically there was one.

Hence, while tacitly admitting that Happiton is a place where they may pray without calling their orthodoxy into question (for people do so without heavier penalty than a joke or two at their expense), shul members stress that, although the two shuls might appear to be alike, the informed insider recognizes crucial differences between them.

Shul members do not limit themselves to informing insiders about such differences. Joint activities with other shuls are shunned because outsiders might then think that if these institutions do things together they might in some way be considered identical. This is especially the case when such activities pertain to Jewish identity–linked behavior. Thus, for example, although both Happiton and Kehillat Kodesh have trouble gathering a daily minyan, they refuse to pool their participants and thereby assure a quorum. Such a union might blur the differences between them. Or both shuls schedule Torah study groups during the week, but at identical times, thereby assuring that no one will be able to attend both classes; thus they are saved from being regarded as having a unified curriculum. Even the topics of these classes are similar, with one group studying the laws of marriage, the other those of divorce. Although members of each shul may not be conscious of this competition, the outsider cannot help but notice it.

Similar efforts at differentiation occur with regard to the Drumlin shul. Here, however, the distinction is made, not with regard to the collective level of participation at the prayer services and the frumkeit which that suggests, but in terms of the actual degree of Jewish behavior and observance on the part of individual members of each shul. With scorn one member of Kehillat Kodesh remarks of the Drumlin shul, "I don't even know for sure if everyone there keeps *shabbos* [the ritual observances of the Sabbath]." Another member goes further and says, "That place is filled with *mechallelei shabbos* [desecrators of the Sabbath and its laws who do not keep even the minimum halakhic observances defining modern Orthodox Judaism]." Indeed, when the members of the Drumlin shul approached the Kehillat Kodesh congregation for financial help in building a mikva in the Drumlin area (suggesting by this that the effort be a joint one), the latter refused, saying, "They have enough money in Drumlin to put up a stained-glass window in the shul but not for a mikve. You know why? Because only about ten people there would use one." Another Kehillat Kodesh man adds, "They claim that they had a mikve in the plans, but that shows that they are only frum on paper." To admit that the Drumlin shul is any kind of modern Orthodox Jewish institution is to admit that the definition of modern Orthodox Judaism does not have to include Sabbath observance or mikva use. It is thus to call into question many Kehillat Kodesh members' activities. Accordingly, shul members reserve what is perhaps their greatest scorn and antipathy for this new modern Orthodox shul. In addition, since it is "new"—younger in institutional life (and also located in Drumlin, an area to which many Dudley Meadows people think of moving)—it is a greater threat than the other shuls, which are older, for it might be identified as illustrative of the modern Orthodox Jewry of the future. This occurrence would threaten not only present but future Kehillat Kodesh identity as well. Indeed, the president has on several occasions publicly announced that he has heard from several former members now living in Drumlin, and all admit to missing Kehillat Kodesh and to wishing they had never left.

Of the three other shuls, Ram Sholom is perhaps the one toward which the Kehillat Kodesh members feel the least antipathy, undoubtedly in part because of the small size of the institution. Moreover, Ram Sholom is neither stable enough nor sufficiently known outside the Orthodox community of Sprawl City to act as a threat by possibly being identified with Kehillat Kodesh. Of the three, it comes closest to traditional Orthodoxy, and many of its weekday members disappear on the Sabbath to attend prayer services at the Sprawl City Yeshiva instead of at the shul. Perhaps the major difference, other than size, that the Kehillat Kodesh membership points to is the fact that Ram Sholom is under the nearly total control of one man. Even one of this man's sons, who attends Kehillat Kodesh, admits that this fact more than any other differentiates the two shuls. In other words, since member involvement is limited at Ram Sholom, it is not considered a shul so much as a shtibble. Identifying it by this latter label removes its threat as an "identical" institution. Once something is defined as different, one need no longer worry about its definition standing for one's own. Such is the case for Ram Sholom.

One can see, then, that the members of Kehillat Kodesh differentiate themselves not only from groups that are obviously different from them in Jewish terms—the less frum and the more frum, who have institutionalized these differences in terms of the sectarian identifications of Reform and Conservative or traditional Orthodox and Chassidic—but also from groups which at first glance seem quite like them. The integrity of the shul is maintained.

Of course they must, lest they succumb to feelings of isolation, identify themselves as part of a larger group that also sees itself in similar terms. Though I have emphasized the distinctions between and feelings of antipathy expressed toward other Jews, I should also point out that much time is spent outlining similarities to other Jews and congregations. Part of this effort is accomplished by Kehillat Kodesh's membership in a national federation of Orthodox shuls, all made up of essentially similar Jews.

In addition to stressing its national affiliation with other modern Orthodox shuls, the members often compare themselves to the members of other Orthodox shuls. The vehicle for such comparisons is often conversations with guests and strangers who have come from another Orthodox shul. One hears, for example, how similar the liturgical style at Kehillat Kodesh is to that of the stranger's shul: "You have kids lead the end of the service here? We do too." One hears comparisons of members' occupations: "We have lots of professors in our shul too." One hears discussion of differences that are seen as minor and as not affecting institutional identity: "You sing this? We say it quietly and later on in the *davening* [praying]." Indeed, strangers and guests are made to feel that Kehillat Kodesh is but one stop like others on the modern Orthodox Jewish railroad, one part of a larger network. It is not alone but is linked inextricably to other like institutions.[8] Only where these institutions, like the local ones, might serve to undermine the identity of

Kehillat Kodesh by presenting a successfully discrepant identity or set of actions is the similarity denied, and is antipathy expressed.

Notes

1. Merton, *Social Theory and Social Structure*, pp. 185–246.
2. Toennies, *Community and Society*, pp. 239–40.
3. Ibid., p. 239.
4. Fichter, *A Southern Parish*, p. 260.
5. Merton and Barber, "Sociological Ambivalence," pp. 92, 95.
6. For a full discussion of reference-group theory, see Merton, *Social Theory and Social Structure*, esp. pp. 286–88.
7. This is often the case when members of Kehillat Kodesh try to explain the difference between them and other Orthodox Jews, specifically Chassidim, to outsiders who see all Orthodox Jews as identical and cannot account for the fact that Kehillat Kodesh people do not all wear beards, satin coats, and so forth.
8. Jews in general and Orthodox Jews in particular tend to be highly endogamous. One of the more interesting ways in which Orthodox Jews of all types express links to other Orthodox Jewish congregations is through kinship lines. The more Orthodox and the more isolated they are from others, the more endogamous they are. Thus members of one Orthodox shul are very often related to members of another. Interestingly, while modern Orthodox Jews have such kin too, these kin are frequently members of Orthodox shuls outside the immediate geographic area. The cosmopolitanism of modern Orthodox Jews does not do away with their endogamy, for many of the things that they value in a spouse are concerned with Orthodox Jewishness; but it does raise the possibility that the Orthodox kin will be located far away. Thus, while much of Sprawl City Orthodoxy is kin linked, Kehillat Kodesh and Happiton, the two modern Orthodox shuls (I do not know about Drumlin) have members whose Orthodox kin are not in Sprawl City but rather in other Orthodox communities—in New York, Boston, Baltimore, and so on. Hence, when members of Kehillat Kodesh express linkage to modern Orthodox shuls elsewhere, they often base such assertions on the fact that they have relatives in these other shuls.

References

Fichter, S. *A Southern Parish*. Chicago: University of Chicago Press, 1951.
Merton, R. K. *Social Theory and Social Structure*. Rev. ed. New York: Free Press, 1968.

————, and Barber, Elinor. "Sociological Ambivalence." In *Sociological Theory, Values, and Sociocultural Change: Essays in Honor of Pitrim A. Sorokin,* E. A. Tiryakian, ed. New York: Free Press, 1963.

Toennies, Ferdinand. *Community and Society.* Translated by C. P. Loomis. New York: Harper, 1957.

Figure 6. Reading the Torah in a prayer service influenced by the Havura movement. (Photo by Daniel Gilburd. Courtesy Novelty Ltd.)

CHAPTER 6

Worship in
the Havura Movement

Chava Weissler

American Jews continued religious trends that had evolved in Europe
but also refashioned them in response to new historical developments.
In this chapter, Chava Weissler presents a case of a *havura,* a form of
prayer group that emerged among young people whose background
was in Conservative Judaism but who sought to create a meaningful
and intimate religious experience that did not depend on large synagogues or on formal institutional affiliation. They drew on traditional
forms of davening (an Americanized form of the Yiddish word meaning to pray) but also expressed the values of the counterculture in the
United States of the 1960s, leading them to introduce innovations in
the formerly standard service. The most prominent change was the
inclusion of women in the minyan, or prayer quorum, and their participation in all the leadership roles of the service. The selection that
follows describes how one woman gradually gained the skills and self-
confidence to lead the *havura* in worship. That achievement implied
ongoing introspection and the gaining of knowledge, both of which
were aided by a close set of ties with individual members of the *havura* and a positive relationship to the group as a whole.

The Problem of Worship

Religious worship is a particularly acute problem for the
modern individual.[1] Since worship services require an axiomatic and

taken-for-granted character to succeed as ritual, they are easily disrupted by the hesitations of the modern consciousness. The modern participant is apt to question them at almost every step, asking: Do I understand what the prayers are saying in their archaic and special language? Do I know how to participate in the ritual, when to stand, sit, or kneel and why? Do I experience the world as the liturgy describes it, as a Vale of Tears, for example? Do I feel the feelings the prayers express, such as gratitude toward God and remorse for sin? Do I believe what the prayers say about the nature of the universe, for example, that it is created by God and operates under divine guidance? And finally, granted that I wish to pray at all, why should I say these particular prayers?

For the American Jewish worshiper, some of these problems are heightened. The liturgy is in a foreign language, Hebrew, which is written in an unfamiliar alphabet. Traditional Jewish worship contains many small ritual acts: bowing, taking small steps backward and forward, kissing the fringes of the *talit,* the ritual prayer shawl. Many contemporary Jews do not know Hebrew or, even if they do, may have an inadequate grasp of the archaic and poetic language of the liturgy. Further, they are often unfamiliar with the ritual of traditional worship and have not been socialized to see it as a means of spiritual expression.

Equally important is the gap between the worldview of the traditional liturgy and that of the modern Jewish worshiper. The liturgy describes a world of exile and oppression that is foreign to the experience of the American Jew. It is infused with a psychology of sin and retribution that is not one the modern Jew seeks to embrace. And it makes statements about the nature of God, history, and the Jewish people that the modern Jew may find difficult to affirm. For Jewish worship to be meaningful to the participant, he or she must bridge the chasm opened up by these difficulties created by modern consciousness and bridge it in such a way as to restore to the ritual some of its axiomatic character.

The effort to overcome these difficulties was the impetus behind the development of Reform and, later, Conservative liturgies and adaptations of the ritual of worship. Both Reform and Conservative congregations strove to create a decorous and inspiring worship service, rejecting what they saw as the hard-to-follow liturgical performance and undignified informality characteristic of traditional Ashkenazic houses of prayer. Further, they coped with lack of Jewish knowledge on the part of the congregants in two ways. First, they provided prayerbooks with vernacular translations of the liturgy and, indeed, recited some of the liturgy in the vernacular. Second, they turned over the leadership of the services to a professional staff of rabbi and cantor. In addition, the Reform movement in particular altered the liturgy, removing or rewriting the portions it regarded as offensive to modern sensibilities.[2]

The Havura Movement

In all these changes, Reform and Conservative Judaism were, of course, influenced by the prevailing intellectual currents and standards of behavior. For example, both the rationalism of nineteenth-century Protestantism and its manner of worship contributed to the evolution of Reform services. Thus, when quite different intellectual currents and social norms became widespread in American society in the late 1960s, it was not surprising that another group of Jews hammered out a different way to approach Jewish worship. These Jews rejected such features of worship as formal decorum and professional leadership, which represented the very solutions arrived at by their predecessors. In turn, they were attracted to some aspects of traditional Ashkenazic worship (informality, broad participation in the ritual) repugnant to earlier reformers. Further, rejecting the literalism characteristic of Reform reading of the liturgy, they developed an allegiance to the traditional prayer book. Yet the liturgy and manner of worship they developed contained many nontraditional features, such as equal participation in rituals for women, circular seating, and readings in English, that were drawn from the surrounding American culture, particularly the counterculture.

These Jews were the founders and members of the *havura* ("fellowship") movement. They made Sabbath services, which they referred to as "davening," the centerpiece of their efforts to reconcile their love of Jewish tradition and their modern consciousness and values.[3] The havura movement arose out of the counterculture and the heightened ethnic consciousness of the late 1960s. Its founders were critical of mainstream American Jewish institutions, both religious and communal, which they regarded as sterile, hierarchical, divorced from Jewish tradition, and lacking in spirituality. Havura Jews sought warm, personal ties in close-knit communities and deepened spiritual experience in less formal styles of prayer. True to their countercultural roots, havura communities are committed to an egalitarian social structure, rotation of social and religious leadership roles, and equal access to such roles for women and men. Yet, true to their attraction to tradition, members of havurot typically have a high level of Sabbath, festival, and dietary law observance. By the mid-1970s, havurot existed in most large East Coast cities, and in some Midwestern and West Coast cities as well.[4]

The Dutchville Minyan

The "Dutchville Minyan," a havura in a large East Coast city, was founded in 1974 by about a dozen people who wanted a less formal, more participatory service than that offered by the Dutchville Jewish Center, the Conservative congregation to which some of them belonged.[5] The membership grew rapidly. By 1979 there were about ninety adult members and about twenty-five children. The Minyan held Sabbath and holiday services, study groups, potluck dinners on occasional Friday nights, kiddushes, picnics, and parties.[6] Members also socialized with each other informally.

The desire for a particular sort of Sabbath morning service, however, was the reason the group was founded, and this service remained its focal activity. The Minyan's service contrasted with that of the Dutchville Jewish Center. On Saturday mornings, in the Center congregation's sanctuary, the rabbi and cantor led a dignified service. The worshipers, sitting in plush seats under a high, vaulted ceiling, quietly murmured their prayers and listened to the rabbi's sermons and the cantor's solos. They used the Conservative prayer book, reciting most of its rather traditional liturgy in Hebrew, and some of it in English. As in most Conservative and Reform synagogues, the congregation was somewhat detached from the main ritual focus: the rabbi and cantor stood on the *bimah,* a raised platform at the front of the sanctuary, about five feet above the congregation. The beautifully carved doors of the Holy Ark, which contained the Torah scrolls, rose behind them. The congregation's dress reflected the formality of the setting: most men wore suits or sport jackets, and the women wore dresses or skirts and blouses.

In the Minyan's service, by contrast, participants met in a small room in the Hebrew school wing of the synagogue building. They sat in a circle, some on chairs, and some on the floor. The Torah scroll was laid on a table inside the circle, covered with a *talit*. Infants and toddlers crawled and played in the back of the room. Some participants wore jeans, and many of the women were in slacks. Some women, as well as men, wore the fringed prayer shawls. Each week, a different member (drawn from those with the requisite skills and knowledge) led the service, departing from the traditional liturgy at times, introducing poetry or other readings in English and his or her own interpretations of the prayers. The service was chanted in the kind of euphonious cacophony typical of Ashkenazic worship, and everyone joined enthusiastically in the singing that punctuated the service. The sermon was replaced by a "Torah discussion" in which participants could react to the biblical portion of the week, expressing doubts and difficulties with the tradition in a warm and supportive atmosphere. It was this sense of warmth, intimacy, and participation that members sought in creating their own service. And it was through the medium of this service that the Minyan sought to bridge the chasm between the modern consciousness and experience of its members and the traditional liturgy. To that end, the Minyan developed multiple strategies for reframing and reinterpreting the liturgy. The remainder of this essay explores these strategies and the meanings they convey.

I shall argue that the distinctive format of Minyan davening—from its circular seating arrangement to its liturgical innovations—embodies the key themes of Minyan worship: the religious character of interpersonal interaction and intimacy and the creation of meaning through personal emotional and intellectual response to tradition. The leader of services bears the chief responsibility for articulating this meaning, made anew each time. As interpretive strategies, he or she may use music, readings, and brief statements, called *kavanot*. Paradoxically, such interpretation allows the worshiper to participate in the davening, while still making manifest the difficulty of that participation. By means of its stress on the interpersonal dimension of worship, and by means of these strategies, Minyan davening expresses modern meanings while making use of traditional language.

The Service: Judi's Davening

To explore these strategies and meanings, I turn to the description and analysis of the preparation for and performance of a particular service. In February 1979, Judi, a teacher in her late twenties, led davening for the first time. Involved in the havura movement since the early 1970s, Judi had moved to Dutchville and joined the Minyan in 1977. For both her warm and cheerful personality and her creative and intensely feminine approach to Judaism, she was a much-loved and central figure in the Minyan.

I have chosen to analyze this particular service for two reasons. First, Minyan members anticipated it eagerly during the week that preceded it, and they evaluated it enthusiastically once it was over. Thus, in major ways it epitomized what members thought a service should be. Second, leading davening for the first time forces the leader to confront and articulate his or her understanding of and attitudes toward prayer. This fact, combined with Judi's thoughtfulness about her Judaism, made her debut as a prayer leader a particularly good occasion on which to observe the construction of Minyan worship.

Judi's decision to lead davening on February 3, 1979, was the culmination of a long process of spiritual preparation. "I've been preparing personally for a year and a half," she related in an interview. During that time, she had approached friends who were experienced service leaders with questions about the liturgy and the mechanics of leading. Part of the preparation had also been to develop "a better sense of davening on my own." For the past several months, she had been reciting the daily prayers privately every morning. "It had been coming more and more naturally," she said.

The pace of preparation quickened. A few weeks before her service, while visiting another city, she had asked an old havura movement friend about "weaving themes—what it meant to have a theme in davening." As we shall see, the weaving of a theme—the creation of an interpretation—is one of the crucial functions of the leader in havura worship.

Judi felt that by that point, the level of her questions indicated that she was ready to lead a service. Interestingly, this readiness was sensed by the community. Thus, rather than Judi's deciding on her own initiative to lead services on a particular week, she was approached by three

Minyan members, Robert, Larry, and Bill, who were on the committee that scheduled service leaders. "They said, 'You're davening next week.' I said I didn't know if I was ready. They said, 'You'll be ready.' And they were potential judgers [of my performance], so their confidence was important to me."

Judi devoted the next week to preparation. She read the weekly biblical portion, thought about themes for the service, improved her grasp of *nusaḥ* (traditional chant), and concentrated on learning to use melody as an interpretive tool. Although her preparations were more intensive than those of veteran leaders and included acquiring skills that such leaders already possessed, some elements were standard. Thus, it was typical that her first act of preparation was to read the *parasha,* the biblical portion for that week, which was *Bo* (Exodus 10:1–13:6). Within it, she found a theme that would occupy her throughout her week of preparations.[7] The verses Judi found most striking were these:

So Moses and Aaron were brought back to Pharoah and he said to them, "Go, worship the Lord your God! Who are the ones to go?" Moses replied, "We will all go, young and old: we will go with our sons and daughters, our flocks and herds; for we must observe the Lord's pilgrimage." But he said to them, "The Lord be with you the same as I mean to let your children go with you! Clearly you are bent on mischief. No! You menfolk go and worship the Lord, since that is what you want." And they were expelled from Pharoah's presence. (Exodus 10:8–11)

Judi paraphrased the passage, bringing out its importance to her: "Moshe [Moses] goes to Pharoah and says to let them go. Pharoah says, 'Who's going, the guys?' Moshe says no, also the sons and the daughters. So, OK, if the daughters are going, I'm going too. This is the issue I grappled with all week—what am I doing leading davening? So it became a feminist issue. On the one hand, I wanted permission to be doing it as a woman, but on the other, I wanted to be just doing it. . . . I didn't want to make it an obviously feminist davening."

From the beginning of the week, Judi also included her friends in the process of preparation. "So you see where the social dimension comes in," she explained. Walking home with her friend Al after a Sabbath afternoon service, she chatted about her preparations.

I said, "I'm leading davening—will you help me?" Al asked, "Did you read the *parasha?*" I said yes and talked about the feminist theme. . . . Then, as we turned the corner onto their street I said, "Now another question—

What to wear?" We both laughed, and then I asked, "Do I wear a *talis?*" I don't wear one usually. He said that a man who doesn't ordinarily wear a *talis* does wear one while leading davening, so I thought *kal va-ḥomer* [how much more so should] a woman.

Judi also needed to learn the *nusaḥ,* the traditional chant to which the liturgy is sung. For help with this, she called on Robert. On Monday night, they spent an hour on the telephone. "I was surprised how much I had already committed to memory—that was something I wasn't really aware of. Robert was a real teacher. He could explain the structure—he taught me the structure through what I already knew. . . . Then he went through the whole thing over the telephone. Then I relaxed about *nusaḥ,* and I could move another *madregah* [level]."

As we have seen, Judi derived from the week's biblical portion what she called a "feminist" theme for the davening, one having to do with what it meant for her as a woman to be leading services. She strove to express this theme through melody. She felt she needed a sense of how to connect words and music, how to know what she wanted something to sound like and how to make it sound that way. She went for help with this and other aspects of the service to Meshullam, a member of the community who possessed musical talent and extensive Jewish knowledge.

"I wanted to do *An'im zemirot* ['I sing hymns']," Judi related. This mystical hymn, a love song to God, is usually sung at the end of traditional services, but is only rarely used by the Minyan.

So, Meshullam said, "Good, so how do you want it to sound?" I was puzzled. So Meshullam said, "What do you want it to look like?" I said, "I want it to be satin," and Meshullam, in his supportive and encouraging way, said, "Satin and what else?" "Like a fabric, soft, and the melody, really beautiful." I wanted something melodic in a soft feminine way, but there was also the constraint of wanting something that I knew.

So Meshullam asked what melody I wanted to use, and I said, "The usual one." But it was too marching. Meshullam tried some Hasidic *nigunim* [melodies], then "Amazing Grace." But Bina [Meshullam's wife] said that was too goyish [non-Jewish]. Then he tried "Dona Dona" but the concepts of that song got in the way.[8] Then he tried more *nigunim*. It was very clear that there was a sense of what sounded right and what didn't. . . . I finally decided to use the melody that I knew, but to sing it a little slower. Even so, it was the process that was important.

Judi felt she had learned a lot from Meshullam. "At Meshullam's, I went furthest in understanding what it means to make it creative, to make it special—how to make the words say what you want." And reflecting after the service about creativity, she said, "I understood, when I took responsibility for interpreting the davening—there's something about the tune for *Borkhi nafshi* and *Ha-El be-ta'atsumot* [prayer introducing the morning service] that has a stately, grand feel—it feels introductory and grandiose. It was what I needed to get where I was going. The creativity flowed from making it say what I wanted to say."

In recounting her experiences, Judi repeatedly stressed the importance of what she called the "social element" of her preparation. Not only did a number of Minyan members—Meshullam, Robert, Al, and others—help her prepare, but also many informal interactions were important to her in the course of the week. She talked with several friends about a variety of questions, from what she would say for her *kavanot* (interpretive statements) to what she should wear to the service.

The "social element" continued to be important as Judi's debut approached. "I went to Alex and Karen's for Friday night dinner, and Larry and Jill were there too. Everyone asked, 'Are you ready?' I talked about it a little, then stopped talking about it—I felt like they had reached the limit of hearing about it." And the next morning, she walked over to the synagogue with Karen, the only person with whom she had discussed her supplementary readings. Judi recalled that when she arrived at the synagogue, she "felt like the hostess, greeting people, realizing how nervous I was, getting my parents oriented to what was going on. I had a sense of, it's my party, I want to greet people."

The preliminaries over, the service began.

Then I sat down, feeling the room fill up and people acknowledging me—Oh, wow, you're davening! I had a clear sense of support and friends, and felt very good about it. I got a nod from different people about when to start—I took a deep breath and began singing *Yedid nefesh* ["Friend of my soul"]. As soon as I began the *nign* [melody] and heard how many people were into it, I was much more relaxed—it was clear by the second syllable that my voice would get lost in it. I felt the strength of people behind me, I was acknowledging friends, checking out who was there—but I also felt serious about it, I could also forget who was there.

After singing this first hymn, Judi spoke briefly. She talked about preparing for leading the service. (Virtually all first-time leaders speak about this in the course of their services.) She said she had worried about all sorts of things, starting with what to wear. Then she had worried about *nigunim*, about what tunes went with what words. Only on Friday night, she said, did she really begin to think about davening, about the service as prayer.

Next, she read a selection from *Your Word Is Fire*, a book of Hasidic meditations on prayer:

> Do not think that the words of prayer
>   as you say them
>   go up to God.
> It is not the words themselves that ascend;
>   it is rather the burning desire of your heart
>   that rises like smoke toward heaven.
> If your prayer consists only of words and letters
>   and does not contain your heart's desire—
>   how can it rise up to God?[9]

She also read a meditation on prayer by Abraham Joshua Heschel. Because she wanted the service to go smoothly, she had clearly marked the pages of the readings. "In my own theatrical way, I made sure I had the place marked with paper clips, so I could open to the place and it would flow, so I wouldn't fumble through pages." Judi proceeded through the service, punctuating it with readings and with songs. "The songs were a way to involve everybody, and I was very aware of that."

Judi also tried to balance the claims made on her as a leader and as a worshiper.

Occasionally, at the end of a *nign*, I was sensitive to the fact that I was looking forward to what to do next. I tried to maintain a balance between being into what I was doing and being aware that I was the leader and would have to be ready for the next thing. There was the theatrical part of me, wanting it to flow. And yet, as a balance to the theatrical, I was aware of not knowing in advance what *tehillim* [psalms] I would do—to trust my gut that it would come to me, and it did. I realized I was doing all the *renanah* ["joyous song"] ones. I didn't prepare in advance—but I picked joy-oriented psalms.

I was comfortable with the reading; I had a sense of not performing.

In certain ways, I felt very much me, and in certain ways I felt very depersonalized.[10] It was a social interaction and not a social interaction. I was doing readings and davening without eye contact. I ceased to be concerned with other people. I was very aware of them at times, but at other times I would really get into davening. Every once in a while I would see someone saying "right on," and supporting me, and then I really got immersed in it all. Until Yaakov came over and said it was 11:45. . . .

"Then, when it was so late, I thought maybe I ought to rush. . . . I didn't realize my timing was so off." (Services were supposed to end at noon.)

However, she only rushed "a little," going through the service as she had planned, not worrying about ending at the prescribed time, and finishing, as she had intended, with *An'im zemirot.* "Then we did *An'im zemiros,* which went well—we really ended 'up.'"

When the davening was over, people crowded around Judi, congratulating her and wishing her well. "People said some really neat things to me. My parents hugged me, and so did my friend Annette—that felt very personal. But at some point, people were talking about how special it was for *them—that* really floored me. Everyone had something neat to say. Meshullam said it was 'seamless.' And everyone looked so happy."

At the end of the interview, Judi summarized her evaluation of the event: "How do you measure what's a big deal? It felt to me and to others that there was something important going on. It was a real special experience."

Notes

1. This essay is based on fieldwork carried out in the group I call the Dutchville Minyan (all names have been changed) from November 1978 until early 1980. I have described the Minyan and its religious life more fully in my doctoral dissertation, *Making Judaism Meaningful: Ambivalence and Tradition in a Havurah Community* (Ph.D. diss., University of Pennsylvania, 1982), from which portions of this essay have been excerpted. I wish to express my appreciation to the National Foundation for Jewish Culture for the Doctoral Dissertation Fellowship that partially supported that research. I also want to thank Yoma Ullman for her helpful comments on an earlier draft of this article.

The quotes from Minyan members in this paper have been "reconstituted" from my written notes and thus are in some cases paraphrases rather than exact quotations. In addition, members use many Hebrew words in conversation. They are not consistent in their use of Sephardic (modern Israeli) and Ashkenazic (Eastern European) pronunciation. Thus, whereas in the text of the paper I have followed the convention of romanizing the Hebrew terms according to the Sephardic pronunciation, in quoted material I romanize them as they were pronounced by the person speaking. I have provided English glosses for all Hebrew terms.

2. See Jakob J. Petuchowski, *Prayerbook Reform in Europe: The Liturgy of European Liberal and Reform Judaism* (New York: World Union for Progressive Judaism, 1968); and Gunther W. Plaut, *The Growth of Reform Judaism: American and European Sources until 1948* (New York: World Union for Progressive Judaism, 1965).

3. *Davening* is an anglicization of the Yiddish word *davenen* (to pray; worship service). In Minyan parlance, *to daven* can mean "to pray" or "to lead the service"; *davening* can mean the service itself or the act of praying. In this meaning, *davening* can refer to any of the three daily services as well as to Sabbath and festival worship. But because the Saturday morning service was the focal liturgical event of the community, *davening* without further qualification usually referred to that service, as in "Who's leading davening next week?" or "Will I see you at the davening?"

4. For further discussion of the background of the havura movement, see Bernard Reisman, *The Chavurah: A Contemporary Jewish Experience* (New York: Union of American Hebrew Congregations, 1977), pp. 3–59; Riv-Ellen Prell-Foldes, *Prayer and Community: The Havurah in American Judaism* (Detroit: Wayne State University Press, 1989); Jacob Neusner, *Contemporary Judaic Fellowship in Theory and in Practice* (New York: KTAV, 1972), passim. I am describing here "independent" havurot, those founded independently of Jewish institutions. "Synagogue" havurot, often founded on the initiative of the rabbi or professional staff of a synagogue or Jewish community center, have somewhat different characteristics. For discussion of synagogue havurot, see Reisman, *The Chavurah;* and Gerald B. Bubis and Harry Wasserman with Alan Lert, *Synagogue Havurot: A Comparative Study* (Lanham, MD: University Press of America, 1983). For an excellent discussion of prayer in a West Coast havura group, see Riv-Ellen Prell-Foldes, "The Reinvention of Reflexivity in Jewish Prayer: The Self and Community in Modernity," *Semiotica* 30, no. 1/2 (1980): 73–96.

5. The word *minyan* means, in this context, "quorum assembled for prayer." Traditionally, public prayer requires a congregation of at least ten adult males; in the havura movement, women also count. Although I have changed the name of the group, the word *minyan* is part of their name for themselves. That members call this group a minyan stresses the importance of worship in its Jewish life.

6. The word *kiddush* means "sanctification." It refers to a prayer recited over wine on Sabbaths and holidays. It can also, as in the present context, refer to a social hour held after services, which is begun by recitation of the prayer over wine and at which cake and other refreshments are served.

7. A portion of the Torah (Pentateuch) is chanted each week in synagogue. In the course of the year, beginning after the High Holidays in the fall, the entire Pentateuch is read sequentially in this manner.

8. "Dona Dona" is a Yiddish song popularized in English by singer Joan Baez. It describes a calf on his way to the slaughterhouse with a swallow flying freely above him through the sky.

9. Arthur Green and Barry W. Holtz, ed. and trans., *Your Word Is Fire: The Hasidic Masters on Contemplative Prayer* (New York: Paulist Press, 1977), p. 51.

10. When she speaks of feeling "depersonalized," Judi means that at times she lost awareness of her own personality and individuality and was swept up in the experience of worship.

Figure 7. An Orthodox Jew guides a younger man in putting on *tefillin* (phylacteries), encouraging him to become more observant. This is a common Habad initiative. (Victor and Edith Turner Collection.)

CHAPTER 7

Turning to Orthodox Judaism

Lynn Davidman

In the United States the 1960s, with its burst of ethnic consciousness, provided the setting for a variety of Jewish expressions. Among them was the activism of the Lubavitch Hasidic movement, with its roots in East European orthodoxy, in reaching out to young Jews and making them come home to Orthodox Judaism (those who have done *teshuva*, from the Hebrew stem *shuv,* meaning "return"). Lynn Davidman has shown the variety within the *teshuva* movement in the 1980s, by comparing women in the process of becoming modern Orthodox, blending their new religious commitments with higher education and careers, with those who have followed the Lubavitch path to orthodoxy. In the following selection she analyzes themes conveyed to young women by a Lubavitcher rabbi in intensive courses on the nature of Judaism and its relation to their lives. Though the success of the Lubavitch movement in part depended on pluralism, which became fashionable in the 1960s, the rabbi downplayed the value of pluralism. Returning to (the movement's version of) Judaism was a return to their true nature as Jews, he argued, which also entailed returning to their nature as women, whose role was to be wives and mothers. These views did not link Judaism to growth in identity and individuality but sought to bring the women to submit to group identity and authority. The central authority figure was the leader of the Lubavitch movement, portrayed by the rabbi as one ready to be revealed as the Messiah.

The Lubavitch Community

DUTY, OBLIGATION, AND COMMITMENT

At Bais Chana the resocializing agents made much less effort to reconcile their religious teachings to modern secular consciousness. They spoke a more traditional language of duty, obligation, and commitment. Rabbi Friedman repeatedly stressed that following the dictates of halakha was not a "lifestyle" that the women could choose but was essential to their own inner natures. As he told the women one morning in class:

Why does a Jew do a mitzvah? For no reason. Because it's natural. They don't need a reason. . . . A Jew by definition wants to do mitzvahs. . . . When God tells us what to do, He's not telling us what to do but what we are. . . . A human being breathes; a Jewish soul mitzvas. That's a verb. . . . God is mitzvas, we are part of God, therefore we are mitzvahs. That's why a Jew who spent forty years living a non-Jewish life and then studied *Yiddishkeit* can be perfectly comfortable as a Jew in one week. . . . If it were a new lifestyle, it would be a struggle. But he's just being himself.

These words recall the accounts of the Lubavitch women, who, as we saw, adopted the rhetoric of compulsion in describing their attraction to orthodoxy. Rabbi Friedman spent a great deal of time emphasizing the utter necessity of their adherence to Jewish law.

The reasons for rejecting evil, for not doing a sin, is that the sin is not true. To sin, a Jew has to deceive himself. And not about something outside himself but about himself. On the grounds that it's crazy. So he rejects sin because it's a lie. On the grounds that it's crazy, not on the grounds of unnaturalness or inelegance.

In these words we can see one of the ways in which the rabbi tried to reverse the assumptions of the dominant society. He challenged the contemporary understanding of individuals as free to construct their own identities by choosing from available options. He sought to minimize the possibly eroding effects of pluralism by presenting adherence to traditional Judaism as inherent in the recruits' own beings. He asserted that people's essential selves were predetermined and that for these women, as for all Jews, being true to themselves—being who they really were supposed to be—meant being connected to a larger community and following the precepts of an ancient way of life. This adherence was not a matter of choice, not the result of weighing the benefits and costs—the basis on which utilitarian and expressive individualism promotes decisions. Rather, the rabbi claimed that following the dictates of these laws was an essential part of the women's inner natures and that if they deviated from this obedience, they would become "insane." Thus, he shored up the worldview of the community by imbuing it with the weight of necessity.[1]

To reinforce this message that the women were really not free to choose or reject this way of life, he asserted that in general people were less free to construct their identities than they thought. As he told the class one evening:

Individuals really have so many options. We have the notion that in America you can be anything. But you can't. If we talk about specific individuals, you'll see that any given individual does not have that many options. . . . We pride ourselves in believing that we can do anything, but we can't. We can only be what we are. What confuses us, and what really sets us off the track, is the seeming endlessness of the options. We have to realize that we don't have endless options. We have a few options. It's because of the openendedness that people don't know who they are and say, "Well, why should I do that?" Why? Because that's what you look like you could do. "Yeah, but I'm free to do whatever I want." You're not free to do whatever you want. You're free to do whatever you can, and you can only do certain things.

The remark "People don't know who they are" reflected the rabbi's belief that identity was not socially constructed but rather inherent in a person. In contrast to the teachings at Lincoln Square Synagogue, which promoted the idea of individual choice and self-fulfillment, the rhetoric at Bais Chana repeatedly challenged the assumption that "autonomy of the self places the burden of one's deepest self-definitions on one's own individual choice."[2] The rabbi reinforced obedience to received tradition by claiming that identity was predetermined.

Paradoxically, however, Rabbi Friedman was aware that it was largely because of this conception of freedom of choice that these women were able to come to Bais Chana and create an alternative to their parents' way of life. Nevertheless, he feared that recognition of choice—awareness of pluralism—would weaken the taken-for-grantedness of the Lubavitch worldview. Thus, he emphasized that this way of life was not a choice; it was necessary and essential. He replaced the value of free choice with the concept of *hashgocha protis* [personal providence], an orientation that encouraged surrender of agency by asserting that everything happened for a reason outside the individual's control.

A similar means of reversing the dominant middle-class ideal of individuals carving out their own identities "free as much as possible from the demands of conformity to family, friends, or community" was the rabbi's frequent assertion that, fundamentally, the women were very much like their mothers and shared a similar destiny.[3] The subject of mother-daughter relationships was a popular theme in the rabbi's classes. Many of the women at the institute described experiencing some tension or conflict in their relationships with their mothers. Rabbi Friedman sought to minimize this conflict. He repeatedly told the women that rather than trying to separate themselves from their mothers, they should acknowledge that their true happiness in life lay in following their mother's footsteps—that is, in getting married and having a family.

When it comes down to what gives you satisfaction in life, it's the same thing that gives your mother satisfaction in life. Young women are really just like their mothers and find fulfillment in the same things: getting married and raising children.

The rabbi was well aware that in becoming Orthodox, these women were in fact choosing to live differently from the way they had been brought up. Yet even while knowing that these women had "left home" to become what he called *themselves,* the rabbi de-emphasized this act of choice. Instead, he emphasized how similar the women were to their mothers, in role if not in ritual behavior. This idealization of their continuity with their mothers had the effect of reinforcing traditional roles as they were cast in the Orthodox mode. It also highlighted the women's ties to the past in the context of a worldview that emphasized obedience to tradition and its history.

DE-EMPHASIZING
CONTEMPORARY RELEVANCE

The Lubavitch teachers were not interested in providing contemporary rationales for the ancient laws, because they did not want to communicate that they were selling a product to a consumer who was free to choose or reject it on the basis of an evaluation of its benefits.[4] Thus, unlike the rabbis at Lincoln Square Synagogue, the resocializing agents at Bais Chana did not emphasize explanations for the various observances or the benefits that individual women stood to gain from following Jewish law. In a guest lecture entitled "Love and Marriage" given at Bais Chana by a Lubavitch woman who worked as a matchmaker within the community, the speaker described the laws of family purity, which, she explained, would govern sexual relations between the women and their husbands when they got married. The following excerpt from my field notes presents a segment of her talk and the discussion that followed. She said:

"Girls, our rabbis have told us that we're allowed to look for rationales in mitzvahs, but we shouldn't do it because it makes sense to us, but because Hashem wants us to. Like *brit mila* [circumcision]. We always did it even though we didn't know the reason. Recently we are finding it can be beneficial."

A woman in the audience asked her, "I heard a woman can't have sexual relations with her husband during menstruation because it's unhealthy for the woman."

She responded, "I wouldn't even want to talk about it. We do it because Hashem says. I'm sure there must be medical benefits, but that's not what we're concerned about."

It is striking how the matchmaker's argument coincides with that of Mary Douglas, the noted contemporary anthropologist, who argues that medical explanations do not suffice to account for kosher laws, which must instead be seen as manifestations of the overall sense of order the ancient Hebrews imposed on the world.[5] The matchmaker was really making the same point: the medical (or other) benefits of the laws of family purity, if extant, were serendipitous; these laws were simply another piece of the organic way of life that the group followed.

PRESENTATION OF THE CONCEPT OF GOD

The Lubavitch teachings on God contrasted with the de-emphasis on God within the modern Orthodox community. The worldview presented by the Lubavitch encouraged the newcomers to submit their wills to God. Rather than upholding the contemporary assumption that individuals should actively construct their own lives to suit their own needs, the rabbi taught the Bais Chana women that their own wills did not count. All the above-mentioned teachings implicitly conveyed this message as well as the instruction that the *ba'alot teshuva* minimize their own needs and preferences and heed the word of God. On the first day of classes during the summer session I attended, Rabbi Friedman laid out the framework for his teachings:

It is important to know that the whole pursuit of *Yiddishkeit,* when it is done properly, is done on a mission. It's not our own. This is the only way we can be sure that it remains holy, uncorrupted. Sometimes we find people who are not very Jewish in their behaviors and attitudes, and they justify it in terms of what they're studying or reading and calling it Judaism, but it's not. How does that happen? Only one way: if they came for their own purposes, on their own motivation, and forgot who sent us. So we must know who sent us and not make it our personal project. If you consider your Judaism a mission from God, you need to ask yourself, What does God want? To put it in other words, you've got no business being here except for the mission. . . . So the project is to find out what the mission is, who is sending us, exactly how we're supposed to fulfill this mission, and then go out and do it.

In this quotation we can see an example of the rabbi's characteristic attempts to negate and reverse the individualistic view of people that predominated in the wider society. Joseph Veroff, Elizabeth Douvan, and Richard I. Kulka's study, *The Inner American,* found that people in the United States used a "personal or individuated paradigm for structuring well-being."[6] Rabbi Friedman challenged this paradigm. Rather than assuming that people should act "on their own motivation" to fulfill their own needs and desires, he explicitly told the women that their wills did not count and should be submitted to God's. This message suited the women who came into this community: they felt that they had already made so many bad decisions and were happy to surrender the responsibility for making their own choices. God, and his human representatives on earth, such as the Rebbe, would guide the women in the correct path.

THE REBBE

The Rebbe, as he is called by his followers, is the leader of the Lubavitch Hasidim. The current Lubavitcher Rebbe, Menachem Mendel Schneerson, is seventh in the line of revered teachers and leaders of this sect. He is believed to have profound spiritual knowledge and insight: his followers claim that "the Rebbe knows all things about all Jews."

The teachings concerning the Rebbe, which were a major emphasis throughout the summer, provided a clear example of the attempt to teach surrender of the self. According to this worldview, all members of the community are in a particular relationship with the man called the Rebbe, who is believed to be "God's representative on earth in this generation." Rabbi Friedman used stories to teach the women the nature of this relationship with the Rebbe. Stories about Rebbes (past and present) were frequently told in this setting by the *madrichot* [counselors] as well as by the rabbis. Some of the stories were about the Rebbe's extraordinary insights, miraculous cures, and so forth. Other stories were about people who had failed to follow the Rebbe's advice and ended up in trouble. One such story Rabbi Friedman told in class provides an example:

A Lubavitcher rabbi from Israel wrote this "true confession" in an Israeli magazine. He came to New York to raise money for his yeshiva. He made a big dinner, raised money. Then he had to collect it, and by then it was late August, so he decided to stay for Rosh Hashanah. But then he thought he had to get back to get school organized for the school year, so he wrote and asked the Rebbe what to do. The Rebbe said the guy should pack, go back to Israel, and get ready for the school year.

But as he was packing, some of his friends had arrived from Israel. They said he was crazy to pack. He said the Rebbe had said it was a priority to go. His friends said, "That doesn't mean you can't stay." So he got confused. He wrote to the Rebbe again. He didn't get an answer. By that time it was a week before Rosh Hashanah, so he stayed.

Between Rosh Hashanah and Yom Kippur, he went to California to raise money. He went with a friend. . . . He arrived in Los Angeles past midnight, took a little motel room on the ocean, so he decided to go for a swim. The beach was deserted. (Now the guy I'm talking about is a young guy, either a year younger or older than me [mid-thirties].) Suddenly the guy got dizzy, got completely disoriented. His friend didn't see him, it was so dark. He started thinking, this is it, he's dead. So he thought, Who will run the school? So he thought, he's not indispensable. Someone else will run the school. So he thought, What will I do when I'm dead? Seek out the previous Rebbes and ask directions.

As he was going through these thoughts, his friend pulled him out. He had swallowed quite a bit of water. It took him a few days to recuperate. He was shaken and made his friend swear not to tell his family.

Back in Crown Heights he was driving a rented car—Hertz. On one corner a policeman stopped the car for a spot check. He asked for a license. The rabbi said he's from Israel. The policeman checks the license, says, "Get out of the car," and frisks him. He puts on handcuffs—the supposed rental car is really a stolen car. He's a very delicate guy, and he's arrested. . . . A couple of hours later a court-appointed lawyer came to see him in his cell. . . . Within fifteen minutes the whole thing was straightened out. . . .

So the guy wrote to the Rebbe to ask why he had suffered so. If it's to make up for his sins, that he accepts, but there's something weird about this. Within an hour he had an answer: the Rebbe had told him to go back to Israel for the school year. These two events happened outside Israel, after the beginning of the school year. Now that it's over you should correct the disobedience and turn it into a virtue to serve God with joy and confidence.

He thought to himself that he could undo the events by publishing his story so others could learn from it.

Through such stories, Rabbi Friedman communicated the group's beliefs concerning the Rebbe—that he knew better than they did what was best for them; therefore, they should submit their wills to his. They were to seek his advice in all major decisions in their lives and follow it. These stories, then, were a didactic means of teaching surrender of the mind and will.

The message in the rabbi's stories about the Rebbe was reinforced by the *madrichot,* who encouraged the women to write letters to the Rebbe for advice concerning important life issues. Thus, the women were taught in practical terms how to relate to a Rebbe. Naomi had been troubled since the first day of the program about how to discern what her "mission" was—did it involve going to Israel next year and following her plan to attend a nonreligious high school there? Or should she move into the Lubavitch community in Crown Heights? The *madrichot* encouraged Naomi to write to the Rebbe about the decision: it was too important to make alone. They sat with her and helped her compose the letter.

The world presented to these women was well ordered and had a beneficent, omniscient father at the head. And not only could this man shape their lives for the better; but he also had the power to change the course of Jewish history. These attributes were taken as evidence that the Rebbe was the Moshiach [Messiah]. In class one day the rabbi presented this understanding of the Rebbe:

The Rebbe feels that for a Jew coming back to Judaism is not a miracle. It's not unusual and it's not strange. It's just natural. But the fact that the Rebbe created a *ba'al teshuva* phenomenon does indicate that he's Moshiach because as far as we can tell, one of the requirements of Moshiach is that he has to bring all Jews back to *Yiddishkeit.* . . . We see someone accomplishing what Moshiach is supposed to accomplish, so we say, "This is Moshiach." And he's going to say, "I'm not Moshiach. I'm just doing what needs to be done." But we'll pester him long enough until he'll accept. He'll agree to be Moshiach. And he will be. So just like Hasidim make the Rebbe a Rebbe, Jews will make Moshiach a Moshiach.

In an interview, Rabbi Friedman articulated the same belief concerning the Rebbe's messianic role:

RF: As far as I'm concerned, who created the sixties was the Lubavitcher Rebbe. Who created *ba'al teshuva* is the Lubavitcher Rebbe. Who created the rejection of materialism is the Lubavitcher Rebbe. Who created idealism among youth is the Lubavitcher Rebbe.

LD: How did he create it?

RF: He generated it. That's what he is, and he just gives off that kind of energy. And that kind of attitude is very contagious.

LD: Is the Rebbe the Moshiach?

RF: He's got my vote.

LD: What does that mean?

RF: That if the Rebbe keeps doing what he's doing, he will change the world, which is what Moshiach is supposed to do. So if we look around and we say we believe that the world can become good, that there's some future for mankind, where is it going to come from? As far as I'm concerned, from Brooklyn. I can't see it coming from anyplace else. Right now it's happening to Jews in increasing numbers and eventually it will spread to the non-Jew and that's it. The world is fixed.

The millenarian cast of these teachings was a powerful way of creating order: the bad old world in which the women "messed up" and "got into trouble" was ending, and the new era was about to begin. And the rabbi assured them that this had to be so.

It's not possible that a bunch of Jews are giving an individual credit that he didn't deserve. People will not give credit to someone unless he deserves it. The Jews, more than most people, are very selective and very stingy with approval, with respect. We don't respect easily. We're great cynics. So what I'm telling you is you should listen exactly to what his Hasidim are saying, and then you'll know exactly what he is. For they will not give him credit for things he's not.

The message that we are on the threshold of a new age is common in sectarian religious groups. In her book about Catholic charismatics, Meredith McGuire describes how "the millenarian dream that the perfect New Order is imminent" operated within the community as a powerful order-creating mechanism.[7] The millenarianism in the Lubavitch worldview similarly served to create a well-ordered universe for the *ba'alot teshuvah*. It reassured them that although the world did indeed seem to be in a critical state, that fact in itself was a sign that change was imminent. And because by joining this community they were allying themselves with "the ultimate source of order"—the Rebbe—they would "have a privileged position in the unknown glorious future."[8]

Within the Lubavitch community the Rebbe was the focus of millenarian beliefs; he would usher in the new era, in which peace and harmony would reign. And each woman would have a role to play in hastening the process:

God wouldn't give people a mission that they couldn't do. The success in this mission produces a greater devotion and deeper commitment to bring more Godliness into the world. This hastens the coming of Moshiach, at which time the world will be perfected. . . . No war, no animosity . . . true peace and lasting peace. And this will come about sooner by each person fulfilling their individual responsibility. When we experience the coming of Moshiach in our days, then we will see the world established on its proper basis.

Through this vision, the *ba'alat teshuva*, who previously had felt at odds with the world, were given a special place in ushering in the new age. Through their actions in following the teachings of the community, they could create order in their lives as well as help restore order in the world.

In an ironic borrowing from contemporary culture, one of the *madrichot*, an earnest young *ba'alat teshuva*, asserted that the existence of technology capable of broadcasting simultaneously all over the world proved that the millennium was near.

It's supposed to be that when Moshiach comes everyone all over the world will know at the same time. How could that be? But now that we can see the Rebbe on cable TV all over the world, that means that we have the technology to broadcast the coming of the Moshiach. So the time must be near.

An understanding of their place in the community and in relation to God and the cosmos was a significant aspect of the new identity taught to these two groups of women. This new self-understanding was a major part of what the women were seeking when they first entered the synagogue. But these *ba'alat teshuva* wanted to be rooted not only in a community of memory but also in the immediate context of a family, a nuclear family. Their desires coincided with the Orthodox Jewish promotion of nuclear families.

Notes

1. Berger, *The Sacred Canopy*, chaps. 6 and 7.
2. Bellah et al., *Habits of the Heart*, p. 65.

3. Ibid., pp. 23–24.
4. Berger, *The Sacred Canopy*.
5. Douglas, *Purity and Danger,* pp. 29–32.
6. Veroff et al., *The Inner American,* pp. 529–30.
7. McGuire, *Religion,* p. 39.
8. Ibid., p. 41.

References

Bellah, Robert N., Richard Madsen, William M. Sullivan, Ann Swidler, and Steven M. Tipton. *Habits of the Heart: Individualism and Commitment in American Life*. Berkeley and Los Angeles: University of California Press, 1985.

Berger, Peter. *The Sacred Canopy: Elements of a Sociological Theory of Religion*. Garden City, NY: Anchor Books/Doubleday, 1969.

Douglas, Mary. *Purity and Danger*. London: Routledge & Kegan Paul, 1966.

McGuire, Meredith. *Religion: The Social Context*. Belmont, CA: Wadsworth, 1981.

Veroff, Joseph, Elizabeth Douvan, and Richard A. Kulka. *The Inner American: A Self-Portrait from 1957 to 1976*. New York: Basic Books, 1981.

Figure 8. A contemporary wedding in America. Women participate in the ceremony by holding the poles of the bridal canopy. (Photo by Rena Diamond.)

CHAPTER 8

Tradition and Innovation in the Marriage Ceremony

Einat Ramon

Some developments within American Judaism have had an impact out-side that country. Einat Ramon is the first Israeli woman to become a rabbi, receiving ordination from the seminary of Conservative Juda-ism in the United States. This religious setting enabled her to com-bine distinct values, including her commitment to rabbinic Judaism and feminism. Merging these influences, however, meant modifying them, and in the selection that follows, Ramon explains how she and her husband preserved some of the basic ideas of rabbinic culture re-garding marriage while altering the specific contents of their *ketubba,* or marriage contract. She describes her detailed engagement with an-cient rabbinic texts, viewed in the context of history, which empow-ered her to formulate new marriage documents. The new formula-tions addressed the economic and day-to-day sides of married life as well as the romantic and symbolic aspects. They also show the close connection between ritual and text in the celebration of life-cycle events. After sharing with us the particulars of her own marriage, Ra-mon discusses how Israeli and American couples with whom she has worked as a rabbi have responded to the innovations that she intro-duced into the marriage ritual.

A Wedding in Israel as an Act of *Tikkun Olam*

When we decided to marry, my husband and I envisioned a ceremony that would embrace our love for rabbinic Judaism as well as our dedication to feminism, liberal values, and secular Israeli culture. Finding theoretical and practical methods to harmonize these sometimes conflicting commitments and traditions was a major challenge. In addition, we anticipated a technical obstacle: we were two newly ordained rabbis—he Reform and I Conservative—who planned to marry in Israel, where Jews can ordinarily marry only via the Orthodox establishment. Our situation necessitated a creative approach both to *halakha* (Jewish law) and to Israeli bureaucracy. On the third of Tammuz, 5750 (July 6, 1989), we were married in Jerusalem, my hometown and the place where Arik and I hope to settle eventually. Planning our wedding was the beginning of what will, we hope, become the enterprise of our life: a constant struggle, to use the words of Rabbi A. I. Kook, for the "renewal of the old and the sanctification of the new," in Zion and in the world.

We understood our marriage through the kabbalistic paradigm, according to which the union of male and female is a catalyst for *tikkun olam* (repairing the world). In an age when women are becoming equal partners in shaping cultures and societies, this paradigm can finally be fully realized. We were guided by the thought of two modern Jewish thinkers, Mordecai Kaplan and Abraham Joshua Heschel, in transforming the wedding ceremony and interpreting the laws of marriage. We also wanted the ceremony to reflect the Bible's vision of marriage as a covenant formed by a man and a woman created in the image of God (Genesis 1:27) who become "one flesh" (Genesis 2:24) and who regard one another as friends and companions (Malachi 2:14). We felt that the literal interpretation of the *halakha,* according to which a woman was symbolically "purchased" by a man through the act of marriage, violated these biblical and kabbalistic visions.

Historical and Halakhic Background

The greatest intellectual and emotional challenge lay in our effort to write our *ketubba* (marriage contract) and *tena'im* (marriage conditions). The *ketubba* is a prenuptial agreement instituted by rabbis in the first century to grant women economic protection within the marriage and in case of its dissolution. In a time when it was easy to expel a woman from her husband's household (Mishnah *Gittin* 9:10), the *ketubba* ensured that "he shall not regard it as easy to divorce her"

(Babylonian Talmud *Yevamot* 89a).[1] The *ketubba* was not a mutual contract but rather the husband's one-sided promise to his wife, witnessed by two men. Traditionally most women were not considered autonomous beings. Until she married, a woman was under the auspices of her father. The wedding of a woman who was not a divorcée or widow marked the transition from her father's to her husband's possession (Mishnah *Ketubbot* 4:5). The Mishnah (*Kiddushin* 1:1) perceived a betrothal partially as a financial transaction through which the man symbolically "acquired" the woman by giving her an object. Though modern scholars and traditional apologists have argued that acquisition of the woman is limited to a husband's claim for exclusive conjugal rights, the "right" and expectation that a wife do housework was also granted by the rabbis.[2]

In the traditional *ketubba,* the groom pledges to provide his bride food, clothing, and sexual relations. He also designates a certain amount of income for the bride in case he dies or divorces her. Last, the *ketubba* assures that the woman can leave the marriage with her dowry and its increment (*Shulḥan Arukh Even Ha'ezer* 1:126). Over time, the Rabbis expanded the range of a husband's duties (Babylonian Talmud *Ketubbot* 51a–52b) so that he became obliged to provide his wife with medical care, to ransom her from captivity, and to bear the costs of her funeral. They also allowed for the addition of *tena'im,* which might add additional financial terms or protections for the woman agreed on by the families of the bride and groom. A woman's obligations to her husband were not the focus of the *ketubba* or *tena'im* and were assumed.

Today, most Conservative and all Orthodox *ketubbot* use the traditional format, written in Aramaic (the everyday language of most Jews in antiquity). Some defend the traditional *ketubba* by claiming that under modern civil governments, which protect women's interests and have jurisdiction over marriage, "the only function of the *ketubba* is to perpetuate an ancient tradition."[3] However, by accepting the traditional *ketubba* or by slightly modifying it within the scope of traditional Jewish marriage law, one is perforce also accepting traditional gender role assumptions. This truth is demonstrated by the fact that the Conservative movement's halakhic "egalitarian" *ketubbot* do not allow the bride to promise to support her groom, except in the event of his illness, or to recite the same words to him that he says to her.[4]

Most Reform and Reconstructionist rabbis, as well as some Conservative rabbis, use egalitarian *ketubbot.* But these documents do not discuss such "mundane" aspects of a couple's life as finances, sex, or division of labor and assets. Thus, they fail to address the concerns that originally gave rise to the *ketubba:* naming responsibilities, protecting the woman, and anticipating problems, including the possibility that the marriage might end. *Halakha* guides us to contemplate and devise respectful solutions for potential conflicts. By using only expressions of romantic love, egalitarian *ketubbot* ignore halakhic cautions to be realistic during the most dreamlike moment of our lives.

Toward a Transformation of the *Ketubba*

Arik, my fiancé, and I felt that perpetuating—or eliminating—an ancient tradition without wrestling with its meaning would betray our own commitment to *halakha*. We relied on modern Jewish philosophy of *halakha* to bridge the gap between ourselves and our tradition. We used interpretation as a means and standard by which to change observances and engage in the traditional halakhic process.

Two major Jewish thinkers set the methodological basis of our reinterpretation: Mordecai Kaplan and Abraham Joshua Heschel. Kaplan's discussion of the principle of "reevaluation" presented a system of reinterpreting *halakha* from a historical perspective.[5] The process of reevaluation requires first a clarification of the values and the religious and psychological needs that a particular observance served in the past, and second, an adaptation of the observance and the creation of a modern *halakha* that remains faithful to those needs and values, as well as to modern sensibilities. Heschel's views on the importance of *aggada* (Jewish lore) in the determination of *halakha* served as another guideline. He held that Jewish law only fleshed out the divine vision set forth by the *aggada*.[6]

Following Kaplan, we tried to outline the original needs that the *ketubba* served: to protect the wife and to regulate obligations that would lead to a dignified marriage and, if necessary, a dissolution of it. We therefore signed and notarized a prenuptial agreement mentioned in our *ketubba,* an agreement that outlined the division of property in case of divorce.[7] To flesh out a renewed vision of the marital union, we established appropriate physical and financial duties for modern men and women. We felt that the modern *ketubba* must spell out a broader range of obligations for both partners. Thus, we incorporated a reference to mutual responsibility in all aspects of life, including housework. We also mentioned commitments to various educational, social, and national tasks that affect our relationship.

The idea of protecting the woman through the *ketubba* presented a dilemma. On the one hand, holding on to this original purpose meant that we would perpetuate a nonegalitarian view of men and women. On the other, the *ketubba* was instituted to mend a world that is not yet mended. Given that our society is still male dominated, it would be hypocritical to pretend that men and women need equal protection. We resolved this tension by having Arik give me our new document and not vice versa. This one-sidedness symbolically stated that in a world where women still suffer discrimination, they need extra protection. At the same time, by making all our pledges reciprocal we stressed that equality and mutuality are the best possible protections for women.

We attempted to preserve the language of the traditional *ketubba* as much as possible. In addition, we incorporated expressions from an ancient *ketubba* found in Aswan, Egypt, including the formula "Thou art my wife and I am thy husband forever." This phrase was disallowed by post-Talmudic rabbinical authorities, because it implied that the groom consecrated himself to the bride as well.[8] We liked this phrase for precisely the same reason that the rabbis decided to eliminate it.

Heschel's thought inspired us to develop nonhalakhic statements that portray the essence of Jewish marriage. One was from the prophet Malachi: "God is a witness between you and the wife of your youth . . . she is your partner and covenanted spouse" (2:14). Another was from the Babylonian Talmud: "He who loves his wife as himself and respects her more than himself . . . about him Scripture says: 'You know that all is well in your tent'" (Job 5:24; BT *Yevamot* 62b). Maimonides turned this *aggada* into *halakha* by incorporating it as a law in *Mishneh Torah Hilkhot Ishut* 15:19. We followed his path by introducing this *halakha* as an explicit mutual obligation.

The traditional concept of *kedusha* (holiness, with a connotation of exclusivity or being set apart) fashioned our understanding of the *ketubba:* The word *kedusha* means holiness; in terms of values, *kedusha* means that we must embrace as holy every aspect of Jewish life, from praying to sexual relations. Maimonides invoked *kedusha* in his description of the appropriate sexual behavior for Jewish scholars and leaders of the community (*Mishneh Torah Hilkhot De'ot* 5:4–5). *Kedusha yetera* (special holiness) is the way we think a husband and a wife should treat each other in their speech and daily behavior.

It is interesting that Jewish tradition viewed sex as an obligation of the man toward the woman. This duty was explicitly mentioned in the traditional *ketubba*. It ensured that moments of intimacy would not be preempted by the husband's potential involvement with other wives (at the time when polygamy was allowed) or by his work. We tried to address the issue of preserving time for intimacy by establishing priorities and principles of mutuality. Intimacy in this sense meant more to us than just intercourse. However, we maintained the tradition of referring specifically in the *ketubba* to sexual intercourse, using a phrase based on Maimonides (*Mishneh Torah Hilkhot De'ot* 5:4–5): "The bride and the groom agree to come to one another when they are both willing and happy," affirming that sexual expression takes place only under conditions of mutual desire and joy.

The following is a generic translation of our *ketubba:*[9]

On the _____ day of the Hebrew month _____ in the year 57 _____ since the creation of the world, according to our way of reckoning here in

_____,

The bridegroom, _____ son of _____ and _____ said to the bride: "Be my partner and covenanted spouse, and I will be your man forever and give you your *ketubba,* according to the law of Moses and Israel." And _____ accepted.

The bride, _____ daughter of _____ and _____ said to the groom: "Be my partner and covenanted spouse, and I will be your woman forever, according to the law of Moses and Israel." And _____ accepted.

The bride and the groom took upon themselves to cherish, honor, support, and maintain each other; to come to one another when they are both willing and happy; to treat one another with special holiness, to respect each other more than themselves and to love one another as much as themselves; to nurture each other's growth, personal development, and joy of living.

In addition they pledged that their home will become their first priority/the fountainhead of their lives, that it will be established on mutual support, equality in responsibilities, and sharing of all aspects of life.

The bridegroom and the bride aspire to build a Zionist home in the Land of Israel which will reflect the striving toward and practice of mending the world and to raise children to do justly, love mercy, and walk humbly with their God.

As part of this *ketubba,* the couple has signed a property agreement.

The authority and contents of this *ketubba* they took upon themselves freely as is the custom of Jewish communities. This contract is not to be considered a non-serious obligation or as mere form. And we have received a token of acquisition from the groom _____ son of _____ and _____ to the bride _____, and from the bride _____ daughter of _____ and _____ to the groom _____, regarding all that has been written and explained above.

And all is valid and binding.

_____ Witness   _____ Witness

A major debate evolved between us concerning the pledge about our home being a first priority in our lives. I wanted this condition, because the setting of priorities was (and is), to my mind, the most important feminist issue facing middle-class Western families. Arik, however, saw himself dedicated equally to family and to *tikkun olam* (mending the world). Clearly, our gender differences came up in this discussion. We finally agreed to use the expression "*berosh ma'ayaneihem*," an idiom with a double meaning: "their first priority" and "their fountainhead." Thus, our home could be understood as our first priority as well as the source from which our lives will flow.

While the *ketubba* outlined the basic principles of our marriage, the *tena'im* document fleshed out their daily implications. We had a *tena'im* ceremony in New York for our friends who could not attend the wedding in Jerusalem. We listed our personal terms for creating a home together. During the gathering we broke a plate following the old practice of smashing a dish on this occasion. Afterward all our guests, not just two males, signed the document as witnesses. We also asked guests to add suggestions on a sheet of paper attached to the contract so that we would not only have their best wishes but also their best advice on staying happily married. Our *tena'im* document reflects the conviction that specific measures must be planned and taken if an egalitarian vision of marriage is to become a reality. It addresses in detail such issues as housekeeping, public service, private time (apart and as a couple), Jewish study, childrearing, vacations, Sabbath observance, and so on. We still find our *tena'im* so meaningful and practical that I encourage couples whose weddings I perform to write their own. To cite some representative clauses:

1. We will clean our house thoroughly once a week for *Shabbat*.
2. We will study Jewish texts together at least two hours per week.

3. We will not continue to rehash unalterable decisions more than twenty-four hours after they are made.

4. We will coordinate a day off once a week where we will spend time doing something unconnected to either of our usual daily activities.

5. Hebrew and English will be the first two languages which we teach our children (should we be blessed with children). We will teach them Arabic at the earliest age healthy for a child to learn a third language.

6. We must compliment each other on something not superficial at least once a day.

7. We will live only in places where both of us have opportunities to engage in meaningful work.

8. Arik will consider going to the barber before the wedding.

We were not under the illusion that all marital issues could be decided in advance, but we believed that agreeing on a set of conditions would anticipate and resolve some of them. Moreover, by jointly writing the *tena'im,* we modeled, for our community and ourselves, both an egalitarian process and a method of negotiating the details and priorities of married life.

The Wedding: Spiritual Preparation

The nuptial festivities began with our signing papers at the offices of a justice of the peace in New York. Ironically, Arik and I, two rabbis, had to follow the procedure of civil marriage at New York's City Hall, because our religious wedding, conducted six weeks later by two non-Orthodox rabbis, would not be recognized by the State of Israel. Though our situation reflected the predicament of non-Orthodox Judaism in Israel, it also indicated that there are ways to circumvent the restrictions of the Chief Rabbinate, because any marriage that is recognized by international law must be recognized by Israeli civil law.[10]

The spiritual preparations that preceded the wedding followed traditional patterns. We went to my grandfather's grave to remember him and acknowledge that his spirit had inspired our union and would be with us under the *ḥuppa* (wedding canopy). As is customary, we separated for a few days to give ourselves time alone, with our families, and with close friends. On the day of the wedding we both fasted. As on Yom Kippur, this is an act of purification and preparation for the new life that is about to begin. We each took time for writing, reflection, and prayer.

On the night before our wedding I went to the *mikve* (ritual bath). Arik too immersed himself in a source of living water, the traditional requirement for ritual bathing, with his three brothers and two close male friends at the beach in Tel Aviv. This "bachelors' party" also fulfilled a spiritual purpose. The ancient observance of immersing in a source of living water was one that I very much wanted to keep, despite the popular Orthodox interpretation that I find offensive, that the immersion in the *mikve* purifies women from the "pollution" of their menstruation. However, ritual immersion is also understood as symbolic of purification and rebirth, and it marks events in the spiritual lifecycle as well as in the menstrual cycle.

My mother offered to accompany me to the *mikve*. Her company was so important to me that it justified abandoning a standing rule in my life—to avoid any unnecessary contact with Orthodox religious institutions. As my mother watched me dip in the water, a peaceful holiness clothed the two of us. It seemed like we had suddenly shared a glimpse of the past thirty years of our lives: From the moment that I came out of the waters of her body, to this moment on the eve of another stage of separation.

Kiddushin (Holy Matrimony)

The wedding itself incorporated as many community and family members as possible. It began with a short prayer service that consisted of selected readings from the Bible, Zohar (premier Jewish mystical text), and modern Hebrew poetry. This service was modeled after similar ceremonies conducted in Israeli Reform *kibbutzim* (communes). The readings were aesthetic expressions that reflected our perceptions of the marital union and of God's presence in it. We read from the Zohar (II:85b) about God's formation of the souls as male and female. According to this passage, the male and female aspects separate from each other as they descend to earth. Only God, The-Holy-One-of-Blessing, knows how to match them properly, and only those "who walk in the path of truth" find their original soul mate. We also read a passage about the rebellion of the labor Zionists against some of the traditional marriage customs and two poems by Israeli poets Raḥel and Zelda. Between the readings, we sang Israeli love songs, and we concluded with a selection from the Song of Songs, "My beloved is mine and I am his" (2:16). Before the procession, we had a private *badeken* (bridal veiling ceremony); only our parents and a few family members were present. In traditional settings, the men dance and sing before the bridegroom and follow him to the place where the bride is seated with all the women, waiting for him. There, the groom puts the veil over the bride's face, while rabbi, groom, and/or guests recite the blessing given to Rebecca before she married Isaac: "Our sister be thou the mother of thousands and myriads" (Genesis 24:60). We deviated from custom in this case, because we preferred to keep this moment short and private in the midst of the public celebration. According to kabbalistic traditions, the veiled bride alludes to the concealed *Shekhina* (close-dwelling presence of God, associated with the feminine), and we felt this awesome image and presence deserved a moment of silence.

The first blessing recited under the *ḥuppa* is that of *erusin* (betrothal), in which we mark the transition from forbidden to permissible sexual relations. We preserved the blessing's reference to the prohibition of incestuous sexual relations but eliminated the reference to premarital sex, because we believe that a modern Jewish sexual ethic should prevail.[11] The traditional version of the betrothal blessing addresses the groom. We changed the language of that blessing so that it would refer both to bride and bridegroom. In general, however, we preferred to retain the basic structure and terminology of the ceremony while giving it new or renewed meaning. The Hebrew term *kiddushin* (holy matrimony) has accumulated layers of sexual discrimination over the years. In rabbinic literature it defines the act of acquiring a wife by transferring a ring or other goods and making a one-sided declaration. We chose not to select a new term because we thought that the rabbinic use of *kiddushin* was a corruption of that word, which comes from the root *k.d.sh.*, meaning set aside as sacred—the same root as *kedusha yetera*. Implementing Heschel's call to find new relevance in religious ritual, we restored the original meaning of the word *kiddushin* by modifying the ritual into one of mutual consecration of and by the bride and groom.[12] Arik and I exchanged rings, and each of us recited the traditional phrase: "By this ring you are consecrated to me according to the laws of Moses and Israel."[13] By making the declaration of consecration a mutual one, Arik and I lifted it out of the rabbinic interpretation of a symbolic purchase of the wife.

A Note about the *Sheva Berakhot* (Seven Marital Blessings)

Perhaps the greatest privileges of the rabbinate is one's continuous involvement in wedding ceremonies. Most of the couples that we marry employ our model of *ketubba* and ceremony that restore the original meaning of male-female unity, rooted in the creation of humanity and founded on equality, love, and mutual respect. Weddings and their preparations have become a central channel through which we pass on to the newlyweds, our students, the fruit of our own struggles with the interpretation of the Torah or marriage. Over and over again we relearn, along with the couples we marry, the texts that served as the basis for our wedding ceremony. The questions, insights, and additional texts that they bring deepen our understanding of the challenges and joys that egalitarian marriage between a man and a woman incorporates.

It is interesting to compare concerns shared by American and Israeli couples that we married over the years. One American couple brought up the question of a feminine God language. The seven blessings under the *ḥuppa* and during the first week of marriage celebrate the unity of masculine and feminine in God and in the world. The paradigm of male-female harmony is revealed in the blessing that honors the creation of humanity, male and female, in the image of God. It is present, too, in the blessings that convey the prophetic, messianic vision of the unification of God, the Father of the people of Israel, with Mother Zion. The concluding blessings focus on the newlywed couple, who manifest this metaphysical male-female harmony. Nevertheless, while male and female are invoked, God is described by the traditional text in exclusively male terms and images that, in a way, undercuts the profound meaning of the liturgy.

In an attempt to incorporate both male and female references to God I altered some of the seven blessings as follows: I substituted the metaphor *melekh* (King) with the kabbalistic term *malkhut* (sovereignty), a name of one of the feminine spheres of the Divine. In *Kabbala* (Jewish mysticism) *Malkhut* is another name for *Shekhina*, Torah, Sabbath,

Zion, and other manifestations of the Divine that are grammatically and metaphorically feminine. I began the blessing with masculine pronouns (*barukh atta adonai eloheinu*) and continued with feminine images and verbs (*malkhut haolam borei peri hagafen*).

Though I share this liturgical alteration with my students and readers, I wish to point out that only one couple I married adopted it. Israeli couples, coming mostly from either secular or traditional backgrounds, chose not to alter the seven blessings (although they do alter other aspects of the traditional ceremony). This fact, I assume, could be attributed to a variety of reasons: they are either not troubled with theological questions, refer to masculine as neutral pronouns, or feel that the richness of female metaphors in the seven blessings (bride, mother of children, and so on) balances the male liturgical metaphors.

For Israeli couples an egalitarian marriage ceremony (even more so with a woman as the officiating rabbi) is not only a personal but also a political statement wherein the couple expresses their objection to a corrupt Orthodox rabbinic establishment with which they refuse to collaborate. Non-Orthodox weddings have become a common phenomenon within certain social circles. Yet, couples that wish to be married by a non-Orthodox rabbi, even more so by a woman rabbi, must often withstand strong family pressure to conform to Israeli norms and have an Orthodox wedding. I therefore find their intellectual and emotional investment in their weddings admirable. Many of the couples I marry demonstrate tremendous maturity as they attempt to prevent legal discriminations that result from the imposition of Orthodox Jewish family law by signing a prenuptial agreement. Some of them participate in a premarriage course on Jewish texts or ask me to teach them biblical and rabbinic sources on marriage. Their preparation for their wedding becomes a prism through which they examine their Jewish identity and moral values.

My standing with a couple under the *huppa* always strikes the audience by surprise that later turns into curiosity and almost always ends with an overflow of excitement and warm feelings. It is not uncommon that the bride or the groom, their family, guests, employees of the wedding hall, or even I shed tears. I once wondered what makes those weddings so emotionally intense. The only answer that I can think of is that egalitarian weddings offer much hope for their Israeli participants. They break the alienation experienced in Israel between Jews and Judaism, but furthermore, they introduce a young generation of Israeli Jews, reclaiming their Judaism and committed in their own quiet way to making the world a better place, to mending the world. As for me, every wedding that I officiate rekindles the bride within me and returns to me the taste of a mended world experienced in my own wedding.

A Glimpse of a Mended World

By the time our wedding ceremony was over, evening had already fallen, and a curtain of stars was spread over Jerusalem, a city that yearns for peace. Unfortunately, the joy of the day was marred by tragedy. A terrorist forced a bus going from Tel Aviv to Jerusalem off the road, causing the deaths of fourteen people. Arik and his brothers had almost taken that bus. When Arik and I broke a glass at the conclusion of our ceremony, we were reminded of the wider world yet to be mended, a world where the line between life and death is so narrow and the boundaries between people so wide. As is customary, before breaking the glass, we recited the verses that commemorate the destruction of ancient Jerusalem: "If I forget thee, O Jerusalem, let my right hand forget her cunning; let my tongue cleave to the roof of my mouth, if I do not remember thee, if I do not set Jerusalem above my highest joy" (Psalms 137:5–6).

Yet, with the breaking of the glass and the exclamations of *mazal tov* (good luck), we began a happy, life-affirming celebration that broke the unnecessary boundaries between people who came from different nations and ethnic groups. Christian, Moslem, and Jewish men and women of many backgrounds and orientations sang and celebrated with one another. This was perhaps a taste of the "world to come," a glimpse of the future Zion, the mountain of God's dwelling which "all the nations shall flow into" (Isaiah 2:2). For me, our wedding was a precious hint of *hit'alut haneshama* (elevation of the soul), a sacred moment in which God and humanity found each other.

Notes

Although I wrote this paper, it really is a product of two people: me and my husband, Rabbi Arik Ascherman, my "covenanted spouse." Thanks also go to Rabbi Debra Orenstein.

1. The Mishnah in *Gittin* 9:10 discusses "sufficient" grounds for a man to divorce his wife. Among these are cooking him a dish that he dislikes or finding a woman who is more beautiful than she. Later decisors of the law, however, maintained a greater compassion toward the woman's vulnerable position vis-à-vis the divorce. See Ben Zion Schereschewsky, "Divorce," in Menachem Elon, ed., *The Principles of Jewish Law* (Jerusalem: Keter Publishing House, 1974), pp. 414–24.

2. See Judith Romney Wegner, *Chattel or Person: The Status of Women in the Mishnah* (New York and Oxford: Oxford University Press, 1988), p. 16; Boaz Cohen, *Jewish and Roman Law: A Comparative Study* (New York: The Jewish Theological Seminary of America, 1966), p. 289; Schereschewsky, "Husband and Wife," p. 385. *Shulḥan Arukh Even Ha'ezer* 80:15 includes women's household work as part of the husband's purchase. See also *Shulḥan Arukh Even Ha'ezer* 64:5.

3. Isaac Klein, *A Guide to Jewish Religious Practice* (New York: The Jewish Theological Seminary of America, 1979), p. 393. His claim is based on Louis Epstein's argument. See Louis M. Epstein, *The Marriage Contract: A Study in the Status of the Woman in Jewish Law* (New York: The Jewish Theological Seminary, 1927), p. 5.

4. After all, according to traditional Jewish law, her wages automatically belong to him, and it is she who is being purchased. An example of such an "egalitarian" *ketubba* is found in Anita Diamant, *The New Jewish Wedding* (New York: Summit Books, 1985), pp. 84–85.

5. Mordecai Kaplan, *The Meaning of God in Modern Jewish Religion* (New York: Reconstructionist Press, 1962), pp. 6–9, 34–39.

6. Abraham Joshua Heschel, *God in Search of Man: A Philosophy of Judaism* (New York: Farrar, Straus and Giroux, 1955), pp. 336–40.

7. A standard prenuptial agreement is available from the legal department of the Israeli women's organization *Naamat* (Pioneer Women of Israel), Strauss 17, Jerusalem, Israel.

8. David Davidovitch, *The Ketubbah* (Tel Aviv: E. Lewin-Epstein, 1968), p. 114. For versions of other ancient *ketubbot* that were more egalitarian than the accepted traditional *ketubba,* see Mordecai Akiva Friedman, *Jewish Marriage in Palestine* (New York: The Jewish Theological Seminary of America, 1980). Thanks to Rachel Adler for referring me to this and other sources on the topic.

9. For the Hebrew text and permission to reprint the English with the Hebrew, contact the authors at P.O. Box 7135, Jerusalem, Israel 91071.

10. Israelis who do not wish to have an Orthodox rabbi officiate at their wedding have three legal options. They can travel to another country (in most cases to Cyprus); sign papers of civil marriage in Paraguay through a lawyer in Israel (a procedure that costs almost as much as traveling to Cyprus); or sign a contract not recognized by the State of Israel as a civil marriage, which nevertheless allows the couple to receive some of the financial benefits that married people enjoy.

11. See Eugene B. Borowitz, *Choosing a Sex Ethic: A Jewish Inquiry* (Washington, DC: B'nai Brith Hillel Foundation, 1966); and Harold M. Schulweis,

"Jewish Silence on Sexuality," in *Jewish Marital Status*, ed. Carol Diamant (Northvale, N.J.: Jason Aronson, Inc., 1989), pp. 81–90.

12. Heschel, *God in Search of Man*, 12.

13. According to traditional Jewish law, it is forbidden for the bride to give a ring to the groom while reciting the same words that he has said to her, since this act throws into question whether an acquisition of the woman has truly taken place. The technical legal problem is that a man could not be consecrated exclusively to one woman, since the law assumes he could marry another wife. Babylonian Talmud *Kiddushin* 4b and the comment by Tosafot there. Maimonides, *Mishneh Torah Hilkhot Ishut* 3:6.

Figure 9. A contemporary ketubbah created by American artist David Moss.

CHAPTER 9

A Bat Mitzvah among Russian Jews in America

Fran Markowitz

The largest demographic change within world Jewry in recent decades has been the emigration from the Soviet Union and the individual states that remained in its stead. The immigrants, most commonly called Russian Jews, have reached both Israel and the United States in the hundreds of thousands. The Soviet Union had prevented them from gaining a systematic religious or cultural education, but many of them still maintained a sense of connection to the Jewish people. After migrating, they came in contact with a variety of religious forms that had developed in their new countries. Below Fran Markowitz describes dilemmas faced by Soviet Jews, as they were called at the time of her research, who lived in Brooklyn. These immigrants wanted to express their Jewishness but were not comfortable with the forms of religiosity common in the organized Jewish community in America. Her essay focuses on one instance of a successful "match" between a family planning a bat mitzvah for their daughter and a Reform rabbi prepared to organize a ceremony in a Russian restaurant frequented by the immigrant community. The ceremony she describes marked the passage of a particular girl into the status of a ritually adult Jew and brought satisfaction to her family, while also celebrating the movement of the Soviet immigrant community into recognizable and mutually acceptable patterns of American Jewish life.

Under the elevated railway, clustered together in aging stone tenements, shiny new shops decorated with multicolored pennants and bright signs in Cyrillic script attract a steady clientele of fur-clad matrons and potbellied men. Flashing gold-toothed smiles, store clerks and shoppers exchange sentences in rapid-fire Russian as herring, caviar, and black bread, along with news items and local gossip, change hands.

These Russian sights and sounds are found not in a faraway Moscow neighborhood but in Brighton Beach, an oceanfront community in Brooklyn, New York. Since the early 1970s, more than one hundred thousand Soviet Jews have made new homes in the United States, and about half of them live in New York City. Brighton Beach, once home to earlier waves of East European Jews, attracted several thousand im-migrant families. Although the area lost a great deal of its residential and commercial population to the suburbs in the 1960s, during the 1970s its low rents, seaside location, and business opportunities made Brigh-ton Beach a hospitable environment for recently arrived Soviet émigrés. Moreover, the neighborhood's long-term residents, elderly Jews who remained behind after their children fled, initially welcomed the new-comers, seeing them as catalysts for rejuvenating and re-Judaizing their crumbling neighborhood. In the 1980s Brighton Beach has indeed been revitalized, but kosher butchers and bakeries continue to shut their doors as Russian groceries, restaurants, fashionable boutiques, and shoe stores spring up in their place. Now long-term residents grumble that their old Jewish neighborhood has been turned into a Russian ghetto.

Soviet émigrés see it differently. They view themselves first and fore-most as Jews, not as Russians, and they are astonished that Americans attach to them a Russian identity that eluded them all their lives in the Soviet Union. Adamantly claiming equal status with their American counterparts, Soviet immigrants recognize as well that having lived in the Soviet Union under the influence of Russian culture has made them a different kind of Jew than their Brooklyn neighbors.

Labeled as different because of their language, their mode of dress, their patterns of consumption, and their food preferences, Soviet émi-grés remain removed from and not quite "Jewish enough" for the main-stream American Jewish community (Gitelman 1984:97; Markowitz 1988). Soviet immigrants thus confront two dimensions of otherness in their postmigration experiences. They face not only the task of learning and adapting to the linguistic, political, and economic workings of the United States but also that of becoming part of and feeling a sense of belonging to the American Jewish community in whose midst they live.

This essay attempts to uncover the dynamics of cultural change among Soviet Jewish immigrants and its effects on their Jewish identity through an examination of one of their lifecycle rituals. The investigation is implicitly guided by two questions: (1) How different in fact are Soviet Jewish immigrants from American Jews? and (2) Through the ritual process, in what ways do these immigrants alter or emphasize particular aspects of their Jewish identity to come closer to—or to delineate themselves from—American Jewish expectations for "Jewish-enough" Jewish behavior?

Rituals, because they encapsulate, demonstrate, and play with central symbols of a social system can be used as keys to unlock the unconscious workings of a culture (see Ortner 1978:1–2). In this essay I describe and analyze Soviet émigrés' bar/bat mitzvahs, describing in detail a bat mitzvah celebrated in a Russian restaurant in 1985. My analysis will show how a close look at the ritual reveals much about the immigrants' specific Jewish identity.

In the Soviet Union, bar and bat mitzvah are rarely celebrated. In a country where religion is viewed as backward superstition, and sometimes even as sedition, there are virtually no ritual specialists to oversee a child's preparation, and the bar/bat mitzvah has become a thing of the past. It is instructive to compare bar/bat mitzah with rituals concerned with the end of the life cycle—death. Ironically, although the Soviet government has shut down churches and synagogues, it has not forbidden the separation of Christian and Jewish burial grounds. Old men stand outside cemeteries and for a ruble intone a benediction over the grave. "You know how my parents are atheists and how dedicated my grandmother was to the Revolution, but when she died, we had an old man say prayers at her graveside." Thus, while Jewish funerals are part of the tradition these immigrants bring with them, the bar/bat mitzvah is a rite that has been introduced only after emigration. My data derive from fieldwork carried out from January 1984 to September 1985 and in June 1986. During that period, I attended two bat mitzvahs and one bar mitzvah ceremony. In addition, many informants described other bar or bat mitzvah celebrations they had been to.

Historical Background

Ashkenazi Jews began settling in Russia during the Middle Ages (Dubnow 1916 1:38, 41; Ettinger 1970:36–37), where they occupied interstitial positions between the Christian nobility and gentry and their peasants. Jews served as tax collectors and moneylenders and sometimes were the focus of hatred in Slavic lands. As their numbers grew, they formed their own communities in which everyday life was regulated by Talmudic law as interpreted by governing boards of local rabbis.

Official restrictions on Jews increased with the consolidation of the Russian Empire (Greenberg 1976 1:4–11; 2:31–54). Jews, with few exceptions, were forbidden residences outside the small towns in the Pale of Settlement, restricted by a harsh quota system in their desire for university education, and denied entry into the civil service and other professions. These official prohibitions notwithstanding, during the nineteenth century the Jewish population of major Russian and Ukrainian cities swelled; either by studying abroad in France or Germany, gaining the few seats available in Russian universities, or by changing their documents, some Jews found their way into the professions and gained the right to urban residences. The 1897 census reveals that 49 percent of Russian Jews were urban dwellers then, and that although 97 percent of the Jewish population claimed Yiddish as their mother tongue, 29 percent were literate in Russian as well (Tsentral'ny Statisticheskii Komitet 1905).

Informants note with a mixture of pride and irony that Jews were very active in the overthrow of the tsars and in the revolution of 1917. During the latter part of the nineteenth century, it was not uncommon for young people to break with the traditions of their families and join secular Jewish movements. Zionism, socialism, and communism in a variety of groups and forms were seen as ways to improve the lot of humanity in general and of the Jewish people in particular.[1] After the revolution, as a literate, mobilized Diaspora (Armstrong 1968:8–9), Jews quickly filled key positions in the new government. Jewish youth took great advantage of the opportunities to receive higher education, and they trained for the professions. In so doing, many freed themselves from what they perceived to be a parochial and oppressive past. In the early days of revolutionary fervor, Jewish radicals staged antirituals on major Jewish holidays, often outside the synagogue doors.

Internal factors within Russian Jewry coupled, of course, with external stresses led to the dissolution of the traditional, religiously based Jewish life in the early part of the twentieth century. Yet it is important to keep in mind that Jews, whether secularized Communists or those who maintained some religious or cultural traditions, did not lose sight of their Jewish identities (Baron 1964:210–14). In 1933, the Soviet state ensured that they never would by means of the institutionalization of an internal passport system. From that time forward, whether a person is born in Georgia, Latvia, Russia, or the Ukraine, his or her Jewish "nationality" was written on line five of his or her passport. Thus, although Jews are urban residents, highly educated native speakers of Russian who have experienced between forty and seventy years of Sovietization, they and those around them are still well aware of their Jewish identity.[2]

By the mid-1970s, Jews were not only hearing loud outcries of anti-Zionism in the official press after the two most recent Arab-Israeli wars, but they were also finding their opportunities in the workplace curtailed. Institutes of higher learning became more difficult for Jews to enter, and an increasing number of Soviet Jews came to realize that "we (as a family, as a people) have no future here in the Soviet Union." For some, this dissonance was pushed to the limit when they found themselves blacklisted, unable to work in their professions because someone with their same last name had emigrated. They were left with no choice but to emigrate themselves, having lost not only their means of livelihood but also their identities.

Once in the United States, these new immigrants were assisted by Jewish social-service agencies that administered resettlement funds, helped them find work and learn English, and encouraged them to take part in American Jewish life. While Soviet Jews did not flock to the synagogues and, with few but notable exceptions, did not become religious Jews overnight, they do take pride in their Jewish heritage. They now celebrate important holidays and key rites of passage in ways they were unable to in the Soviet Union.

Bar/Bat Mitzvah

Survey data from several cities in the United States consistently show the commitment of immigrant parents to keeping their children within the Jewish fold (see Simon 1983), with a significant proportion of children attending Jewish schools (Federation of Jewish Philanthropies 1985:34–35—35 percent; Gitelman 1984:97—49 percent; Gilison 1979:21—39 percent). After coming to America, many parents have increasingly opted to have bar/bat mitzvah celebrations to mark the passage of their children into Jewish adulthood (38 percent of those questioned in New York City by the Federation of Jewish Philanthropies 1985:30–31). For many of these parents and their guests, these ceremonies are their first encounter with Judaism in a public arena.

In New York City, particularly in Brighton Beach, immigrants have the option of celebrating their childrens' bar and bat mitzvahs in any one of eleven Russian restaurants. Despite some differences in decor, menu, and orchestra, the restaurants are very similar to one another: dining on weekend nights is by reservation only. The six-hour meals combine Russian conviviality—food, drink, and song—with American opulence. Even the most modest of the restaurants provides an impressive table of *zakuski* (appetizers) and several additional courses throughout the night. There is no shortage of vodka and brandy, and spirits already high are made more so by the orchestra's repertoire of Russian, Ukrainian, Georgian, Uzbek, Jewish (Yiddish and Israeli), Italian, and American popular melodies.

Many of these restaurants advertise, "Have your birthday, anniversary, wedding, bar mitzvah here with us!" None of the restaurants is kosher, and although Jewish specialties (such as gefilte fish and *ptsha*) are always served, they are placed on the table along with crab salad and pork-based cold cuts. Establishment owners provide a list of rabbis who will perform Jewish ceremonies in their restaurants. Not surprisingly, however, the list of participating clergy is small and confined to liberal Reform rabbis. Nonjudgmental about the everyday life of the immigrants, the rabbis allow and even encourage them to express their Jewishness in a style appropriate to their own background:

You know, the main reason, one of the reasons, I picked the Russian restaurant is because I felt—I can't go to a synagogue and then put on a face like I lived this way my whole life. Do you see what I mean? Like our temple— it's Conservative, and I didn't feel I could go there and have the ceremony there because that's not me. And I couldn't ask that rabbi to come to the restaurant because it's non-kosher. So how could I go to a synagogue and do it there if it didn't feel right?

This rabbi . . . was on the list [the restaurant owner] gave us of rabbis who work with them. He was the third one I called. As soon as I talked with him on the phone I liked him. I want to tell you that he is a great businessman too, because he understood that in a Russian ceremony you shouldn't get too involved and you shouldn't mind is it kosher or not. He knew that this is the only way to deal with us.

When I met with the rabbi I was very uptight, and I was afraid he would ask all these questions [about religious practices]. But he didn't, and after he came to the house and talked to me, my husband and the children, he understood what we wanted. We did it exactly as we wanted.

In another case in which the parents chose to separate the religious ceremony, held in a synagogue, from the celebration, held in a Russian restaurant on Rosh Ha-Shanah eve, the rabbi, this time Orthodox, instructed the child in his *haftara* reading (the portion from *Prophets* a boy chants as part of a traditional bar mitzvah service) without posing questions about how, when, and where the family would have a party to celebrate this event.

Immigrants select a rabbi to instruct a child in preparation for bar/bat mitzvah not according to his credentials as a scholar and teacher but according to his personality and his attitude toward the family's manner of observance of religious traditions.

To many Soviet Jewish immigrants, celebrating the bar or bat mitzvah is not only a rite of passage for the child but a rite of expurgation for the entire family, ridding them of a negative Jewish identity and receiving in exchange a positive one: "You know, I told you this, in the Soviet Union being Jewish is something you hide. Here I know that being Jewish is something to be proud of. Now I am a little less outspoken about this than right when we came and I don't broadcast so much that I am Jewish, but I am very proud of this and I want my girls to be proud too. . . . You know I'm not religious, but that's not the point." The ceremony itself promotes among parents and children not only pride in a still shaky identity but also a sense that this newly rediscovered religion can be fun.

How is this done? Below, with slight modifications to ensure the privacy of the family, I will describe a bat mitzvah that was celebrated in a Russian restaurant on a Sunday afternoon during the summer of 1985.[3]

With a four-piece band set up on stage, a clean-shaven, gray-haired rabbi stands at the far end of the dance floor dressed in a black robe, a black yarmulke, and a thin *talis* (prayer shawl). He stands behind a table on which a white-and-red frosted cake, decorated with a gold facsimile of the Ten Commandments in its center and several large glass candleholders filled with tall white candles placed around it, is on display.

The rabbi, standing alone, says, "Please take your seats." Then, with a strong American accent, he repeats this phrase in Russian. He continues in English, "The ceremony is about to begin, and there will be no talking during the ceremony."

"I would like to welcome you to the bat mitzvah celebration of our beautiful, wonderful bat mitzvah girl, Leah (using her Hebrew name instead of the Russian, Lina). Let's give her a big hand!" and Lina walks out to join the rabbi as the orchestra plays a melody in a minor key. "And now—her wonderful parents—Bella and Alex!" who walk in side-by-side as the orchestra plays "Sunrise, Sunset."

"Today, in celebrating her bat mitzvah," the rabbi continues, "Leah is confirming her commitment to live by the laws of the Torah, to live as a member of the Jewish people. Now, in her sweet, beautiful voice, she will recite the *Shema Yisroel*—our statement that there is one God and no other gods before Him. Now to you, Lina!" And Lina chanted this one-line proclamation in Hebrew and immediately recited it in English, "Hear, O Israel, the Lord is our God, the Lord is One."

The rabbi resumes, "Let's have a round of applause for this wonderful girl, for her sweet voice. Let's hear it for her!" And all two hundred or so guests applaud.

"Now very close friends of this beautiful bat mitzvah girl, Irene and Danny, will bring the Torah scroll to us." These children walked in together, accompanied by Jewish music, carrying a small, velvet-covered Torah. The rabbi instructed them to place it on the table and then asked for "some applause for these sweet, wonderful friends— Irene and Danny!"

As the guests clapped and the children unceremoniously took their seats, the rabbi took off its velvet cover and unrolled the scroll. "Now, with your sweet little finger, touch the place in the Torah where we are going to read," the rabbi instructed the bat mitzvah girl. "Now she will kiss her finger to show us all how much she loves the Torah, the gift of God to the Jewish people. Now our lovely, beautiful, wonderful bat mitzvah girl will sing her bat mitzvah prayer over the Torah." This is a short Hebrew chant, after which the rabbi again asked for "a round of applause for her sweet and wonderful voice."

"Not only is this girl beautiful and sweet, she is also smart," he continues. "Now she will read to you a speech she has prepared for the occasion of her bat mitzvah celebration. I give to you now—Lina!"

Lina begins reading in a clear, deliberate voice, "My dear parents, family, and friends. I am very happy that you all came to be with me to celebrate my bat mitzvah. I am very happy today to celebrate my bat

mitzvah and to show my belonging to the Jewish people." The speech
is short, three or four more sentences, focusing on family, friends, and
her gratitude to America for being able to express pride in being Jewish. At its conclusion the rabbi asks, "Wasn't that a wonderful speech
from our beautiful, wonderful bat mitzvah girl?"

"Now, Leah, bend your head. I am now going to give her the bat
mitzvah blessing, to confirm her, as her mother, her grandmothers, and
great-grandmothers, as a Jewish woman. *Barukh ato* . . . ," and he
touched her on the head and intoned this Hebrew blessing. "Now this
beautiful, wonderful girl has become a Jewish woman. Papa, today I
will ask you to say something," the rabbi continues, addressing Alex.
"Mama, today you have nothing to say, because on all other days you
do all the talking and papa stays quiet." The audience laughs and ap-
plauds at this remark. "Papa," the rabbi continues, "come here and repeat after me," and he intones a short Hebrew chant, translating it into
English for Alex to repeat, "And today—I am no longer responsible—
for the Jewish education—of my daughter. I *am*—still responsible—
for her support—until the day—that she gets married," to which he
adds "*kin ayne hore*" and spits over his shoulder three times, "tfu, tfu,
tfu," for which he receives appreciative laughter from the audience.[4]
"Let's have a big hand for Papa Alex—and what a wonderful papa he
is! And for Mama Bella! It is no wonder that their daughter Lina is so
sweet, smart, and beautiful—look at her wonderful parents! Let's have
a round of applause for these wonderful parents—Bella and Alex!"

"We will now conclude the religious portion of the ceremony by
making the final blessing—the *shehehiyanu*." The orchestra strikes up a
fanfare and accompanies the rabbi as he sings this blessing. Then they
play and sing the festive Yiddish song, "*Mazel tov, simen tov*." The rabbi
sings in a loud voice, and the guests join in rhythmic clapping.

"We have now concluded the religious portion of the bat mitzvah
ceremony, and Leah has taken her place as a Jewish woman, like her
mother, grandmothers, and great-grandmothers," the rabbi resumes.
"A bat mitzvah is also a birthday celebration, and now we will call upon
family and friends to help light the candles on this beautiful birthday cake for our wonderful birthday, bat mitzvah girl. First, I want to
call *bube* Khane and *tante* Mila to join us.[5] We have a wonderful grandmother and beautiful aunt to light the first candle on our wonderful
birthday cake." As the rabbi speaks and hands the taper to the grandmother, she starts to cry and dabs at her eyes as he says kind things

about her. She lights the candle and kisses her granddaughter, crying all the time. "Let's have a round of applause for this wonderful grandmother and beautiful aunt!"

Several more names are called until all thirteen candles on the cake are lit. The band plays Jewish melodies throughout the candle-lighting ceremony. The parents' close friends and business associates, as well as family members, are called on to participate. When all the candles have been lit, the rabbi asks all the guests to join in singing "Happy Birthday to our beautiful, bat mitzvah girl." The orchestra plays, the guests all sing, and Lina blows out her birthday candles. The band then strikes up a reprise of "*Mazel tov, simen tov*," all the participants in the candle-lighting ceremony take their seats, waiters remove the cake and table from the middle of the dance floor, and the rabbi disappears just as dinner is to begin.

This bat mitzvah ceremony elicited strong emotional responses from all the immigrant guests: "I was all choked up. It was really touching, moving, being up there. I cannot explain how or in what way—it just was—very touching." Another, through her tears, was able to explain the emotion she felt: "This was the first, the very first, bar or bat mitzvah I've ever been to. It was really nice to see—especially for us who, you know, in the Soviet Union were Jewish but hid it. We just wanted to be like everyone else. So we had no ceremonies, no rituals. This was really beautiful." "It was great! Wasn't the rabbi terrific?" exclaimed Alex and several of the guests.

Why did this ceremony elicit such positive heartfelt reactions? This bat mitzvah is radically different from those held in synagogues, and on the surface at least, has little connection with normative Judaic practice: although the bar mitzvah ceremony has deep roots in Jewish religious practice, bat mitzvah is a recent innovation, and its popularity is limited to Conservative and Reform synagogues, which unlike the Orthodox provide identical initiation rites for boys and girls. The rite signifies one's initial participation in prayer and in the Jewish community as a full-fledged adult. At age twelve for girls and thirteen for boys, the child is assigned a place of honor in the synagogue for all to see and takes part in the Sabbath service wrapped for the first time in a prayer shawl. During the normal course of prayer, the child, who has prepared many months for this moment, is called to the Torah to chant that day's portion of the *Prophets* and thus becomes a son or daughter of the law (bar/bat mitzvah). At the conclusion of the service, the child's family usually sponsors a reception for the congregation. That night after the Sabbath, parents often throw gala birthday parties, spending thousands of dollars to celebrate their son's or daughter's passage into Jewish adulthood.

American bar and bat mitzvahs separate the sacred from the secular. At the last two bar mitzvahs I attended, one Reform, the other Conservative, I remember thinking that with these celebrations American Jews were sending messages to themselves that say: although our daily lives are no longer intimately connected to the precepts of Judaism and the obligations of Jewish law, we have not forgotten our religion. In New York, Jews play a major role in all spheres of social, economic, political, and cultural life. Being Jewish is not only unstigmatized, but aspects of Jewish ethnicity, such as Yiddishisms and Jewish food, have found their way into the cultural mainstream. Judaism, however, remains the sole provenance of Jews.

For Soviet immigrants, religion is not the linchpin of their Jewish identity. Jewish ethnicity or "nationality" remained stigmatized in the Soviet Union, although Soviet Jews are, in the main, not religious. A rite that emphasizes the retention of Judaism in the face of the acculturation and acceptance by American society of secular ethnicity would only be a painful reminder that they, lacking Judaic knowledge, are not in fact "Jewish enough."

The bat mitzvah ceremony that Soviet Jewish immigrants perform in their restaurants works as ritual precisely because it blends and reconciles, rather than disconnects, three powerful aspects of their sense of self—their Jewish, Russian, and American identities. The rabbi, as a key symbol of Judaism, plays a crucial role in this identity resolution. As a modern, clean-shaven English speaker willing to come to "their" restaurant, he embodies Judaism in a positive and accommodating light, both as a committed Jew as well as a man of the world. Indeed, the rabbi represents precisely the way Soviet Jews see themselves—as educated, cosmopolitan, and Jewish. Moreover, the rabbi also possesses knowledge of Judaism and its ritual practices, something the immigrants recognize they have lost and would like to regain (through their children).

The bat mitzvah ritual itself, combining English prose with Hebrew chants in a public setting, is for the girl and her parents a cathartic experience that symbolically frees them from the stigma that their Jewish identity had in Soviet society. The girl's mother said, "In Russia every night I used to sleep with a kerchief tightly wrapped around my head to get rid of this Jewish [curly] hair of mine." Others told of their children's dread of going to school on the day they had to bring in their birth certificates for fear that "now everyone will know that I am a Jew." One girl, after insisting to no avail that she was not Jewish, became "blood sisters" with a Russian friend. She returned from school and demanded that her parents now change her birth certificate because now she had "Russian blood." The rabbi's frequent use of the words, "beautiful," "wonderful," and "sweet" in reference to the bat mitzvah girl and her family confirmed and reconfirmed that Jews are indeed good, nice people.

The bat mitzvah was as much a rite of explication as it was an individual rite of passage. It reviewed the meaning of a tradition dating back thousands of years, a set of holy laws, sacred texts, and an ancient language that unite Jews throughout the world. The rabbi's restructuring of the bat mitzvah into a rite of explication allowed Soviet Jewish immigrants to understand and appreciate these traditions. It also made the rite a common ritual, a group rite of passage. The rabbi's explanations included the guests in the ritual. Without condescension, he fed them knowledge to foster their identification with the bat mitzvah girl, her family, and the entire Jewish people.

This ceremony, it must be kept in mind, took place in a specific context—a Russian restaurant in America. Not only was the bat mitzvah a proclamation of Jewish identity, but it was a demonstration of being both American and Russian as well. By means of the ritual in this context, these three facets of the self were reconciled and relegated to their proper places.

Although the restaurant is "Russian," its staff and musical repertoire proclaim that it is also Jewish, and its luxurious furnishings and the opulent dress of its patrons testify to its being in America. Performance of the rite in English underscores the Americanness of the event and of the people involved. While most immigrants are at least competent in English (Federation of Jewish Philanthropies 1985:15), there is no doubt that they feel most comfortable expressing themselves in Russian. Knowledge of English is a source of pride, especially the "perfect English" spoken by their children. The children's display of being "real Americans" through their language is read by the parents, who readily concede that they themselves will always feel themselves to be strangers, as confirmation of the fact that they did indeed make the right choice by coming to America.

Thus, Jewish identity as expressed through the bar/bat mitzvah is one in which cosmopolitanism and modernity take their places alongside the traditions and symbols of Judaism. It is a rite of confirmation, not only for the child involved but for the guests as well, because their image of themselves as Jews is publicly and joyfully acknowledged. It is a rite of acceptance—not only the child's acceptance of her Jewish identity but also the acceptance of American Jews, represented by an American Jewish rabbi, of Soviet immigrants as Jews, legitimate bearers of this ethnic-religious identity.[6] It is also a rite of expurgation—a symbolic passage from a stigmatized identity to a positive identity. It is this combination of highly charged passages that make the bat mitzvah of one girl into a cathartic moment for all those involved. In clarifying and resolving competing strands of the identity for these immigrants, the bat mitzvah tells them that they did in fact achieve the goal that many cited for having left the Soviet Union in the first place, "to live normally, to be rid of that fear (of anti-Semitism), to breathe easy, to be free, to be myself."

Notes

Funding for the research reported herein was generously provided by a FLAS fellowship from the Center for Russian and East European Studies, University of Michigan, a Grant-in-Aid from the Wenner-Gren Foundation for Anthropological Research, and by a predoctoral fellowship, NRSA No. 3 F31 MM09168-01S1, from the National Institute of Mental Health.

I am very grateful to all the gracious people who patiently answered my many questions, especially to those who included me in their family and friendship networks. A special word of thanks goes to Zhenya, *dorogaya podruga moya*. Aram A. Yengoyan, Sergei Kan, and Jack Kugelmass read earlier drafts of this essay. Their careful readings and helpful comments added much to the final version of this essay.

1. Two other important social movements were occurring at this time as well, *Haskala,* or the enlightenment, which modernized but did not always challenge Orthodox Judaism, and, of course, mass emigration to America.

2. According to the 1979 census of the U.S.S.R., more than 80 percent of the Jewish population claimed Russian as its native language. The westernmost portions of the Ukraine and the Baltic republics did not become incorporated into the Soviet Union until 1939. It was not until after World War II and the near annihilation of the Jewish population of these areas that they fell under Soviet sway.

3. Throughout the course of this essay, names and in some cases family composition have been changed. Both remain true to the spirit of these people, however; for example, some common Russian first names such as Ivan and Nikolai, which are rarely if ever used by Jews, were not chosen to disguise informants.

4. Both the Hebrew verbal incantation and the Russian custom of spitting three times are devices to ward off the evil eye. Informants laughingly tell me that Russians—or is it Russian Jews, no one is really sure—believe that a little devil sits on everyone's left shoulder. And if you mention a good quality or happenstance about someone that you hope will persist or if you express the hope that something good will happen to them in the future, spit three times over your left shoulder into the face of this devil and then, automatically, the evil eye is blinded as well.

5. Yiddish kin terms for grandmother and aunt.

6. As I have discussed in greater depth elsewhere (Baskin 1985), Soviet Jewish immigrants have been challenged, or at least feel that they have been challenged, by American Jews about the legitimacy of their Jewish identity. Having a bar or bat mitzvah performed by a rabbi who is himself an American Jew helps to cancel out their self-doubts.

References

Armstrong, John A. 1968. "The Ethnic Scene in the Soviet Union: The View of the Dictatorship." In *Ethnic Minorities in the Soviet Union,* Erich Goldhagen, ed. New York: Praeger, pp. 3–49.

Baron, Salo W. 1964. *The Russian Jew under Tsars and Soviets.* New York: Macmillan.

Baskin, Fran Markowitz. 1985. "Jewish in the USSR, Russian in the USA: Social Context and Ethnic Identity." Paper presented at the 84th Annual Meeting of the American Anthropological Association, Washington, D.C.

Dubnow, S. M. 1916. *The History of the Jews in Russia and Poland from the Earliest Times until the Present Day.* 3 vols. Philadelphia: The Jewish Publication Society of America, vol. 1.

Ettinger, S. 1970. "Russian Society and the Jews." *Bulletin on Soviet and East European Jewish Affairs* 5:36–42.

Federation of Jewish Philanthropies/Fran Markowitz Baskin. 1985. *Jewish Identification and Affiliation of Soviet Jewish Immigrants in New York City—A Needs Assessment and Planning Study.* New York: Federation of Jewish Philanthropies of New York.

Gilison, Jerome. 1979. *Summary Report of the Survey of Soviet Jewish Emigrés in Baltimore,* rev. ed. Baltimore: Baltimore Hebrew College, Center for the Study of Jewish Emigration and Resettlement.

Gitelman, Zvi. 1984. "Soviet-Jewish Immigrants to the United States: Profile, Problems, Prospects." In *Soviet Jewry in the Decisive Decade, 1971–1980,* Robert O. Freedman, ed. Durham: Duke University Press, pp. 89–98.

Greenberg, Louis. 1976. *The Jews in Russia.* 2 vols. New York: Schocken Books.

Markowitz, Fran. 1988. "Jewish in the USSR, Russian in the USA." In *Persistence and Flexibility: Anthropological Studies of American Jewry,* Walter P. Zenner, ed. Albany: State University of New York Press, pp. 79–95.

Ortner, Sherry B. 1978. *Sherpas through Their Rituals.* Cambridge: Cambridge University Press.

Simon, Rita J. 1983. "The Jewish Identity of Soviet Immigrant Parents and Children." In *Culture, Ethnicity, and Identity,* William C. McCready, ed. New York: Academic Press, pp. 327–39.

Tsentral'ny Statisticheskii Komitet. 1905. *Relève général pour tout l'Empire: Des résultats du dépouillement de la population en 1897.* 2 vols. St. Petersburg, vol. 1.

Figure 10. An Israeli boy from an Italian family lights a large Hanukka lamp, which comes from a synagogue in Italy. (Reproduced courtesy of the U. Nahon Museum of Italian Jewish Art, Jerusalem.)

CHAPTER 10

Books as a Path to Jewish Identity

Claudio Segrè

Alongside migration, the Holocaust was a major external factor re-
shaping Jewish life in the twentieth century. Its impact reverberated
far beyond the experiences of those whom it touched directly. Claudio
Segrè was the son of an eminent physicist who left Italy for the United
States in the 1930s, under the pressure of Fascism. He grew up in
Berkeley and Los Alamos, in a milieu of international scholars, and
was barely aware of his Jewish background. Eager as a child to fit into
normal American life, he first saw himself as Protestant but later, after
sampling different American religions, reclaimed his identity as a Jew.
More than through any links to organized religious life, Segrè arrived
on a highly individualized connection to his past by virtue of his study
of modern European history. He viewed himself as similar to other
secular, educated, but Jewishly aware Italians and devoted himself to
a life of scholarship and teaching that would not let people, neither
Jews nor Gentiles, forget the daunting questions that the Holocaust
raises. It is these questions that Segrè explores in this selection.

In one way, at least, I was sure that I was solidly mainstream American. As I wrote on school forms under "religion," I was
"Claude Segrè, Protestant." What else could I be? I wasn't excused
from school once a week for religious ed., so I wasn't Catholic. I didn't
spend Sunday in the living room listening to blue-suited white-haired
gentlemen, as the Perry boys did at Los Alamos, and my family and I
didn't socialize at the church across the street from our home in Berke-

ley, so I wasn't a Mormon or an Episcopalian. I couldn't see any connection with the "Israeleets" of the Bible stories my mother read me, nor did I wear a little skullcap (that reminded me of Brownie Girl Scout beanies) or pray in Hebrew. So I wasn't Jewish. "Protestant" was fine with me; my parents never told me otherwise, and it *seemed* to make sense.

How "Protestant" I really was did not emerge until after my father's death. Going through his papers, inside a plain white envelope, I found a card that read, "This certifies that Claudio Giuseppe Giorgio Segrè, child of Emilio Gino Segrè and his wife Elfriede Hildegard Spiro, born on the 2 day of March 1937 at Palermo, Italy, received CHRISTIAN BAPTISM on the 7 day of April 1943 at Berkeley, California." The seal on the certificate indicates that the minister was from the "Northbrae Community Church." Even today, the sight of the certificate with "CHRISTIAN BAPTISM" in large, florid Gothic type shocks me.

That certificate, I suspect, was largely my mother's work. Even in the land of the free, even with an ocean between her and the madness of Nazi rallies and Italian Fascist racial manifestos, my mother did not feel entirely secure. Almost forty years later, I understood my mother's uncertainties. The occasion for my epiphany was a retirement dinner for a colleague of mine, a distinguished German-Jewish émigré historian. In reminiscing about what it had been like starting his academic career in the United States just after the war, he quoted from the letter of recommendation his professor—a well-known American scholar—had written for him: "Mr. X is a competent historian. He does not have the abrasive manners of the Jewish race."

"Claude Segrè, Protestant," was fine with me as a child. If anybody asked me about my religion, I had an answer. For the most part, however, nobody asked. My friends who went to church on Sundays envied my freedom. My parents seemed to pay about as much attention to religion as they did baseball.

Yet I wasn't entirely comfortable. From time to time, I heard my parents remark that someone they had just met, or perhaps someone they had passed on the street, was *ebreo* or *ebrea*. I thought I caught them exchanging knowing glances, as if they'd identified a member of a secret brotherhood. I tried to fix that man or woman in my mind. For the most part, I saw only the usual adult, dressed more or less as my parents did, and perhaps speaking with an accent—but so did nearly everyone else among my parents' friends. What set these *ebrei* apart? What were my parents talking about? Could it be that we had something in common with them after all?

My father was not much help. For him, I gradually understood, religion was like music: he didn't have much of an ear for it. As he noted in his memoirs, he "never had a religious crisis." In matters of faith, however, as on most other topics, he was a person of the book. He read about religion and he read religious works because he read everything. That was part of being an educated man. So he devoured Descartes, Galileo, Tolstoy, some of Plato's dialogues. He read the nineteenth-century French historian-philologist Ernest Renan's *Life of Jesus*. He plowed through explications of Buddhism and Judaism and other major religions. He read the Bible—the Old Testament, at least the parts he could get through. Some he found "sublime and rich with moral teachings; others seemed barbarous and cruel." The varying images of "Adonai" impressed him. In some cases he found them "so churlish and vindictive as can be conceived only in the mind of a priest."

Reading, however, did not lead him to faith. What religious feelings he had he recognized as "childish." He cherished them, and they comforted him, for, as he wrote, "they remind me of people I once loved and of old times." On the rare occasions that he did attend religious services, he sometimes found them moving because of "the traditions they evoked, from family history and from feelings rooted in the subconscious." On an intellectual level, he wrote, he regarded religion much as Einstein did. As a scientist, Einstein believed that the laws of nature determined what took place in the natural world, and thus he could not accept that prayer, or some address to a Supreme Being, would influence events. Nevertheless, he recognized that believing in the laws of nature as an explanation for the world was in itself an act of faith—though one often justified by the successes of scientific research. And yet in doing scientific research, Einstein recognized the existence of some spirit in the universe vastly superior to that of man—a spirit "in the face of which we with our modest powers must feel humble." Thus, Einstein recognized, "the pursuit of science leads to a religious feeling of a special sort, which is indeed quite different from the religiosity of someone more naive." When I came across that passage, it struck a familiar chord. I thought of my father—aloof, apart, elitist. Whatever religious feelings he had were those of the *gente colta* [cultured people].

Yet my father certainly considered himself Jewish, probably more in a cultural than in a religious sense. His upbringing was almost entirely secular. He was not bar mitzvahed. He did not know Hebrew. His family did not generally observe the High Holidays. When he was doing his military service, he was not even aware that he had a right to a leave to celebrate Yom Kippur. "Being Jewish," however, did mean marrying within the faith, even though my mother was not at all religious.

In his education and his attitudes, my father was typical of his generation of middle-class Italian Jews. As my grandfather's story attested, emancipation for the Jews in nineteenth-century Italy came relatively easily, and there was a great trend toward secularization and assimilation. By the time of my father's generation, in Italy, as the memoirs of contemporary Italian writers such as Primo Levi and Vittorio Dan Segre (no relation) illustrate, whatever it meant to be Jewish was fading rapidly. Without Mussolini's anti-Semitic legislation in 1938, without the experiences of the Holocaust, the Jewish tradition in Italy would have dimmed even more.

With such a secular father, my seeking faith, tracing the outlines of a religious identity, was like groping around in a cave. At times, as I grew up, I came across movies or novels with a Jewish theme. I envied the son in the clichéd scene when the father thunders, "My son, have you forgotten the Sabbath?" or "If you marry her, you are no longer my son." My scenes with my father were far more nebulous. In my scenes, the son was uncertain whether to follow the father. Is the father leading? Or is he standing apart, his critical eye on the son's fumblings? I often felt that my father, as the English essayist Charles Lamb put it, was determined that his "children shall be brought up in their father's religion if they can find out what it is."

From time to time, as I groped about in the cave, my father handed me a torch—usually in the form of a book. In 1950, for my thirteenth birthday, for example, he gave me a Bible. Its tan leather cover and gold lettering were neither elegant nor memorable; I think he ordered it from Sears Roebuck. By now the pages are the color of a tobacco-stained finger. It was evidently a wartime edition, for it included a letter from President Roosevelt "commending the reading of the Bible to all who serve in the armed forces of the United States" and assuring me that "Throughout the centuries men of many faiths and diverse origins have found in the Sacred Books words of wisdom, counsel and inspiration." My father filled in the presentation line, which reads, "A sacred token to _____ from _____" with "Claudio Segrè" from "Papà."

What was I to do with it? Was the Bible to take the place of a bar mitzvah? (At the time, I wasn't even sure what a bar mitzvah was.) Had he chosen it *because* of President Roosevelt's words, "men of many faiths and diverse origins" had found inspiration in the Bible? I didn't know what to make of this torch or of my parents' silences. When I joined a Congregational Church youth group in high school, they said nothing. I edited the organizational newspaper and wrote mildly Christian and pantheistic editorials praising nature, peace, brotherhood. I celebrated the richness of a busy life of schoolwork, dates, and sports, leavened with Christian moments of prayer or devotion.

At home, at Christmas, we celebrated a kind of secular winterfest, more out of my mother's nostalgia for the snow and fir trees and carols of her childhood than for any religious content. I went to midnight services at Christian churches selected at random. On those cold, foggy Berkeley nights, I loved hearing the joy and affirmation of the carols, the grand swelling of oratorio choruses. I tried earnestly to absorb—and then to spread—the message of "Peace on earth, goodwill toward men." Occasionally my mother came to the services with me. We spent one Christmas at a ski cabin in the mountains. My mother, my sisters, and I sang carols. "It was worth it just to see the smile on Papà's face and the way the singing seemed to draw out many German carols that Mamma sang as a little girl," I noted in my journal. I liked being "Claude Segrè, Protestant." It was a nice, generic, American whitebread way to reach God. As far as I could tell, I was not in disharmony with my upbringing and family traditions.

In college, I discovered that I wasn't nearly as free to search for my own religious creed as I had imagined. I left for college with high hopes. Maybe I'd have an experience like Paul's vision on the road to Damascus or Luther's fit in the choir or Saint Francis's dream of Lady Poverty. That didn't seem likely in Portland, Oregon, among Douglas firs and spruce, azaleas and rhododendrons, in Tudor-style dormitories fronted by huge English-style lawns. I thought I might become Episcopalian; instead, I turned Jewish.

I wanted to come to my faith, that of the People of the Book, through books, as my father had come to his beliefs. That didn't happen. I read about Christianity and Stoicism and noted in my diaries that "they don't provide a very good outlet for pent-up emotions [read 'sex']." Somerset Maugham's *The Razor's Edge* excited me about mysticism and the spiritual life for a while, but not enough to find a clear spiritual direction. Disappointed with books (combined with long freshman and sophomoric discussions of religion with roommates and friends), I decided to settle matters the American way. I went shopping.

Sporadically I sampled various Christian denominations and explored the limits of organized religion. My critiques read a bit like restaurant reviews. "Plain on the outside, plain on the inside." So much for a Methodist service I attended during a summer I spent at Woods Hole on Cape Cod. "Very unattractive and devoid of religious feeling. The people were there because they had to go, not because they were inspired. The altar had many flowers and was cluttered up with the instruments for the service, but everything was puritanical in comparison to European cathedrals." So much for Catholics. Episcopalians and New York City's Riverside Church rated more favorably. The Episcopalian minister quoted from Somerset Maugham's *The Summing Up*. I was pleased with his "nice bedside manner" and that he was "not a bigoted holy man." At Riverside Church, "the service went smoothly and beautifully, all except for the guest preacher who was pretty much of a dud and overly pedantic."

Initially, Judaism did not fare much better. As a small, nondenominational liberal arts college, with a reputation for radicalism, Reed attracted many Jewish students, especially from Los Angeles and New York. In the spring, I attended Reed "community" Passover seders in the college Commons, and in the fall, Yom Kippur services. My "reviews" continued ruthlessly:

Service long and not very interesting. Operatic cantor. Responsive readings much like any Christian Church service. . . . Didn't like the tribal aspects of the service. No love expressed for *all* men as in Christianity. . . . Tradition seemed ego-centric, selfish. I like the Christian concept of a brotherhood of all men and a "love thy neighbor" attitude better. It is more mature, I think.

A girlfriend during my sophomore and junior years precipitated more of a spiritual revelation than my shopping expeditions had. My family might be secular, even areligious; nevertheless, a web of implicit assumptions bound us. The girl's name was Esther. I proudly showed her picture to my parents and to my relatives during a summer trip to Europe. I noted the nods, the smiles of approval. Suddenly the questions became more explicit. "Oh, what about her family? Orthodox? Ashkenazi?" I felt increasingly embarrassed at my answer: "No, she's a Unitarian from Oregon." After Esther and I broke up (not over any religious matter), I continued going out with girls from a variety of religious backgrounds. Yet when I went out with Jewish girls, though I could not explain why, I began to feel that they were more "my crowd."

I stumbled onto another part of the family web—the Holocaust. I happened to see *Border Street,* a movie about the Warsaw ghetto, at Christmastime during my junior year. Afterward I attended an open house at a girl's dormitory. The candlelit rooms with the fir boughs on the mantel and bookshelves, the softness and good cheer of the girls, the sweetness of the punch and cookies, the joy of the carols shocked me. "I kept thinking that it [the Holocaust] had taken place just thirteen or fourteen years ago. . . . I could only sing as fervently as I could, 'Peace on Earth, Good Will to Men,'" I wrote in my diary.

My own family's story I knew only dimly. Mainly through relatives, like my mother's sister, my Aunt Lilli, and through family friends, I learned something about it. Whenever I tried to broach the subject with my father, he shied away. "Nazi *und* murder," he usually muttered. The odd mix of German and English sounded like a sorcerer's spell, as if my father were talking about a vicious fairy tale. He claimed that stories of the Holocaust gave him nightmares. At other times, like a clever child, he recited a little doggerel from the comic strips of his boyhood in which a European lectures a black cannibal:

Quessa lezione elementar,
Che è cattiva educazione
Carne uman divorar.

This lesson is elementary,
that it's bad manners
to devour human flesh.

It was a lesson, he claimed, that the Germans under Hitler had not learned.

Almost half a century later, he brooded over scars from the Holocaust. He imagined a conversation with his grandfather and told me about it. In the conversation, my father explained about Fascism and how "they kicked [him] out of Italy." Even worse, my father described "a great persecution of the Jews . . . in Germany, they have killed millions of them, and many also here [in Italy], including Mother." The grandfather protests in disbelief: "We are not in the Middle Ages. What kind of nonsense are you telling me?" "Unfortunately, what I told you is true," my father replies sadly.

At other times, I uncovered the depth of his feelings quite by accident. Movies or television programs about the war, especially the Italian partisan struggle against the Nazis, moved him deeply. In one movie, at the last moment, the SS officer refuses to give the order to shoot hostages, including Jews. He could go so far and no more. It was one of those rare moments when tears welled up in my father's eyes and his voice broke. Even among the Nazis there were limits, he murmured, as if he needed the comfort of at least that bit of faith.

I pondered his unwillingness to probe the darkness of the Holocaust. For once, I thought, I had found a topic too enormous, too frightening for him to grapple with. For my part, I wanted more. I was not satisfied with the Holocaust as a story of "Nazi *und* murder," of monsters in a nightmare. Germans were real. My maternal grandparents had lived among them. Nazis were real, thugs, politicians, criminals who ate, slept, perhaps even loved, as I did. What had gone so terribly wrong with them? I was determined to find out. When I embarked on an academic career, I studied modern European history, especially the story of Fascism and Nazism. Gradually, very slowly, I came to understand how the Holocaust had come about, how, in the historian-philosopher Hannah Arendt's phrase, "the banality of evil" was possible, in perspective how easy (though in no way inevitable) it all was when men of goodwill abdicated their responsibilities or lost heart.

Israel served as another one of those periodic paternal flash points. During the summer of 1960 I visited the Jewish state for the first time. I felt the bite—and the tug—of Zionism, as I noted in my diary:

On that ridiculous slice of swampland and desert . . . you can hold up your head and be proud of David and Saul, Maimonides and Hillel, as the Italians brag of Caesar and Columbus and Leonardo, the English of Shakespeare and Churchill, the Americans of Washington and Franklin. After 2,000 years, they've come back to hold up their heads, to build their nation on that bit of waste sand with a terrier-like defiance. There's something between the cute and the pathetic about it—until you feel like crying over it because it's a dream come true. "If you will it, it need not be a dream," Herzl said.

I had my doubts about contemporary Israeli society. The Promised Land, the dream of the Millennium looked suspiciously like American suburbia—except that people spoke Hebrew. For me, I decided, the Messiah was

just a plain old healthy child in a T-shirt, shorts and sandals, looking for all the world like a product of American suburbia, without a mark on him, growing up in a clean, modern apartment with a Daddy who doesn't wear a tie. That's the meaning of Israel. That's what everyone has been working and praying for for these two millennia. The Messiah is that little kid playing in the park.

Perhaps Israel had fallen short of the Zionists' lofty visions,

but better that they should worry about too many PTA meetings and too much leisure, as Jews under the star of David flag, than that they should worry about Bund meetings.

Each in his own way, my father and I became involved with Israel. Toward the end of his career, my father joined the board of Governors of Tel Aviv University. He regularly attended board meetings and served on a prize committee. When I settled on an academic career, I went to Israel for conferences, spent part of a sabbatical there, and collaborated with an Israeli scholar. Since my sister Amelia married an Israeli and made her home near Tel Aviv, the trips also became an opportunity for family visits.

On the rare occasions when we all met there, I listened to my father grumble and complain about Israel and Zionism. My father admired the bravery of the Zionist pioneers, as I did. They had the courage of their convictions. He admired, yet he also wavered, and he could even be snide. "Everybody knows that he [an Italian Zionist leader] ran off to Israel because he got a girl pregnant," he snorted. Naturally, he worried about the safety of my sister and her family, and the *cacadubbi* in him regularly generated gloom-and-doom scenarios about the future of the tiny Jewish state, surrounded by a sea of hostile Arab neighbors. Yet I also thought I noticed a peculiar gleam of satisfaction in his eye as he, like a proud biblical patriarch, posed with us all—children, in-laws, grandchildren—for a family picture.

Identifying as a Jew, empathizing with Israel wasn't enough, I discovered. What kind of Jew was I? I had never gone to Sunday school. My mother had never joined Hadassah; my father had never spent a Sunday on the phone raising money for the UJA. If anything, he was dubious of those who congregated there. So where did I belong? How observant should I be?

I tried to sound out my father. The echoes came back confused, disorienting. When my sister Amelia considered marrying the son of a Russian Orthodox priest, my father objected strongly. Yet when my sister Fausta married an English Gentile, there was no protest. When I married a Jewish girl, I heard no comment, for or against. When I observed the Jewish holidays and told my father, he would sometimes reply, "Bravo!"—but little more. Later I would learn that he, too, had been to services or had attended a seder.

A book finally gave me my bearings, and it was my father who first told me about it. It was a novel about an Italian Jewish family. When I first read Giorgio Bassani's *The Garden of the Finzi-Contini,* shortly after it appeared in 1965, I seemed to have discovered a story that summed up the traditions and experiences I knew best. In the nostalgic and tragic tale of Giorgio and of Micòl Finzi-Contini, I found a Judaism that I could identify with: Italian and patrician, a Judaism in which secular learning was more important than religious study. I also felt a personal tie to the story. Distant relatives—my father's second cousins—lived in the little Renaissance town of Ferrara, halfway between Bologna and Venice, where the novel is set.

Yet when I looked about the book more closely, I wondered if my yearning to identify with it wasn't forced. What did I really have in common with Giorgio and with Micòl Finzi-Contini? I'd lived in Los Alamos and Berkeley, never—despite my relatives—in a small town like Ferrara. I knew nothing, really, of the aristocratic ways of the Finzi-Contini family. I didn't even know many of the Hebrew expressions that they used. Why should I identify more with them than with German Jewry? After all, my mother was German.

Yet I did. Perhaps subconsciously I was hearing my father: "If you're going to be Jewish, my son, do it my way." I was the reflection of my father's dominance over my mother, her rejection of her homeland and culture. I also found that the traditions of Italian Jewry—as I understood them—presented a relatively painless path to Judaism. The Italian Jews I knew were largely nonreligious. According to their model, I didn't have to discipline myself seriously and follow ritual and dietary laws. Without overlooking the shabby, vicious, and cynical anti-Semitism of Mussolini's regime, I could still identify with the long tradition of religious tolerance in Italy. If I felt uncomfortable with Malamud, Roth, Bellow, and the American Jewish literary and intellectual tradition, I felt at ease with contemporary Italian Jewish writers: Primo Levi, Natalia Ginzburg, Giorgio Bassani, Vittorio Dan Segre. They fit into my father's ideal of *gente colta.*

In identifying with Italian Jewry, I discovered an added bonus—especially in the United States. At *oneg shabbats,* the festive gatherings over cakes and punch or coffee after Friday-night services, I relished the furrowed brows and the quizzical expressions when I told fellow worshipers about my background. "An Italian Jew? I didn't know there were any." Or the reaction among the connoisseurs of the multiplicity of Jewish traditions, especially marriageable women or matchmakers: "Italian Jews? Oh, they're the best kind! Are you married?" The Italian tradition set me apart from most of my coreligionists in the United States. As in so many aspects of my life, I belonged—but not quite, I concluded.

But I did belong. The central historical factor in my life, I realized, was the Holocaust. Hitler, and to a lesser extent, Mussolini, had been determined to snuff out the Jews. The enormity, the audacity, the obscenity of their crimes took my breath away, then filled me with rage. My immediate family had been relatively fortunate; yet we bore our scars and remembered our dead. Without the Holocaust, most likely I would be living in Italy. Without the Holocaust, I would have known grandparents; without the Holocaust, I would have mingled with aunts and uncles and cousins more than I did.

For a while, I felt helpless. My father's and mother's silences, the Holocaust as "Nazi *und* murder" left me uneasy, hungering for something more. I decided to fill in the voids and the silences. I did so with every service I attended, with every prayer I uttered, with every class I taught, with every lecture I gave, with every piece I published about the Holocaust. I was also honoring my dead, and the millions I didn't know, Jew and Gentile alike. Against the enormity of the evil, my efforts appeared minuscule; without them, I knew, men of goodwill would have no chance at all.

Figure 11. *In Fitting Memory*. A sculpture in cast stone, stainless steel, and glass by Hungarian-born Marika Somogyi. A commemoration of *Kristallnacht* in Nazi Germany, 1938, when organized violence was perpetrated against Jews, their shops, and their synagogues. (Courtesy Judah L. Magnes Museum.)

CHAPTER II

Memory and the Holocaust: Two Perspectives

Ismar Schorsch and Jackie Feldman

The Holocaust took not only the lives of its victims but also their cultural creativity and religious sensibilities. What we are left with is major questions about the *memory* of that rupture in human history. How is it to be remembered, made sense of—if at all—and who is to guide future generations in giving an adequate place to both the pain and resolve for the future evoked by its recollection? This chapter presents two personal accounts that confront these questions. Both are written by people whose parents knew well the developments of Nazi-dominated Europe and against the backdrop of the authors' visits to sites on that continent.

Ismar Schorsch escaped the town of Esslingen in Germany with his parents and sister in 1938, but his grandfather remained there to serve as director of the local Jewish school and later died in Theresienstadt. In 1994, when Schorsch was Chancellor of the Jewish Theological Seminary of America, he was invited to Esslingen to commemorate the anniversary of his grandfather's death and to witness how the town restored the memories of its Jewish past. Schorsch's scholarship enabled him to place this highly local event on the broad canvas of Jewish history in Germany, which began in the Middle Ages. His address in the town, delivered in German, blends the personal, the intellectual, and the spiritual in a manner that draws lessons of general human relevance from a particular family history.

Jackie Feldman, whose father escaped a train headed toward a death camp, was born in the United States but decided to make his home in Israel. An experienced tour guide, he began to explore the educational trips of Israeli youths to Poland, which were becoming a common feature of the pupils' high school years. He describes how these trips work to impart a very specific set of Zionist messages amid the very visceral reactions that the voyages elicit. He also points to the limitations of these messages, both with reference to specific familial experiences in the Holocaust that some of the youngsters seek to know and to the universal questions raised by its perpetually distressing events.

The Sword and the Book

Ismar Schorsch

On July 3, 1994, the town of Esslingen (near Stuttgart) commemorated the fiftieth anniversary of the death of my grandfather, Theodor Rothschild, in Theresienstadt. I delivered the following address (in German) for the occasion.

When my sister and I visited Esslingen briefly in July 1977, we came unannounced. It was our first visit since we had fled Germany in December 1938. We made our way to the building that had once housed the well-known Jewish boarding school run by our grandfather for forty years and our great-grandfather for twenty-six. It had been plundered by Nazi zealots on November 10, 1938, and closed for the last time at the end of August 1939, just before Hitler invaded Poland.

My sister recognized the stately house instantly, because it remained basically unchanged from the place she had roamed as a young girl on summer vacation. My own memories, those of a three-year-old, had long evaporated. When no one answered the door, we made our way inside and slowly walked around without ever meeting a soul. Indeed, the building was still a school, now run by the state, clean, bright, and airy. What saddened us no end was the obliteration of the institution's Jewish past. Its public spaces held no trace of any photographs, plaque, or memorial to make the students aware that this school had not always been what it presently was.

I relate this visit to underscore how much has changed for the better. Not long after, a number of local residents mounted an arduous campaign to rename the school after its prominent last Jewish director that culminated in victory in November 1983. Inside, the walls of the school now recount the history and fate of the Jewish school, which was founded in 1841, and a trove of documents and pictures are assembled in the director's office to instruct any curious student or visitor who might wish to know still more. And today, the city of Esslingen has chosen to commemorate the fiftieth anniversary of my grandfather's death in Theresienstadt because he was unwilling to abandon his children while his school was still permitted to stay open by the Nazis.

I do not make light of these gestures. They are reflective of a ground-swell across Germany during the last fifteen years for reconciliation, often spearheaded by the younger generation. While the past cannot be undone, it can be mastered through honesty, understanding, and contrition. These are the sentiments motivating many hundreds of university students every year to take courses in Jewish studies, even to the extent of learning Hebrew and spending a year at the Hebrew University in Jerusalem. These are the sentiments moving curators to mount major Jewish exhibitions such as the one in Berlin in the winter of 1991 to 1992 and minor ones in local communities. These are the sentiments prompting many towns and cities to bring back, at their expense, Jewish former residents for a visit, to erect monuments to memorialize what was destroyed, and to care for Jewish cemeteries. The media prefer to focus on the outbursts of extremists; they utterly fail to note how deep and diversified and mainstream has become the German effort to confront the Holocaust and turn its grisly lesson into a force for good. Surely Germany has done far more in this regard than any other modern nation guilty of genocide. It is critical for Jews to recognize and celebrate that the Germany of 1994 is not the Germany of 1944.

Theodor Rothschild was a teacher and author, a lover of books, and a transmitter of culture. In his school he had created two libraries, one for the children and one for the teachers. Reading aloud in small groups was part of the culture of the place. He personified the love of learning and addiction to books that has long marked Jews as the people of the book. In Judaism sacred works are not discarded but buried, as if they were human. And indeed they are, because it is the written word that makes us most human.

When the Nazi mob plundered his school on the afternoon of November 10, 1938, it assaulted civilization itself. Besides brutalizing its teachers, the thugs took out the Torah scroll from its synagogue and the books from its libraries and torched them in a bonfire in the courtyard. In Esslingen they wildly reenacted the bonfires fed with Jewish books that were lit across Nazi Germany on May 10, 1933, by university students bent on cleansing the Germany spirit. In Berlin, Goebbels had blessed the violence with a personal appearance and announced the end "of a period of excessive Jewish intellectualism (Zeitalters eines über-spitzten jüdischen Intellektualismus)." In the flames he professed to see the spiritual foundation of the Weimar Republic reduced to ashes.

The spectacle of torching Jewish books brings to mind the luminous line written by the young Heinrich Heine on the burning of the Koran by the Spanish grand inquisitor: "That was merely a prologue. There where books are burned, people will also be burned in the end." What Heine caught in this unforgettable epigram is that books are not a mere symbol but the very essence of civilization. To burn books is to repudiate the instinct-renunciation, sublimation, and rationality that separate the jungle from civilization. It is, to move from Heine to Freud, the revolt of civilization's discontents ever ready to rip off the constraints vital to producing culture. Once unleashed, the repressed urges of the id move quickly from pyres of books to mass murder, from Kristallnacht to the Final Solution.

As Freud already intuited, Judaism epitomized the triumph of spirit over the senses and intellect over instincts. Goebbels was not wrong: Judaism did revere the mind. Long before, a Palestinian rabbi of the second century had imagined that the book and the sword once descended from heaven locked together in eternal combat. With its devotion to study and religious practice, Judaism called for self-conquest rather than the conquest of others and literacy rather than license. Even when vanquished and forced into exile, Jews did not become homeless. The sacred written text became their portable homeland. They persisted in spinning webs of words that transported them to tranquil realms of lasting meaning and inured them to the harsh conditions outside. They based their Shabbat liturgy on the annual reading of the Torah, the Five Books of Moses, and marked the passage of time by their location in the text. Above all, Jews grew into masters of textual analysis, putting a premium on slow, reflective reading with commentary as the quintessential mode of Jewish literary expression.

Moreover, it is this cerebral religious tradition that uniquely prepared Jews to embrace modernity, even before emancipation freed them from their shackles. Barely out of the ghetto, Moses Mendelssohn and Heine became masters and models of German prose and poetry. By 1886 to 1887, Jewish students represented 10 percent of all students studying at Prussian universities, and by 1912, 8.5 percent of all students at institutions of higher learning in the Russian Empire where Jews had still not been emancipated. And there can be no doubt that the extraordinary achievement of a new nation like Israel to govern itself effectively and democratically owes much to the affinity of Jews for education. The first official act of the Zionist movement in Palestine in 1918 after having received the Balfour Declaration a year before was to lay the cornerstone for the Hebrew University on Mt. Scopus. And today Israel publishes annually more books per capita than any country in the world except Iceland, in a language that a century ago was barely living.

When the Nazis came to power in 1933, German Jewry took up the pen in a heroic five-year struggle of spiritual resistance. They published books to nourish the mind and comfort the soul, such as the daring *Schocken Bücherei*, a series of nearly one hundred titles, both old and new, drawn from the entire range of Jewish creativity and printed in inexpensive pocket-size editions. Beginning with the lyrical prophecies of Second Isaiah in the gritty Buber-Rosenzweig translation, the series included German renditions of talmudic and midrashic texts, medieval Hebrew poetry and modern Yiddish literature, as well as works of Jewish history written long ago and in the 1930s.

The shattering of emancipation also prompted my grandfather to take refuge in the world of the spirit. Along with two other Jewish educators, he published in 1936 a splendid anthology of modern Jewish poetry whose title, *Not und Hofnung* (Need and hope), indicated its purpose. Its contents covered broad topics: Jewish history, days of holiness, the land of Israel, and resistance to oppression. In the foreword, the authors stressed the solace to be found in the poetry evoked by earlier experiences of persecution. "If prejudice and persecution have accompanied us throughout the millennia, so have our poets and singers, faithful companions who illuminated our pain in their works." The Nazis regarded the pathos and power of the book as subversive and immediately confiscated the entire edition.

The medieval history of the Jews in Esslingen also offers remarkable testimony on the bookish nature of Judaism. It is the home of the oldest Hebrew manuscript from Germany with a recorded date. Just a few decades after Jews had settled in Esslingen, Qalonimos ben Yehudah noted in a postscript (colophon) to his *mahzor* (prayerbook) for the fall festivals of Rosh Hashanah, Yom Kippur, and Sukkot that he completed his work on the Hebrew date of 28 Tevet 5050, that is, January 12, 1290. An illuminated manuscript with decorations typical of thirteenth-century Ashkenazic (German) manuscripts, the fragmented *mahzor* of Qalonimos has just recently been reunited. Evelyn M. Cohen, a young and sensitive Jewish art historian, in a moment of drama, recognized that the incomplete section in the Bibliotheca Rosenthaliana in Amsterdam derives from the same patrimony as the truncated one preserved in the library of my own institution, the Jewish Theological Seminary. Moreover, on the basis of the Esslingen *mahzor,* scholars are beginning to identify other medieval Hebrew manuscripts as originating in Esslingen, making it an important transmitter of Jewish culture.

In Theresienstadt, two books served to fortify the faith, good humor, and indomitable will of Helene Rothschild, Theodor's only sister. Like her, they came through the horror of this "model" camp and are today among my most treasured possessions. The first is a pocket-sized traditional prayer book for weekdays and Sabbath with Hebrew text and German translation. The inside cover bears the inscription of her name. What else makes this *siddur* uncommon is the fact that according to its title page, it was printed in Frankfurt am Main (Rödelheim) in 1939, long after any hope German Jews might still have harbored for an accommodation with the Nazis had vanished. It must surely be among the last Jewish works printed in Nazi Germany. To me, it has always symbolized the flicker of eternal light in the midst of total darkness, the book that in this instance denied the sword its victory.

The second spiritual bulwark of Tante Helene, as we knew her, was an equally small and slender volume of prayers in German for Jewish women for all occasions. Edited by Fanny Neuda a century earlier and reprinted many times, this particular edition of *Stunden der Andacht* (Moments of meditation) was published in Prague in 1873. It was intended to bring edification and solace to women who could not read Hebrew. On the inside front cover is a list of some seventeen first names of family members, including my mother's, with the birthday of each one alongside. More poignant still, on the back inside cover is recorded the day of death of Tante Helene's two brothers, who died in Theresienstadt in rapid order after the bitter winter of 1944. Karl died on June 2 and Theodor on July 11 (actually July 10). In each instance the Hebrew date is given. The women endured adversity better: Theodor's sister, wife, and sister-in-law survived. One can only imagine the comfort they drew from sending their anguish aloft in the sacred vessels of these two fragile links to eternity.

In every generation, civilization hangs by a thread. Neither culture nor morality is imprinted in the genes; every child must be socialized afresh. As a teacher, Theodor Rothschild protected that which makes us most human. His being was filled with compassion for children, with love for the forms and values of Judaism, and with wonder at the marvels and mysteries of nature. I knew him only through the person of my father, who came to Esslingen at a tender age from a broken home, and for whom my grandfather became a lifelong model. For both of them the immediacy of God's presence was a daily reality experienced in the countless miracles of the ordinary. I am convinced that my father's doctoral dissertation at Tübingen entitled, "The Teachability of Religion" (*Die Lehrbarkeit der Religion*) came right out of my grandfather's school, where Judaism was lived and learned unself-consciously. Its pattern of daily prayer and sacred days determined the rhythm of the school. My father went on to become the rabbi that my grandfather, as a gifted teacher and genuine religious personality, had always been, even without the title.

Theodor had two daughters, my aunt Berta and my mother, Fanny. My aunt and her husband left Germany in August 1938 to resettle in the United States, and my family followed in December 1938. I still have the many letters that Theodor wrote to his children in the two years before Pearl Harbor. Obviously self-censored and laced with family matters, they nevertheless convey the robustness of his unbroken spirit. By December 8, 1938, almost a month after his school had been closed for the first time, he had come to realize how misguided had been his belief that by not applying for a visa number from the American consulate, the school would be allowed by the Nazis to remain open. "That we did not permit ourselves to get a number is an act of neglect that we can never make good. We must simply adjust to it and hope that the many numbers ahead of our own will be quickly disposed of." It is heartrending to follow in this correspondence from the world of insanity the interminable delays and dashed hopes that marked the tireless efforts of our families, without financial resources, to secure the emigration of Theodor and his wife, Ina. As late as November 4, 1941, he wrote with renewed optimism about soon getting an American visa, after a telegram from us that held out the prospect of passage to Cuba.

He used the time to deepen his knowledge of Hebrew and to master English. On September 5, he declared proudly from Esslingen: "In English I have come so far that I can read and understand quite well simple stories, which gives me great joy. By the time we get to you, we will surely understand some English and even be able to speak a bit." At the time he was teaching twenty-six hours a week, including math and geometry, the only teacher well enough to carry such a heavy load.

Once removed to Stuttgart, he continued to teach, conduct religious services, and serve on the executive committee (*Der Oberrat*) of the organized Jewish community. On November 27, 1941, in one of his last letters, he admitted: "It is right now very tough. He who visits this upon us, also gives us the strength to bear it. Particularly unpleasant for us is that we needed to vacate our apartment and have still not found another. But also in this instance we hope for a solution. All this means that we approach our holidays in low spirits. But I don't want to be disheartening and will offer in the services as much comfort and strength as I possibly can." Ina and Theodor finally found a one-room apartment that required them to share a common kitchen and bathroom with four other families.

In Theresienstadt, spiritual nourishment sustained his declining physical strength. He never missed a chance to hear a lecture. After the war, Ina reported to us that he used every free minute for study. "A Czech doctor studied Hebrew with him. English books cluttered his workplace. It was well known that anything to read would give him the greatest joy." It is true that he finally succumbed to the brute force of the sword, but only after prolonged spiritual resistance. Less than a year later, Hitler's vaunted thousand-year Reich was to fall after a twelve-year reign of terror. Theodor Rothschild's inspiring legacy of humanity in the face of inhumanity personifies the very essence of Judaism and the secret to its extraordinary survival.

"Roots in Destruction": The Jewish Past as Portrayed in Israeli Youth Voyages to Poland

Jackie Feldman

Introduction

Walter Benjamin wrote that the storyteller is the one who comes from afar in space and in time to tell what is very near. The storyteller is a native who comes back to the circle. From Benjamin we learn that the native is confined to his circle not necessarily in that he never leaves, but in that he must return in order to tell the story (Gurevitch 1997: 203).

My father was born into a Hasidic family in Hungary, and when taken away from his home, west to the camps, he jumped off the train. I was born into a modern Orthodox family in New York. When I left my home, it was by subway, at least until the day when I ascended on a plane and came on aliya to a new-old home I claimed as my own, Israel. After my father died, I took another train, eastbound across Europe to his hometown, once Hungary, then part of Soviet Ukraine. There, with the help of a diagram constructed from the account of my last surviving aunt and of an old caretaker of the Jewish cemetery, I found the house of his youth and the tomb of my grandmother who died before the war. My grandfather was killed at Auschwitz.

After finding the remains of my dead I took my child's *kippa* out of my pocket and walked the streets of Ungvar, searching doorposts for vanished *mezuzot,* in the hope that some live person, Jew or anti-Semite, would acknowledge my presence, and I would know I'd come home. But the Russians, Ruthenians, and Hungarians who inhabited the gray Soviet town gave no sign of recognition. And I had to continue, to search for that home elsewhere.

Subsequently, when I encountered Israeli kids traveling to Auschwitz, my first instinct told me that they were all traveling, en masse, on my pilgrimage. On my return to Israel, I decided to investigate these voyages further and began by reading about Jewish memory, memory of the Shoah, and Holocaust education in Israel.

Jewish Memory, Israeli Memory, and the Shoah

In Jewish culture, the memory of common origins, the sense of common destiny, and the practice of commemorative rituals enabled the people to retain a sense of common identity in the absence of a territorial base or common spoken language. Memory, *zekher,* is not so much the content of intellectualized, individual reflection as "a matter of . . . evocation and identification; . . . a series of situations into which we can somehow be existentially drawn" (Yerushalmi 1982: 44). One of the most important metaphors that shape the way the past is understood has been *mi-hurban li-geulah,* the destruction of the Temple leading to an exile, which would terminate with the coming of the Messiah and the final redemption. Although the State of Israel was built upon the experience of Jews in exile and nourished by (secularized) Messianic hopes of redemption, the founding fathers of the State sought to distance themselves from the Jewish society in exile, which, for them, represented passivity, humiliation, obscurantism, and suffering. These founders saw the establishment of the State as a return to the biblical, pre-Exilic period; exile stood for the loss of the physical bond to the land as well as the loss of the Jews' collective experience as a nation. Thus, the Shoah could be seen as a "natural" end to Exile—an inevitable consequence of the vulnerability and weakness of Jewish life outside the homeland. Until 1967, most Holocaust survivors were looked down upon by the pioneering settlers, the Israeli elite, as those who went passively as "sheep to slaughter." Only the ghetto fighters and partisans were listened to and valorized. Yet, in spite of its oppositionist stance, the dominant Zionist view of its own recent history *mi-shoah li-tekumah*—from utter destruction (Shoah) to revival (through the State)—was an adaptation of the paradigm of *mi-hurban li-geulah*.

In the weeks preceding the Six-Day War in 1967, the existential anxiety of the State, and the isolation of Israel in the world community, brought Israelis to identify their situation with that of the Holocaust victims. The Yom Kippur War, in 1973, emphasized the vulnerability of Israel and further strengthened this self-perception. As a result, the memory of all Holocaust victims was assimilated to that of the Israeli soldiers who sacrificed themselves on the altar of the State. Once the Holocaust was incorporated into the Zionist narrative in this way, subsequent historical events served to "confirm" this understanding of the relation of the Shoah to the State of Israel, while the Shoah provided an interpretative model for current events. Symbolic equations were constructed: Israel = Jew, victim; Arab = Nazi, oppressor; Gentiles/world opinion = indifferent bystander.

The post-1967 period was marked by growing criticism of formerly sacred institutions. While the conquest of East Jerusalem and other biblical sites in the 1967 war led to a renewed alliance with mythic-religious centers in some circles, it also engendered disillusionment among those who did not share that messianic fervor. The Yom Kippur War, the Lebanon War (1982), and the Intifada (Palestinian uprising, 1987 to 1993) dimmed the faith in the wisdom of Israel's generals and the justice and inevitability of its wars (Bilu and Ben-Ari 1997: 232–33). The overall demythologization process included questioning the sacrificial role of the Shoah in Israel's self-understanding. During the last fifteen years, different approaches to Holocaust memory have become part of the larger ideological struggle over Israel's identity and the foundations of the Jewish State and an important influence on students' understandings of the past.

Since 1973, young Israelis have shown greater interest in the Shoah and felt a greater identification with its victims. This change is certainly due to aging of the survivor generation; many youngsters are eager to hear, while they can still tell them, the untold stories of their elderly grandparents. The growing interest in the Shoah also reflects the decline in the appeal of the two exemplars of the native Israeli—the soldier and the pioneer kibbutznik-farmer as well as the rise of a hedonistic individualistic ethos. These trends have led to a wide variety of root-searching phenomena among diverse groups in Israeli society: the repentant return of youths to Jewish orthodoxy (Aviad 1983), the sacralization of development town shrines (Bilu and Ben-Ari, 1997), ethnic festivals (Dominguez 1989), and many others. This same impetus may have directed descendants of survivors to search for their repressed roots in the Holocaust past. The State has promoted the memory of the Shoah as a uniting force. The potentially divisive force of the Shoah (as a catastrophe that befell primarily European Jewry) is offset by the perception of the event as fundamentally separate from any specific Diaspora Jewish past. The Shoah is depicted as part of common Jewish destiny. As the Education Ministry's guidebook states: "Even if there were amongst us social, ethnic and ideological differences—in Treblinka, Majdanek and Bergen-Belsen these differences disappeared . . . there they made us one nation—the nation that was murdered!" (Keren 1993: 103).

Changing Israeli attitudes toward the Shoah were reflected, with several years' delay, in Israeli education. At first, the Holocaust had been ignored, and the little attention it received focused on the ghetto fighters and partisans. In the 1970s and 1980s, the number of hours devoted to the Shoah in the curriculum increased. Teachings about the Shoah centered on its uniqueness, its connection to Jewish history, and its link to the State of Israel. In general, the universal implications of the Shoah were never an important part of Holocaust education. While traditionally the primary means of teaching the Shoah were textbooks, readers, and the performance of Holocaust Memorial Day ceremonies, since 1988, voyages to Poland have become an increasingly important part of Shoah education. In 1998, almost 15,000 students, about 10 percent of the national class size, traveled on school trips to Poland. More than a quarter of them traveled on trips organized by the Ministry of Education, trips that serve as a model for other groups' voyages as well.

The stories and pictures of the returning students have become an important influence on their classmates and friends.

The Structure and Significance
of the Voyages to Poland

To understand these trips better, I enrolled in the Ministry's preparatory course for tour guides to Poland. My participation familiarized me with the subject material of the voyages—the Shoah and prewar Polish Jewry—and enabled me to guide groups myself, thereby allowing me to learn the organization and structure of the voyage from the inside. I traveled to Poland four times as a guide with Ministry of Education youth groups before accompanying a fifth group as a participant-observer. On that voyage, I sat with the students, recorded the guide's narrative and the students' reactions and conversations, and filmed the ceremonies and visits. At the end of the trip, the students agreed to let me copy their trip diaries, which offered invaluable insight into their thoughts and emotional reactions to sites, recorded in real time.

During the preparatory course, Oded Cohen, the moving force behind the Ministry's Poland voyages, explained their origin as follows:

I was supposed to go to Chernobyl that day, but the Holy One Blessed Be He helped me, and the explosion took place that day and I didn't go there . . . And (the Polish representative) asks me if the gentleman has any suggestions about the program. . . . and I say, "You know, for us Jews . . . on Shabbat we read, 'it is my brothers whom I am seeking.' I am not interested in the congress, I am seeking my brothers." . . . And so, for seven days, I did about the same itinerary that you're doing . . . anyway, from Auschwitz you don't return the same . . . Like fire in our bones, one of the main things we decided then was that we have to bring the youth of Israel to Poland.

In this account, national identity is all that matters. It is expressed through family metaphors—"my brothers." Modern-day Poland is of no interest. The juxtaposition of "I was glad it happened (to someone else) so that I didn't have to go to Chernobyl" followed by "It is my brothers I am seeking" suggests that the strong opposition of "us" and "them" was built into the voyage from its inception.

Although the Ministry's declared goals combine particularistic national lessons ("the need for a strong, autonomous Jewish state") with universal ones ("the obligation to struggle against all forms of racism"), the priorities of the voyage can be discerned from its structure and from the things that are characterized as *en brera* (lit. "no choice") during the trips themselves. The elements seen as absolutely unchangeable— *en brera*—reflect the often unstated but unquestioned understandings at the heart of the voyage. For example: "The security personnel give us orders; not we them. They have information that we don't. Important: we must arrive at places on time. Your guides will push you in the back—*en brera* . . . Nothing to be done." This demonstrates that security is the supreme authority on the voyage, and must be seen as such by the students. Another example was the course instructors' and teachers' unanimous agreement that: "*Hatikva* (Israel's national anthem) is prescribed at the end of every ceremony. Always." The assertion of national Israeli identity provides the closure for every ceremony in Poland. Still another example is the "impossibility" of changing the itinerary or schedule to visit a site where a participant's grandparents lived for reasons of schedule and security. Nationalized memory of the Shoah takes precedence over individual family memory. Finally, during the guide course's pilot trip to Poland, the head administrator/guide rushed the participants to curtail a conversation with one of the few old Jews of Ger in order to arrive on time at another cemetery. One of the participant guides said: "No, wait. Maybe this Jew has something to say, even if he's not dead yet!" The memory of the murdered Jews of the Shoah seems to be of greater interest than the lives of Jews remaining in Poland today.

I learned how the messages of the Ministry of Education's Poland voyage are built into the voyage's personnel structure, its construction of time and space, and its commemorative ceremonies.

PERSONNEL STRUCTURE

The groups are organized into delegations of 120 to 150 participants, made up of four to five buses, each containing thirty students, two to three teachers, an Israeli guide, and a Polish bus driver. In addition, three survivor-witnesses, two to three security persons, two Polish guides, a doctor and nurse, and a delegation leader and assistant are attached to each delegation. While the Israeli guides are to provide "the facts," the accompanying "witnesses" are Holocaust survivors who tell of their personal experiences. They are not so much a source of information as an incarnation of the dead. They testify not only through their narrative but also through their physical presence at the sites. These survivors are the undisputed heroes of the voyage.

The Israeli security personnel carry out security briefings, check the buses and hotels for suspicious objects or persons, guard the group while touring, and patrol the lobby at night. Students must never leave the sight of the security guards. By living under these tight constraints for a week, students are constantly reminded that as Jews and Israelis in the Diaspora, they are subject to hostile, potentially murderous forces and that only the agents of the State can provide them with protection. The decision to travel in large delegations heightens the group's visibility, which, in turn, necessitates greater security measures, further increasing the group's isolation and visibility.

TIME AND SPACE

The environment in Poland is insulated and intense, since the group spends an average of twelve hours of touring a day. Almost every minute of the voyage and every site on the itinerary are determined in advance. All activities are done as a group. The space in Poland is clearly divided between encompassing, homey inside spaces and alien, alienating outside spaces. The polarity of these spaces may be summarized in the following list:

Inside the bus or hotel	*Outside the bus or hotel*
Encompassing environmental bubble of the home world	Alienation of the foreign terrain
Warm temperatures	Cold temperatures
Hebrew spoken / Israeli food and music	Polish spoken / Unfamiliar food
Security	Danger
Fun and socializing	Mourning, serious demeanor
Present and future	Past
Israel	Holocaust Poland / Diaspora Jewry
Life	Death

In their travels through Poland, students come to associate the bus and hotel with Israel, the center of life and hope, whereas the "outside" world of Poland comes to stand for the Holocaust and death. The outside sites may be divided into Jewish death sites (for example, Auschwitz), past-Jewish-life sites (like synagogues preserved as museums), and several non-Jewish Polish tourist sites, included for "ventilation." The most time is allotted and attention paid, however, to the death sites.

Furthermore, even the "Jewish-life sites" are empty of living Polish Jews and speak of death. The itinerary provides no meaningful encounter with contemporary Poles or Diaspora Jews, which might moderate the picture of the world outside Israel as the place of Holocaust death.

The voyages follow a standard itinerary. Though some itinerary considerations stem from logistic constraints, the main determinant is the construction of a pilgrimage experience. The inner rhythm of the itinerary is determined by the theme *laga'at ve-livroah,* to touch and recoil. The voyage rhythm alternates between contact with Holocaust death in the Polish landscape and socializing and having fun in the bus and hotel. On a typical, eight-day voyage, the "heavy" days of visits to the death camps of Auschwitz-Birkenau, Majdanek, and Treblinka (days two, five, and seven) alternate with "lighter" days, of visits to sites of the Jewish past (days six and eight), Polish tourist sites (day three), or shopping and rest time (day four).

COMMEMORATIVE CEREMONIES

The site visits are punctuated by ceremonies. These ceremonies are designed to create unity in feeling and a sense of community through repetition of central symbols and songs; they manifest strength and survival through massive common presence on Polish soil. They offer participants an opportunity to summarize and bring closure to what was previously witnessed through active commemoration and provide liturgical "triggers" for the accumulated emotional charge. The ceremonies take in the fragmentation of the sites, absorb it, tame it, and turn it into a collective expression. They communicate the themes through a dense, compelling ritual language of symbolic display and dramatization. Although many types of ceremonies take place, two delegation-wide ceremonies (with 150 participants) are always held: one over the crematoria at Auschwitz-Birkenau (to identify with the dead and proclaim the students as their victorious heirs) and the other at the Warsaw Ghetto Memorial at the end of the voyage (to proclaim heroism, struggle, and victory as the gateway to the home world, Israel).

The Performance of the Poland Pilgrimage

How, and to what extent, are the messages built into the time, space, and ritual of the voyage, absorbed by the students? How students may contemporize their experience with those of the survivor-victims is illustrated by three things: 1) the testimony of the witness at Auschwitz-Birkenau, 2) the visit to the barracks of shoes at Majdanek, and 3) the raising of the flag in the delegation ceremonies.

THE TESTIMONY AT AUSCHWITZ-BIRKENAU

The visit to Auschwitz-Birkenau takes nine hours. The morning is dedicated to visiting the exhibits in the restored concentration camp of Auschwitz 1, which include models of the crematoria, piles of hair, and mounds of suitcases and prostheses. The afternoon is spent in the preserved barracks of the Birkenau extermination camp (Auschwitz 2). There students are squeezed into the long, narrow space of the quarantine barracks between the wooden bunk beds to hear the Israeli witness-survivor testify. Most voyages take place in the fall or early spring, and it is often quite cold. Students curl up against one another atop the bare brick heating duct to keep warm. They huddle in the cold, as the witness, the incarnation of the dead, recounts his or her story of suffering and survival. On one not atypical visit, the witness pointed to the objects, which completely surround the students, designating them as authentic material witnesses to his story. He told the students:

It moves me to tell you all I went through in the terrible years of the Shoah at a time when I was your age, seventeen years old, fifty years ago . . . Imagine, a boy of your age that thought he would be something in life. I was the son of a wealthy family, I had many plans, and I found myself here [points to bunk beds], alone at Auschwitz.

More than the content of the narrative, the ritual of common presence with the witness in the camps enables students to visualize that they could have been imprisoned there, on the bunk bed that the survivor designates as his own. As a student wrote in his diary:

In Birkenau, things were so real . . . all of a sudden you see the reality of the things and someone comes and tells you exactly where he was and what he did and who talked to him and . . . It really affected me.

The survivor continues his narrative outside:

Look, here was the iron ramp. This earth is soaked with blood and tears of innocent people . . . There was a selection. For life or death . . . and at that time I was skinny and weak. The selection: where you're standing now, there were the officers and they pointed left or right. There [the witness points] to the crematorium, or here [he points again] to work. And the officer stood there . . . And I passed at a run. That way, I could show that I was fit to work, and he directed me to the left and I joined the group. And maybe it was my fate, so that I can tell you the story today.

He concludes:

You know, it is you who give me the strength so that I can go on, even until nightfall. E (delegation leader) said, "H, you're exhausted"; maybe he thinks that I don't have the strength to transmit things that were hidden for fifty years. But I see that you're thirsty to know, and that's why we came, so that you can be witnesses to what they did to our people . . .

   You who are here in this place know that you are the correct answer to Nazism and anti-Semitism. On the one side are the ovens, in which hundreds of thousands were burnt. And now children, girls and boys, bring many new sons to the nation, so that we live forever.

The students are told that they empower the survivor to give his testimony and provide the redemptive close to his story, his victory over death. Students and witness are enclosed in the same bubble and share the same roles: survivor, victor, witness. Through their common presence at Auschwitz, students become "witnesses of the witnesses" and associate their experience of Auschwitz with that of the survivors.

THE BARRACKS OF SHOES AT MAJDANEK

   Within the memorial site at the Majdanek death camp are three adjacent wooden barracks containing huge, cagelike bins, filled to the brim with old shoes of the victims of the Shoah. As one enters, the floorboards creak. The buildings are badly lit and poorly ventilated. The stench of old, decaying shoes fills the dark. The light is dim, and the intense smell of the putrefying shoes evokes death and rotting corpses. One girl wrote:

As you go further inside, among the rows of shoes, it gets darker and darker, somber, more damp and dark—and dangerous. Everything closes in on you inside there. . . . Suddenly an unexplainable urge took hold of me, unexplainable but really strong to touch one of the shoes, as if only then I'd know that all the thousands of pairs of shoes really exist, are tangible, and not some hallucination. But I was scared. . . . But the urge to touch, to feel, was too strong, so I stretched out my hand; . . . but then, the shoe moved . . . and to see the past move before your eyes, . . . it almost finished me off (*gamar oti*) . . . Apparently when the past becomes present and they join up at the same spot—this was my breaking point . . . it struck me as nothing else ever did and frightened me more than anything in my life until then.

The authenticity of these relics is conveyed through their exposure in darkened barracks, isolated from the surrounding world and by the overwhelming sensory stimuli of the shoes' feel and smell. The students breathe and embody the experience of the site. Often they burst into tears or choke. The students' desire to experience, the expectation of "experiencing the horrors as they were," and the anticipation surrounding the barracks of shoes and personal effects at Majdanek is so great that the look and smell of the shoes and prisoners' uniforms serves, for many, as a final verification of "having been there." Another girl wrote:

It was unbelievable, what happened there: finally I am "worthy" to see with my own eyes an authentic prisoners' barrack, complete, with the beds, the bunkers and the clothes of the prisoners lying upon them. It was simply like returning back in time and all of a sudden simply to see everything—in reality—without the need to imagine the place, the details. Here is the barrack, here are the bunks and here are the prisoners themselves, and I almost suspected that they would appear before my eyes and "fill" the old striped clothes on the bunkers . . . it was a most powerful experience.

The isolating darkness and the sounds of some participants crying often bring forth tears. Crying, the overpowering of oneself by one's own expression (Plessner 1970: 56) is seen by many organizers and students as an index of the profundity and authenticity of the students' experience of the camps. The crying out loud (in the language of the voyagers—*shevira*—breaking), confirms, for many students, that the desired transformation has taken place and that they have "been broken"; they have "experienced" the Shoah. In the language of the organizers and guides, "the coin drops."

THE RAISING OF THE FLAG
IN THE CEREMONIES

The ceremonies performed by the groups at death camps and memorial sites are not just acts of identification with the dead; they are also a symbolic act of appropriation—of the memorial site (from the Poles) and the memory of the dead—for the State of Israel. The visual redundancy of central national symbols (in flags, blue-and-white sweatshirts, and ceremony text folders) and the frequent repetition of texts, songs, and symbols are designed to "create an emotional state that makes the message incontestable because it is framed in such a way as to be seen as inherent in the way things are" (Kertzer 1988: 99–100). They also create optimal conditions for the "contagion" of emotion. The students see one another becoming emotional and perceive that the State, made present through its symbols, is the "natural" precipitant of the emotional charge, the unifying force of the physically discrete bodies. The ceremonies do not merely express the sense of community, connection to the dead of the Shoah, and dedication to the nation of Israel; they may create them as well.

The sequence of obligatory ceremonies is a reflection of the stages of transformation promoted by the voyage: from child to victim to victorious survivor to *oleh* (immigrant/ascender) to Israel to empowered "witness of the witness." The overall structure of the voyage is, however, sufficiently flexible to enable the transformation to occur to different participants at different stages. As delegation leader E said, "The coin drops for everyone at a different time."

Religious texts, such as the Kaddish and *El Mole Rahamim,* are a standard part of the repertoire, but within the ceremonies, these texts serve exclusively as mourning prayers for the dead. Religious expressions represent primarily the dead pre-State past; the triumphant singing of the *Hatikva* (Israeli national anthem) and the raising of the flag, which conclude each ceremony, evoke the future. The national anthem resounds through the camp; students, wearing blue-and-white flag sweatshirts hold large flags aloft. The flag and anthem unite the participants and offer common uplift and hope for the members of the group, who have been pulled down by the intense gravity of the camps. One teacher commented:

I linked up (to the experience) at the closing ceremony at Birkenau. I saw one of the guys there with an Israeli flag raised as high as he could hold it, passing it from one hand to the other, and not giving up and holding it as high as he could. And at the *Hatikva,* another few raising the flag as high as they could. And I first heard *Hatikva* at a volume that comes out of the soul. In school we perform many ceremonies. I hear murmuring during *Hatikva,* students moving around, and here I feel, at *Hatikva,* how it uplifts everyone and connects us from a collection of individuals to a single conglomerate, to one nation. And here I felt this power. And we have power. And this force should accompany us everywhere.

The raised flags and shared singing of the *Hatikva* also provide a declaration of "who we are" to the Polish passersby. Through the students' performance, rising to their feet, and raising the flag over the death pits, they become embodiments of memory for both their fellow participants and for outside onlookers. They bodily link the symbols of past death in exile with those of current and future life in the homeland. Voyage initiator Oded Cohen writes:

As we stand by the crematoria . . . our heart sorrows and our eyes shed tears for the terrible destruction of European Jewry, and Polish Jewry among them. . . . But opposite the flag of Israel raised on high and over the death pits and ovens of destruction, we stand erect and our lips whisper—the people of Israel live! . . . And we swear to the millions of our murdered brethren—If I forget thee, O Jerusalem, let my right hand forget its strength! In the ears of our spirit we hear their souls calling to us—through our death we have commanded you to live! Guard and protect the State of Israel like the apple of your eye! And we answer wholeheartedly—long live the State of Israel forever!

The nation, presented by the anthem and flag, is framed as the response to death.

Conclusion

During the voyage, the Holocaust is seen as the natural outcome of Jewish life under Gentile rule, and under the Poles in particular. The only witness to the Shoah that the students encounter during the voyage is the Israeli survivor, whom students identify as "one of us." There is no significant encounter with an "other," such as a non-Jewish victim, a Polish Resistance fighter or Righteous Gentile, who could serve as a subject of identification and empathy. The glorification of the survivor as hero has the consequent risk that the life of the nation may be understood as an eternal struggle for physical survival against hostile forces. The larger ethical questions—about the fragility of culture and humanistic models of conduct in face of political bestiality—become practically impossible to raise given the impermeable boundaries between "us" and "them" in the voyage construction.

In spite of the Ministry's declared aim of "showing the wealth of Jewish life," the voyage glorifies Jewish death. Consequently, although they strongly identify with the Shoah victims, students see little link between the past Jewish life and current Jewish identity and do not identify with Diaspora Jews (Lev 1998: 94, 96).

The voyage to Poland is a rite of transformation, designed to transmit understanding, not through intellectual analysis, but through experience, embodiment, and identification. At a pivotal stage in their development, when they are most susceptible to romantic ideals and shortly preceding their mobilization into the army, Israeli teenagers perform an intensive, week-long pilgrimage that performs the history of the Jewish people, as schematized in the Zionist master narrative. This pilgrimage is constructed as a ritual reenactment of survival. The students leave the life world, the Land of Israel, for Poland, the land of the Shoah, where they "witness" the destruction of the Jews of the Exile. But there they survive, to return with the triumphant survivor to Israel. The movement through space, the sequence of ceremonies, the texts within the ceremonies, the positioning of performers: all describe a cycle of transformation from child to victim to victorious survivor to *oleh* and witness of the witness. The students do not experience these transformations as biological descendants of survivors. Rather, it is in their capacity as members and future defenders of the State of Israel that they become spiritual heirs to the legacy of the now-dead exilic past.

Upon their return, the travelers appreciate Israel, not as the taken-for-granted birthplace of the native Israeli, but as the object of yearning and choice of the *oleh*. As one teacher put it: "I traveled thousands of kilometers to find the beautiful Land of Israel." Their successful pilgrimage empowers the participants to be responsible embodiments of Jewish memory and peoplehood—they are "witnesses of the witnesses."

On the other hand, the closed, triumphant and triumphalist nature of the voyage and the emphasis on the drawing of final lessons also involves risks—that the incommensurability and openness of the Shoah event be lost and the moral, theological, and existential questions that reverberate in the void left by Auschwitz may be silenced completely. There is a danger that "the dialogue with the mute God may . . . be drowned out altogether by the growing noise of the merely spectacular" (Friedlander 1992: 22).

Epilogue

The pilgrimage of Israeli school groups to Poland, as I came to know it, was not my pilgrimage. My voyage was limited by the fragmentary nature of family memory and the difficulties of finding that past imposed by the passage of time and the change in the human landscape of Eastern Europe; theirs was limited by the Israeli construction of the organized voyage. And yet . . .

The night before I was to present a lecture on my research, I had a dream. In it, I was wandering around my grandfather's house in Ungvar, a house that (in the dream) also contained his tombstone and those of the extinct Jewish community. A group of young Hungarians were performing some activity at the new swimming pool built on the site. I slinked around trying to find my grandfather's tomb, with no success. In a second dream scene, I sat at a long wooden picnic table somewhere in the house, along with the participants of the training course for Israeli tour guides in Poland, listening to a young Hungarian female guide explain something. She then turned to me and said, "And now, I thought you would tell us the story of your father." I stammered, "I'm sorry, I wasn't taking notes." In the last scene, I left Ungvar with my wife in a New York subway car. Suddenly, I realized that I did not succeed in finding the tomb of my grandfather and that my voyage was incomplete; I would have to return.

Israeli teenagers, when they reach a point in their development when they begin to ask themselves who they are and where they came from would like to be able to rummage for an answer in the houses and dusty attics of their grandparents. But the houses are often also their tombs. Many homes don't exist any more. The way back, for many young Israelis, leads through Auschwitz. It is this search for roots, for a tie to Jewish history that leads many—myself included—to Poland. Yet, when students or guides publicly re-present our pasts before the representatives of the nation, in the context of the organized mass trips, some part of our search is lost along the way. The multiplicity of personal meanings arising from the Shoah cannot all be contained within the narrative *of mi-shoah li-tekumah*—from Holocaust to redemption. So either we close our eyes, join in the chorus of Kaddish and *Hatikva,* and try to focus on our dead and our living, or we stammer, "Sorry, I wasn't taking notes." If, in my research, I represent the voyage as merely the latest stage in the Zionist appropriation of Jewish memory, my story is incomplete as well.

In a 1986 interview Claude Lanzmann, producer of the film *Shoah,* explained: "When does the Holocaust really end? Did it end the last day of the war? Did it end with the creation of the State of Israel? No. It still goes on. These events are of such magnitude, of such scope that they have never stopped developing their consequences. . . . When I really had to conclude I decided that I did not have the right to do it. . . . And

I decided that the last image of the film would be a rolling train, an endlessly rolling . . . train" (Lanzmann, quoted in Felman 1992: 242).

The New York subway train taking me out of Ungvar is not the cattle car that brought my grandfather to Auschwitz. That train and the one I'm on travel in opposite directions. And yet, the two trains are, in some way, coupled. Often, quite often, the way back is the only way forward.

References

Aviad, Janet. 1983. *Return to Judaism*. Chicago: University of Chicago Press.

Ben-Ari, Eyal and Bilu, Yoram, eds. 1997. *Grasping Land: Space and Place in Contemporary Israeli Discourse and Experience*. Albany: State University of New York Press.

Dominguez, Virginia R. 1989. *People as Subject, People as Object; Selfhood and Peoplehood in Contemporary Israel*. Madison: University of Wisconsin Press.

Felman, Shoshana. 1992. "The Return of the Voice: Claude Lanzmann's Shoah," in Felman, Shoshana and Loeb, Dori, eds., *Testimony: Crises of Witnessing in Literature, Psychoanalysis and History*. New York: Routledge, pp. 204–83.

Friedlander, Saul. 1992. "Introduction," in Friedlander, Saul, ed., *Probing the Limits of Representation: Nazism and the "Final Solution."* Cambridge: Harvard University Press, pp. 1–22.

Gurevitch, Zali. 1997. "The Double Site of Israel", in Ben-Ari, Eyal and Bilu, Yoram, eds., *Grasping Land: Space and Place in Contemporary Israeli Discourse and Experience*. Albany: State University of New York Press, pp. 203–16.

Keren, Nili, ed. 1993. *"It Is My Brothers that I Am Seeking": A Youth Voyage to Poland*. Jerusalem: Israel Ministry of Education and Culture, Youth Division.

Kertzer, David. 1988. *Ritual Politics and Power*. New Haven: Yale University Press.

Lev, Michal. 1998. *The Influence of the Youth Voyages to Poland on Students' Attitudes towards the Shoah in the Cognitive and Emotional Spheres* (in Hebrew). M.A. Thesis, Bar-Ilan University: Ramat-Gan.

Plessner, Helmut. 1970. *Laughing and Crying: A Study of the Limits of Human Behavior*. Evanston: Northwestern University Press.

Yerushalmi, Yosef Hayim. 1982. *Zakhor: Jewish History and Jewish Memory*. Seattle: University of Washington Press.

Figure 12. An overall view of the Western Wall plaza, with the Muslim Dome of the Rock on the level above. (Victor and Edith Turner Collection.)

CHAPTER 12

Meanings of the Western Wall

Danielle Storper Perez and Harvey E. Goldberg

The Holocaust has become a factor in contemporary Jewish identities because of its powerful external negativity, but expressions of rebuilding a sense of Jewish peoplehood have also grown from within. One of these was Zionism, a political movement that developed in the late nineteenth century claiming that Jews, despite their Diaspora existence in diverse regions, were in fact a nation and should have a country of their own. Although there were Jews who opposed Zionism, and there were vigorous debates among pro-Zionists, the idea of a return to a revived center in the Land of Israel struck chords in the imaginations of Jews around the world. One of the symbols of this new vision was the Western Wall in Jerusalem, a remnant of the supporting wall of the Temple Mount built at the time of Herod. In recent centuries, Jews came to the Wall with special prayers, despite its location in a Muslim neighborhood in Jerusalem. In the nineteenth century the image of the Wall became widespread in Jewish folk art; it seemed to stand for both the exiled condition of the people and their survival and steadfast prayers for a "return to Zion." In the twentieth century, Jewish prayer at the Wall became a matter of fierce contention between Jews and Palestinian nationalists, and when East Jerusalem was ruled by Jordan between 1948 and 1967, Jews were barred from visiting the Wall. This prohibition reinforced its importance in the eyes of Israelis and Jews abroad, and the Israeli government, razing the buildings near the Wall, made it available as a prayer and pilgrimage location soon after the eastern city was conquered. The following selection by Danielle Storper Perez and Harvey E. Goldberg, based on field research done in the early 1980s, stresses the wide range of meanings that the Wall assumes to the variety of people who visit it.

The Kotel Plaza and Its Social Ecology

The Herodian wall was built of massive rectangular stones, most of which weigh between two and eight tons each and lay side by side with startling precision. The base of the original wall lies far below the present level of the Kotel plaza, and seven layers of the Herodian stones that are now visible constitute the lower portion of the contemporary Wall. Above that, four or five layers of large stones from the Umayyad period are to be seen. These support additional layers, from different periods, which make up the upper portion of the Kotel, but it is impossible to distinguish between Fatimid, Crusader, Mameluke, and Ottoman contributions. The very top three layers were added relatively recently, probably by the Muslim Religious Council, bringing the Kotel to a height of more than sixty feet above the newly fashioned plaza.

The Kotel stands against the background of the golden-tinged Dome of the Rock, which is situated directly behind the area that has been made into a synagogue. To the south of this area, a ramp leads to the *Haram ash-Sharif,* through an opening still known as the Mughrabi gate.[1]

The synagogue area at the base of the Kotel is about two hundred feet long and seventy feet deep and is partitioned by a metal barrier approximately five feet high, into a men's section and a women's section, with the former covering about two-thirds of the rectangular synagogue floor. To the right of the women's section is a small room reached by several stairs, in which prayer books are found along with chairs for those who wish to escape the elements and where some light candles, despite the guards' instructions not to do so.

The monumental Wall continues to the left of the men's section, with access to it available within a large chamber that houses prayer books, Bibles, and the sainted Torah scrolls, which are opened and read several times a week. While there is often a minyan (prayer quorum of ten men or more) or two in this chamber as well, it is preeminently a place for individual religious expression. In the innermost section of the hall, candles may be lit as a token of the fervent wish or vow made by a single petitioner. Some archeological soundings have been made inside this chamber, regulated by the Ministry of Religious Affairs, but because the chamber is found at the bottom of several layers of building this work is carried out very slowly.[2]

Since the Kotel has officially been given the status of a synagogue, benches, prayer books, lecterns, and Torah scrolls are available and may be used during prayer services. Cardboard skullcaps for men, and scarves for women, also are provided for those who arrive improperly attired. The other items are housed in the chambers at the side, described above, but during the day, in good weather, prayer books lie on tables outside and can be picked up by any visitor. Behind (to the west) of the synagogue area is a large open area in which various amenities for the visitor are located. Near the entrances to the synagogue section are drinking fountains. At the northern side of the square are washrooms, first-aid facilities, and telephones, which have recently been installed. Moving to the left of these, one can find the entrance to a yeshiva (house of Torah study) in which the office of the "Rabbi of the Kotel" may be found. On the western edge of the square is an office, adjacent to a small police station, where arrangements for bar mitzvahs or other celebrations can be made. At the southern end stands one of the main entrances to the Kotel esplanade through which arrive passengers of Bus No. 1 and visitors who have parked outside the Dung Gate.

Visitors and pilgrims may choose to reach the Kotel by various routes, with each route carrying different cultural connotations. Bus No. 1 passes through the whole town, and many people headed to the Kotel board in the ultraorthodox neighborhood, Mea She'arim.[3] After the Mea She'arim stop, the appropriate dress code and the separation of men and women can already be noticed. The Dung Gate entrance links up with traffic, which crosses the Armenian quarter and skirts the newly rebuilt Jewish quarter. Those who wish to reach the Wall from the Jewish quarter itself descend steps that pass by several of the reconstructed yeshivot that overlook the Kotel plaza. Many visitors come through the Arab part of the city, entering at Jaffa Gate, where they descend David Street bordered by tourist shops. Less usually they enter via the Damascus gate, which has the atmosphere of a traditional Middle Eastern city. Probably the least common way of arriving at the Wall is through the Mughrabi gate, after having reached the *Ḥaram ash-Sharif* by another route.

Within the area defined by these various entrances, each of which serves as a focus for different conceptions and loyalties, the paths of diverse people cross: tourists, pilgrims and local Arabs make their way from one side of the Old City to the next. Not everyone is oriented toward the Western Wall and some visitors go directly to *Ḥaram ash-Sharif,* either as worshipers or as tourists. In any event, this crisscrossing of persons and cultures turns the Kotel into a public area, with the dynamics of many other public places.

The Kotel as Public Place

KOTEL REGULARS

As a public place the Kotel plaza has to be cleaned, controlled, and managed, and services are provided, both officially and informally, for the many worshipers and visitors. These requirements are the basis for the presence of a variety of people and Kotel "types" regularly to be found there, helping to meet these needs and also deriving some gain, both spiritual and material, from their activities.

Each week on Thursday afternoon a massive clean up for the Sabbath takes place. The water from the hoses of Arab workmen often forces back the women attempting to gain access to the Wall. Periodically, too, charity boxes, placed in various spots in the Kotel compound, are emptied, and the money is gathered up and carried away in an armored car. Security is maintained by policemen and middle-aged Israeli Jews doing military reserve duty, who have to check handbags and parcels at the entrance to the plaza. This reflection of current political tension perhaps provides the element of danger found in all pilgrimages, while serving as a ritual crossing of the threshold into the numinous zone.

In addition to the security guards are Kotel guards, employed by the Ministry of Religious Affairs, who are located mostly in the synagogue area. They pay particular attention to the nonobservant and non-Jewish visitors, ensuring that the men don a cardboard skullcap upon entering the synagogue area. Visitors have different reactions to this imposition, and they find themselves in a sea of motley head coverings. Similarly, shawls and kerchiefs are available to cover heads, shoulders, or even legs when entering the women's section. The provision of these ritually appropriate items also marks the openness of the Kotel to all, for Israeli synagogues, normally frequented by defined regular congregants, usually do not take the trouble of making these appurtenances available to guests.

Beggars, both male and female, benefit from the opportunity they give visitors to perform a mitzvah (religious duty) and feel acknowledged by the tradition stating that the Western Wall of the Ancient Temple was constructed by the poor. The beggars, like the two regular "camera people" who circulate on either side of the metal divide with Polaroids around their necks or the "pigeon ladies" feeding the birds, have their own territory. It is not unusual for a tiff to break out if one trespasses on "the turf" of the other. Other women bring fresh herbs, particularly on Fridays, for people to sniff after they have pronounced the appropriate blessing, thanking God for the creation of fragrant herbs. Visitors who take the herbs will give these women some coins in exchange. The sweet smell may help inaugurate the Sabbath on Friday night or become a charm to augment one's livelihood, if placed in the pockets. Begging, or the "sale" of blessings, does not take place on the Sabbath when the use, or even the carrying, of money is forbidden. These regular denizens of the Kotel know one another, just as they are known by some of the steady visitors to the Wall.

The Ministry of Religious Affairs has put up metallic plaques, in several languages, giving instructions about the behavior appropriate to the place. These include the prohibition against begging. Thus a daily dynamic between the Kotel guards, sporting their special badges, and the beggars who carry out works of charity while formally breaking the rules is created. A similar situation is created when brides and grooms enter the women's section, with a male photographer, and the guard provides a white shawl so that the bride can be dressed in a manner fitting this nonpermitted occasion.

Among the regulars are also men who can be found at the Kotel daily, in search of prospective "born-again" Jews (cf. Aviad 1983: 29). These men are quite young, in their late twenties or early thirties, and several of them frequently hang around the Kotel square, looking for "a hit," in their words. Most are English speaking, on the lookout for young Americans who have come to visit the Wall. Representatives of yeshivot attempt to recruit young seekers who may have come to the Kotel after visits to shrines in other countries. Another well-known figure is Zechariah the Yemenite, who attracts visitors by sounding the ram's horn (shofar) and takes the opportunity to instruct children in the blessings or to spread a prayer shawl over those willing to enter his ludic world of a messianic shadow play.

Other men, Hebrew speakers, make themselves available to help organize a prayer service in which a bar mitzvah is celebrated or during which a blessing is recited for an ailing relative or friend. Such unofficial "organizers" will lead the prayers or read the Torah, calling up various men to recite the appropriate blessings, and will generally see to it that the occasion runs smoothly. Worshipers familiar with the traditional service do not need this aid, so the organizers expect remuneration from those who accept their assistance.

DIVERSITY AND INTERACTION

Along with the uniformity embodied in established Kotel roles and their incumbents, exists an active, but partially predictable, diversity. Open to the sky, the region adjacent to the Wall is divided, unofficially but regularly, into recognizable areas. It is said, in an anthropomorphizing way, that there is never a minute when the Kotel is completely empty, and its openness encourages all sorts of daily behavior and interaction as well as individual religious expression. These are not rigid divisions of sanctified territory, but conventional working arrangements. Time, too, is divided informally as people move smoothly and rapidly from mundane to sacred activities and back again.

Outside the synagogue plaza is mainly informal. Children play together and disturb the pigeons being fed by the old beggars. In this area men and women part, each going to their separate places of prayer. They plan to join one another later on. Couples also come to promenade, as do students, soldiers, and old ladies of a senior citizens club. For some of these, a visit to the Kotel is a rare privilege, and those from a Middle Eastern background may express their joy by playing tambourines and dancing.

The presence of foreign tourists adds to the atmosphere of informality. These visitors may rest in the shade while writing a postcard or eat snack food purchased in the old city. In groups, they gaze on the worshipers in the synagogue, while receiving an explanation of the site's significance. Many tourists attempt to immortalize this exotic episode in their world travels with the aid of a camera, their memento destined to become part of middle-class existence at home. Some foreigners, in search of the authenticity of other traditions, will pray at this spot through which, it is said, all prayers rise to heaven. They, like other visitors to the Wall, play many roles: they are all part pilgrim, part tourist, part seeker.[4]

In addition to interaction, a fair bit of avoidance, born of close attention, takes place. Arab residents of the Old City walk by quickly, without turning to the Wall, and Muslims look down on the Jewish pilgrims from the ramp leading to the *Ḥaram ash-Sharif*. Visitors and passersby of all backgrounds stop at the same fountains to drink and to wash their hands.

There is also, as stated, great diversity among the Jewish/Israeli visitors to the Wall. The nonreligious or merely traditional commingle with the yeshiva students who visit the Wall daily or with the few extremists who insist on trying to conduct Jewish prayer on the Temple Mount (Offenbacher 1985). Other Jews are Kotel shy and visit the Wall infrequently and with hesitation, claiming that the promise of the shrine materializes slowly and in undramatic ways. Some even espouse the view of the late philosopher Yeshayahu Leibowitz, that the Kotel is a place of semi-idolatry (1977: 404–5). This range of approaches is evident in the variegated styles of dress and gesture at the Wall.

Near the Kotel one can find Jews of different visages and visions whose identities receive expression in speech, apparel, and behavioral approach, all of which convey varying attitudes and significance. The Hasid with a fur *shtreimel* on his head may enter the synagogue area alongside a man in shorts using a cardboard skullcap made available to secular visitors.[5] American youngsters in jeans may ponder Israeli soldiers their own age dressed in uniform and wonder what their lot might have been if they had been born in another country. Women from Yemen, wearing embroidered trousers under their dresses, edge close to the Wall, as do women in contemporary styles whose religiosity may have been filtered through a modern education. Among men, modern religious views are often signaled by the wearing of a small knitted skullcap, a practice adopted by many Jews from abroad when visiting Israel. The North African–born Israeli, uttering a personal prayer with his forehead against the Wall, becomes an object of comment for a European tourist. Pious women, with heads covered for modesty, instruct their children in the decorum appropriate to the prayer situation. People from many parts of the country, nay the world, meet unexpectedly.

Diversity thus becomes more than a sociological fact and itself takes on cultural import. The heterogeneity of the Jewish people, who are brought together in a single space, is captured, condensed, and highlighted, giving cause for individual and collective reflection (cf. Babcock, 1980). Each must admit, happily or begrudgingly, that he or she is part of a larger national whole. The stage is set for the symbolic interdigitation and confrontation of many themes of Jewish life, spanning the centuries and the traces of the lands on which Jews have lived. This is the material from which new personal and communal identities can emerge and be asserted. The following section describes some occasions in which this "identification of individual and collective discourse" (Nora, 1984, p. xxxix) may take place.

Time and the Integration
of Person and Collectivity

KOTEL RHYTHMS

The Kotel, a physical space that has been invested with a special ritual status, is also subordinate to the Jewish ritual calendar and the daily divisions of time, which regulate religious behavior. Within these time-space coordinates, which are in phase with Jewish celebrations throughout the world and throughout history one is able to link his or her existence to wider identities. Examples may be seen by considering different time frames significant to activities at the Kotel.[6]

The Kotel knows diurnal, weekly, and seasonal rhythms. Morning prayers are most comfortably recited early, when the Kotel's shadow offers coolness to much of the plaza. Jewish law demands prayer three times daily, and those who are knowledgeable are aware that the latest time at which *minha*, the afternoon prayer, may be said can be correlated with the call of the Muslim *muezzin* toward evening. In the summer, students from abroad, visiting Israel for the first time, will be brought to the Wall at midnight, enhancing the contemplative mood that it evokes.

Monday and Thursday mornings are times for bar mitzvahs, as are the longer Sabbath morning prayers. The latter day brings about intensified activities by the Kotel regulars as the end of each week is approached. One does not expect to see many married women near the Kotel on Friday afternoons, as Sabbath preparations at home receive their final touches, but some observant young girls make a point of praying there on Friday night adorned in their Sabbath best.

Some women frequent the Kotel on the new moon, so that this minor holiday, long compared to the biological cycle that characterizes womanhood, carries implications of reproduction and thus becomes imbued with an element of peoplehood. The fact that tradition restrains women from hard work on this day gives them the opportunity and legitimation for an extradomestic visit.[7] The new moon itself is also a day on which the Torah is read and is thereby another day when the Kotel is filled with bar mitzvah celebrants.

Mass visits to the Kotel take place during the three Festivals, linking the present to the pilgrimage celebrations of ancient times. On the intermediate days of Passover, in the spring, or on Sukkot, at the end of the summer, when travel is permitted, modern pilgrim-tourists from all over the country visit their capital and the special Wall that stands in its midst.[8] The "appointed times" of Jewish tradition form the grid upon which Jews, as individuals and as groups, can bring the Kotel into their lives and connect their personal concerns and joys with one of its many facets.

DIFFERENCES IN ETHNIC STYLES

The relation of an individual to the Kotel, of course, is molded by his or her version of Judaism and the social network of which he or she is a part. Different styles of coordinated minyan behavior are in evidence: Sephardim will form a procession to fetch the Torah Scroll from the Ark when the reading service begins.[9] Young Ashkenazic yeshiva students seem to like close corporal contact with their teacher-rabbi. Thus, in addition to the official division of the synagogue into areas for men and women, with the former about twice as long as the latter, there seems to have emerged a loosely defined ethno-religious allocation of space. In the left half of the men's section, close to the Wall, ultraorthodox Jews of Eastern European provenance are normally concentrated.[10] Other minyanim are spread out facing the Kotel to the right, lining themselves parallel to the women's section or backed against the outer rail that guards the Kotel floor. In these prayer groups, Sephardic Jews, with their own melodies and distinctive customs, are prominent. The latter two positions, near the male-female divider and near the back, enable women to place themselves in relative proximity to the central prayer activities. This is crucial during bar mitzvah celebrations (which will be discussed further below), when female relatives and friends ululate and throw candy upon hearing the blessings indicating that a young man has reached religious majority. The closeness of women to the ritual taking place on the other side of the divider helps mark the young male's step away from the family and toward manhood. Communal distinctions are thus reflected in differing emphases in gender roles and family life.

DEVOTIONAL EXPRESSION
OF MEN AND WOMEN

In addition to the communal celebrations, people also can give individual expression to their religious feelings. There are differences between men and women in this regard that can be seen, among other ways, along spatial lines. Among men, private devotion often takes place in the underground chamber to the left of the men's prayer section. In the innermost section of the hall, we may observe candles, which are lit as a token of a fervent wish or a vow made by a single petitioner. Here, too, may be found Hasidim, or other traditional Jews, totally immersed in private prayer or study, as if all the Kotel were at their disposal to process their pleas and submissions. At specific times this den of personal devotion is open to women. The illuminated darkness provides both a sense of shelter and the glimpse of a prayer that may be answered.

Men have the option of praying with a minyan or individually, and they are often invited to join one prayer group or another. The women, on the contrary, usually pray individually, just as they arrive singly and leave on their own. On some occasions they may strain and attend to a minyan on the men's side. Even for women who know no Hebrew, the taking out of the Torah Scroll, and its ceremonial lifting up in front of the congregants, is a high point in the service. In the absence of a minyan of males, however, the fervor of women can only be given an individual outlet, nurtured by the sense of communion that the Kotel engenders. Although the women may be more crowded together than the men are, a gathering of women near the Kotel has no formal communal structure but reflects a collection of individuals intensely concentrating on their own prayers while reinforced by parallel sentiments shoring them up from all around. These moments of intense concentration may follow, or be followed by, pleasurable episodes of casual socializing with other women who have come to the Wall.

Loosened from the bonds of formal minyan participation, women often exhibit a deep sense of the divine at the Wall. According to tradition, the *Shekhina* (Divine Presence), the feminine aspect of God in exile from Himself, followed His people into exile and can always be found at the Kotel.[11] Though the focus on the mystical is confined, among the men, to nocturnal devotees (often sitting on the floor) who read from kabbalistic tracts, some women place themselves directly under a caper bush growing out of the Wall, which is said to be the precise seat of the exiled, but compassionate, *Shekhina*. Women in general try to place themselves close to the Wall, either praying from a book or crying with abandon as if in the arms of a beloved one. This sense of physical presence is evident when on leaving the Kotel plaza, women (like some ultraorthodox men) do not turn their back on the sainted place but remove themselves slowly, facing the Wall for as long as possible.

Though the ability to physically approach a central shrine such as the Wall to the same degree (although not in precisely the place) as the men is a new experience for many women, it does not release them from their age-old definition as being responsible for family care and socialization. Many women come to the Kotel with infants and young children, bringing food with them to feed the youngsters. They will also encourage the young to take a prayer book in hand so that the child will become familiar with its appearance and texture. Often the young are directly encouraged by their mothers to kiss the Kotel.

The differences separating Ashkenazic and Sephardic traditions also have their impact on the religiosity of women. While it is rare for an older Sephardic woman to be able to read the Hebrew prayers, it is not unusual among Ashkenazic women, but both will place themselves in close proximity to the Wall in their attempt to connect with the Divine. Younger Sephardic women who have received standard religious education in Israel will not differ in outward behavior from their Ashkenazic age mates, but others, who have had secular schooling, will exhibit the more popular religiosity of their elders.

One of the most common forms of individual religious petition at the Wall is the insertion of notes into its crevices. Again, this is particularly important among women but may be carried out by anyone, even those who doubt its efficacy or tourists who are not quite sure how to go about this "authentic" experience. Old, illiterate women may ask younger ones to write out their notes on a piece of paper but generally one does not reveal the contents of this written prayer.[12]

LIFE CYCLE CEREMONIES: THE BAR MITZVAH

One way in which the Kotel is woven into the lives of individuals and their families is by the marking of life's milestones there. An occasional Hasid may be seen giving his three-year-old son a first haircut at the Kotel before he takes him to visit the tomb of Rabbi Shim'on Bar Yohai in Meron.[13] Religious schools organize a ceremony, at the end of the first grade, in which each child, having mastered the fundamentals of reading, is presented with a prayer book at the Wall. A standard route of picture taking has developed in Jerusalem, for brides and bridegrooms on the afternoon preceding their wedding, with a picture at the Kotel being an important station in this procession. At the close of elementary education the Kotel becomes prominent, since bar mitzvahs are often celebrated there.

In addition to private family bar mitzvahs, (to be discussed shortly), communal bar mitzvahs are organized there as well. An entire class of seventh-grade males, who have passed their thirteenth birthday, may celebrate the attainment of religious majority together. Secular schools, with less commitment to the details of religious tradition, may organize a "class Bar and Bat Mitzvah," including girls, in the square behind the synagogue area itself. During such a ceremony each pupil may receive a pen (or each girl a candlestick) with his or her name engraved on it. One may find a bat mitzvah near the Kotel itself, in the women's section, but this is a new form of celebration separated from the standard prayer service.

The more common bar mitzvah is organized by a family inviting relatives and friends. These take place at the Wall on the days during which the Torah Scroll is opened and read, and they reveal details of different Jewish ethnic traditions. In all groups they mark the attainment of religious majority, emphasized on weekdays by the donning of phylacteries for the first time, and highlight the links between family and community. The practice of having this celebration at the Wall is prominent both among Jews of Middle Eastern background and among tourists from abroad, such as the United States or France. Perhaps these groups, for somewhat different reasons, are those whose communal frameworks are most uncertain and who are therefore in greatest need of "places of memory." [14]

Bar mitzvah ceremonies begin to take place at about 7:00 A.M. continuing until about 1:00 P.M. Approximately fifteen lecterns are available, so it is conceivable that fifteen bar mitzvahs will be celebrated simultaneously. The males among the bar mitzvah boy's family and friends huddle around the lectern conducting the morning prayer service, which normally lasts about half an hour. When it's time for the Torah to be read, the ceremony begins to change, in an obvious manner, according to the practice of each ethnic group. Frequently, immediate members of the family enter the room to the left of the men's section of the Kotel and bring out the Torah, very often followed by the bar mitzvah boy being carried on the shoulders of a relative, amid singing, as the high point of the bar mitzvah ceremony approaches.

The apogee of the bar mitzvah celebration is the association of the "child-becoming-man" with the Torah, but not all communities include the same festival procession with the Torah. Sometimes the young man himself carries the Torah on this occasion. The text read from the Torah is the same for all groups, and the ceremony, in terms of calling people to honor the Torah, is basically the same as well. There are, however, distinct differences in the pronunciation of Hebrew, in the melodies, and in the dress of the participants.

Throughout the bar mitzvah, women stand alongside the partition, or at the back of it, while tending to the food for the festive gathering that will take place at the close of the prayer service. They also hold candies to be thrown at the bar mitzvah boy when he successfully recites the appropriate blessings. The women ululate at this point, a custom practiced at almost all bar mitzvahs, except for those following Ashkenazic tradition. Women often now combine these traditional practices with playing the role of photographer, while the men signal to them the best times to take snapshots, depending on what is transpiring in the ceremony. Bar mitzvahs are often colorful events, filled with visual and auditory stimulation: embroidered skullcaps, or multicolored and golden cloaks, and the music of goat-skin drums or tambourines. Some groups who have immigrated to Israel recently still possess the instruments they brought with them. The musical accompaniment of other groups, who have been in the country for a long time, may be a large tape recorder that plays popular songs outside the Kotel area until the time of the bar mitzvah ceremony proper and again at the end of the ceremony. Modern technology thus comes to the support of waning "memory" (Nora, 1984, p. xxvi). When the prayer service ends, the young man may once more be lifted to the shoulders of the dancing adult men while the women, on the periphery, clap hands in joy.

Having a bar mitzvah on a weekday (that is, Monday or Thursday) as opposed to on the Sabbath, allows the full use of technical accompaniment, both traditional and modern. Musical instruments may not be played on the Sabbath, and no electricity may be employed. Taking pictures is similarly forbidden by strict law, and the prohibition against motorized travel would limit the number of guests to those who could walk to the Kotel on that day. While the spiritual joy of the Sabbath undoubtedly would add to a celebration, the Sabbath laws restrict the elaboration of festiveness in which each family seeks to make its own mark.

The bar mitzvah, like pilgrimages to saints' tombs or henna celebrations (the festive application of a vegetable dye cosmetic) before a wedding, is a way for Middle Eastern Jews to express and develop their ethnic identity. These groups who, in the mass immigration of the 1950s, suffered the heavy loss of their way of life, are able to recoup their communal traditions without the strict control of established orthodoxy while taking upon themselves a new national self-definition. A comparison of celebrations at the Kotel with other sites of familial and ethnic gatherings in Israel (cf. Shokeid, 1974; Deshen and Shokeid, 1984) or with comparable "places of memory" in which loosely bound communities can receive firm expression (Nora, 1984) would highlight the delicate process whereby expressions of distinctiveness are limited by a sense of common commitment to Judaism and Jewish peoplehood. Each ethnic tradition, with its preferences and peculiarities, can form a community at the Kotel, side by side with other communities from which it is distinct and to which it is bound.

Space and the Annual Cycle Linked to Histories

FESTIVALS ANCIENT AND MODERN

Just as the Kotel sets the stage for the integration of time, person, and collectivity, it is also the setting in which the annual cycle, individual and communal histories, and consecrated space come together. In ancient times, the Temple was the focus of mass pilgrimages, three times during the year, as prescribed by biblical law. Pilgrims from all over the land came to the spot chosen by God to "place His name there" (Deuteronomy 16), and during the Second Commonwealth both pilgrims and contributions reached the Temple from the Diaspora. Although the Temple has not been standing for close to two millennia, the memory of these events has been preserved in the synagogue liturgy, particularly in the "additional prayer" of the Festivals, which recalls the former sacrifices and the ascent to the Temple.[15] The fact that the Pilgrimage Festivals are a major occasion for present-day visitors to the Kotel places ancient expressions of collective memory in metonymic relation to a contemporary "place of memory," creating a sense of continuity, and perhaps even identity, between their devotional visit and that of their ancestors.

Each festival attracts thousands to the Wall, but each takes on a special atmosphere reflecting the requirements of the holiday. The first night of Passover represents the most intense ingathering of the family during the ritual year, and travel to the Kotel later in the week is preceded by careful preparations to bring food from home that has been made according to the strict Passover rules. Even when the Wall is not the focus of celebration, as during Lag Ba'omer, thirty-three days after

Passover, when more than one hundred thousand Israelis flock to Meron, it stays in contact with the ritual pace of the people. It also accommodates, easily, modern festivities and solemnities; the sameness of place provides a persuasive link between the old and the new.

The Kotel thus appears to be the natural setting for modern celebrations such as Independence Day or Holocaust Day, even as the forms of these recently established celebrations evolve amid debates over their significance. In some of these ceremonies religious themes are given prominence, while in others the national component clearly dominates. In the energetic Friday evening dance to the Kotel from the Jewish quarter, on the part of young male yeshiva students, it is difficult to untangle the political overtones from the religious commitment. The meshing of modern Israeli identity and traditional religious symbols is salient at military swearing-in ceremonies, which have become more frequent at the Wall since the previous favorite site, Masada, has relinquished its primacy. In these ceremonies the recruit, after his basic training, holds a Bible in one hand, a rifle in the other, and is told that without the Book he is nothing but a murderer. Other ceremonies reflect current political events as in the case of demonstrations concerning distressed Jewish groups in Russia, Syria, or Ethiopia. A particularly impressive event takes place on the eve of the anniversary of the reunification of Jerusalem, when thousands of yeshiva students from all over the country, stirred by the ideology of the Gush Emunim movement (Aran, 1991; Sprinzak, 1991, esp. chap. 8), come to the Kotel carrying torches.

SUKKOT

Two traditional sacred days, Sukkot and Tish'a Be-Av, coming at the outset of the liturgical year and toward its end, have been given additional emphasis by proximity to the Kotel.[16] The weeklong Sukkot holiday serves as a bridge, both in terms of the seasons and the sacred yearly cycle, between one year and the next. During the intermediate days of the festival, when travel is permitted, modern tourist-pilgrims from all over the country visit Jerusalem and the Wall, which is now its symbolic center. Sukkot, the Feast of Booths, commemorates, historically, the wandering in the desert and, in terms of the cycle of time, marks the end of the harvest, the transition between the summer dew and the autumn rains. During this week, large segments of the population eat and even sleep in the temporary shelters, which are covered by palm branches between which one can glimpse the stars.

A great Sukka (booth) is constructed near the Wall, enabling the pilgrims to eat there. At the end of the weeklong holiday it may receive the drops of rain that the pilgrims have prayed for, from Sukkot until Passover in the spring.

Toward the end of the week, on the festival of Hoshana Rabbah, the esplanade of the Kotel begins to fill up, after a night of study during which all the books of the Bible and other sacred texts are reviewed.[17] Orthodox men, women, and children begin to arrive at dawn, a dark flow running from West Jerusalem along the streets of the Old City until reaching the open plaza of the Wall. The devotees carry a palm branch and *etrog* (a lemonlike fruit), the "four species" (including also a myrtle and willow) signifying the integrity of the land and of the people, and fill the entire area of the esplanade.[18] While the sun rises above the massive stones of the Wall, the palm leaves are beaten against the stone, as a grassy wand sweeping in all directions and encompassing prayer group after prayer group. On the last day of Sukkot, men dance with Torah scrolls in their arms, while the women look on.[19] The scrolls are bedecked with veils and kerchiefs, like a bride on the eve of her wedding. This form of rejoicing, which for generations has signaled the renewal of Jewish life through books (Goldberg, 1987), is especially poignant when placed in counterpoint to the surviving Wall.

THE FAST OF THE NINTH OF AV (TISH'A BE-AV)

Tish'a Be-Av, which falls in mid-summer when the sun has dried up vegetation everywhere, is a Fast Day that commemorates the destruction of both the First and Second Temples and has become a fundamental observance at the Kotel. Dressed in slippers, sneakers, or other footwear without leather, observant Jews come to spend part of the day and night at the Wall. Heightened solemnity intermingles with pronounced intimacy. Fathers and sons, mothers and daughters, boyfriends and girlfriends, yeshiva students or women from a traditional *moshav* share mats or blankets spread out both inside and outside the synagogue plaza.[20] On this night (and day) all the Jewish communities and ethnic groups, all the religious tendencies—including the Lubavitcher Hasidic "mitzvah tank," which provides phylacteries for the afternoon prayers—are present.[21] Individual and collective, communal and national, can be found, compounded with one another.

The police guard the area all night long. Ultranational groups may try to reach the Temple mount, while pseudomessiahs and would-be prophets both lament the existence of the Diaspora and announce the imminent reunification of the people. Inside the synagogue area and outside, pilgrims read the biblical Book of Lamentations, chant dirges, or fraternize in this unique setting of a foodless picnic in which daily needs are hardly a distraction. A mourning ceremony animated by a pervasive but disorganized sociality, Tish'a Be-Av, since the retaking of the Wall, has emerged as a point in time and space in which the meeting of messianic aspiration and national sentiment has been crystallized. This process is reminiscent of the famous conceit of the talmudic sage, Rabbi Akiva. When asked why he laughed upon seeing a fox running through the Temple ruins, Akiva assured his puzzled colleagues that his mirth stemmed from his witnessing the evidence of the prophecies of destruction and the implicit certainty that this guarantees the fulfillment of the prophecies of redemption.[22]

Summary and Conclusion

It is possible to view the Kotel as a physical space, suffused with history, in which the story (or stories) of contemporary Israel are condensed. A clearly circumscribed area in the midst of an eminently Middle Eastern setting, the Kotel proclaims Israel's deep roots in the past, even as its newly expanded plaza and the care with which it is guarded are evidence of the political will and conflict that created and maintain the new state. To an equal extent, the internal components of that state and society come into relief at this shrine in their harmonious and potentially tense diversity.

While eminently a "place of memory," socially constructed by the exigencies of a modern national state, the Kotel effortlessly merges with traditional modes of commemoration. It thus has "naturally" become a popular shrine, both religiously and nationally, exuding a resonance rarely achieved by sites that have been singled out by governmental fiat. It also has no formal standing in rabbinic law except insofar as the decision has been made to use the Kotel plaza as a synagogue. At the same time, it has not developed in popular opposition to established norms but works in conformance and complementarity to them. Official and informal pressures placed on visitors to the Wall to act in accordance with its sanctity provide the framework for the range of mutually reinforcing religious, national, and ethnic expressions that characterize its ambience.

Beyond the specific norms guiding and restricting behavior at the Wall there appears to be a general correspondence between widespread attitudes concerning the Kotel and basic Jewish conceptions, another factor that may underlie its taken-for-granted symbolic centrality. Judaism, as reflected in the biblical text and later, has been uncomfortable with the notion of sanctity inherent in a physical place, except as the result of Divine choice operating within a historic situation. The unknown burial place of Moses is one example of this phenomenon, and some scholars suggest that the unclear location of Mt. Sinai in the biblical narrative is another expression of the same apperception (cf. Davies, 1982). The celebration of the Wall, which is not the Temple itself, but a historical reminder of the Temple, may be in line with this general conception. At the same time, it is clear that Israel's control of the Kotel has become a symbolically central statement of the importance of political and territorial sovereignty associated with modern nationhood and that this control, once established, has opened the door for concrete aspirations toward physical *cum* spiritual "redemption" of all the Temple Mount. The range of views defined by the (small but vociferous) "Faithful of the Temple Mount," who would like to be able to conduct Jewish prayer on the *Ḥaram ash-Sharif,* and critics such as Leibowitz, who deny all religious value to the site, outlines a dialogic field within which can be located the majority of Jews and Israelis who find the Western Wall an appropriate setting for their own mixture of religious and national identities.

The Kotel has become a reinvigorated *axis mundi,* a spot where heaven and earth may be connected in the eyes of the faithful or of those seeking faith. Equally, it connects past, present, and future for those with little interest in the supermundane. In this setting opposites and divergencies, expressed in particular Jewish forms, may be united. Individual and local histories may merge with Jewish and Israeli myths through the parallel collapsing of time and space. Religion and secular nationalism may be linked, peppered with specific ethnic overtones. The tourist becomes a pilgrim, and the pilgrim an onlooker; and the cycle of individual lives may be harnessed to the expression of collective identities. Catharsis and communion stand side by side; memory, consolation, and hope are bound up in a single act. Just as these diverse elements are brought together and, as it were, bounced off one another, so they may be sorted out and isolated in accordance with private wishes and communal sentiments. Jews, the "People of the Book," have transformed the stone rows of the Kotel into a giant writing tablet upon which distinct individuals and groups may inscribe their own stories.

Notes

1. In the winter of 1985 to 1986, changes were made near this ramp, slightly reorganizing access to the Kotel, but our description reflects the period of fieldwork.

2. A complex series of subterranean passageways runs under the buildings adjacent to the Kotel, and under the *Ḥaram ash-Sharif,* that hint tantalizingly at links to ancient structures. Muslims and the Muslim authorities have been extremely sensitive about attempts by Jews to explore these passages.

3. A Jewish quarter founded in the 1870s that later became the center of the ultraorthodox community in Jerusalem.

4. On relations between tourism and pilgrimage, see Graburn (1977, pp. 17–32) and Turner and Turner (1978, p. 102). Cohen provides a typology of phenomenological attitudes associated with travel to distant lands but points out that often the different attitudes appear in the same individual (Cohen, 1979, pp. 179–201).

5. See Mintz (1968), including photographs, on Hasidim.

6. On the Jewish calendar, see the *Encyclopaedia Judaica,* vol. 5, pp. 43–53.

7. See the *Encyclopaedia Judaica* (1971), vol. 12, p. 1039.

8. See the *Encyclopaedia Judaica* (1971), vol. 6, pp. 1237–46.

9. See the *Encyclopaedia Judaica* (1971), vol. 3, pp. 450–58.

10. Mira Zussman, in a conversation with the author, reported that in the days after the 1967 War, when the Kotel was first accessible to Israelis, she saw ultraorthodox European Jews physically displace Yemenite Jews who were congregating at this spot.

11. See the *Encyclopaedia Judaica* (1971), vol. 14, pp. 1349–54.

12. Van Gennep (1914, p. 57) describes a petition at a traditional Jewish pilgrimage shrine.

13. This practice usually takes place in Meron on Lag Ba'omer. While the custom is to give the haircut on this minor festival, it was not the date on which we observed it at the Wall.

14. On the Middle Eastern Jews, see the end of this section.

15. See the *Encyclopaedia Judaica* (1971), vol. 6, pp. 1245–46 and Hertz (1948, pp. 530–3).

16. The liturgical year begins with Rosh Ha-Shanah on the first day of the month of Tishri, in the autumn, and Sukkot falls on the fifteenth of that month. The month of Av, in mid-summer, is the eleventh month, and the twelfth, Elul, is treated, liturgically, as a prelude to Tishri.

17. See the *Encyclopaedia Judaica* (1971), vol. 15, p. 501.

18. See the *Encyclopaedia Judaica* (1971), vol. 6, pp. 1448–50.

19. See the *Encyclopaedia Judaica* (1971), vol. 15, p. 502.

20. A smallholder's cooperative. This type of settlement was established for many of the immigrants from Middle Eastern countries in the 1950s (see Weingrod, 1966).

21. The Lubavitcher (Habad) Hasidim are known for their activist approach in influencing other Jews toward greater religious observance. One promotional attempt involves a mobile vehicle ("tank") containing the ritual paraphernalia used in this effort.

22. See the Babylonian Talmud, Tractate *Makkot 24b*.

References

Aran, G. "Jewish Zionist Fundamentalism: The Bloc of the Faithful in Israel," in M. Marty and S. Appleby, eds., *Fundamentalisms Observed*. Chicago: University of Chicago Press, 1991, pp. 265–345.

Aviad, J. *Return to Judaism*. Chicago: University of Chicago Press, 1983.

Babcock, B. "Reflexivity: Definitions and Discriminations," *Semiotica* 30 (1980): 1–14.

Cohen, E. "A Phenomenology of Tourist Experiences." *Sociology* 13 (1979): 179–201.

Davies, W. D. *The Territorial Dimension of Judaism*. Berkeley and Los Angeles: University of California Press, 1982.

Deshen, S. and M. Shokeid. *The Jews of the Middle East* (in Hebrew). Tel Aviv: Schocken, 1984.

Encyclopaedia Judaica. Jerusalem: Keter, 1971.

Goldberg, H. "Torah and Children," in H. Goldberg, ed., *Judaism Viewed from Within and from Without: Anthropological Studies*. Albany: State University of New York Press, 1987, pp. 107–30.

Graburn, N. "The Sacred Journey," in V. Smith, ed., *Hosts and Guests: The Anthropology of Tourism*. Philadelphia: University of Pennsylvania Press, 1977, pp. 17–32.

Hertz, J., ed. *The Authorized Daily Prayer Book*, rev. ed. New York: Bloch, 1948.

Leibowitz, Y. *Judaism, the Jewish People and the State of Israel* (in Hebrew). Jerusalem: Ma'ariv, 1977.

Mintz, J. *Legends of the Hasidim*. Chicago: University of Chicago Press, 1968.

Nora, P. *Les Lieux de memoire*. Paris: Gallimard, 1984.

Offenbacher, E. "Prayer on the Temple Mount." *The Jerusalem Quarterly* 36 (1985): 129–40.

Shokeid, M. "An Anthropological Perspective on Ascetic Behavior and Religious Change," in S. Deshen and M. Shokeid, eds., *The Predicament of Homecoming: Cultural and Social Life of North African Immigrants in Israel*. Ithaca: Cornell University Press, 1974, pp. 64–94.

Sprinzak, E. *The Ascendance of Israel's Radical Right.* Oxford: Oxford University Press, 1991.

Turner, V. and E. Turner. *Image and Pilgrimage in Christian Culture: Anthropological Perspectives.* New York: Columbia University Press, 1978.

Van Gennep. A. *En Algerie.* Paris, 1914.

Weingrod, A. *Reluctant Pioneers.* Ithaca: Cornell University Press, 1966.

Figure 13. Women praying at the tomb of Rabbi Shim'on bar Yohai in the Galilee Shrine of Meron. (Victor and Edith Turner Collection.)

CHAPTER 13

A Moroccan Jewish
Shrine in Israel

Yoram Bilu

Zionism called for the movement of Jews from their Diaspora communities to the Land of Israel. The State of Israel now contains about 40 percent of world Jewry. Migration to Israel, however, did not mean that people abandoned their cultural and religious attachments, but rather, they often reinterpreted familiar religious forms to take on new meanings in the Jewish State. Below Yoram Bilu provides a detailed example of this process with regard to Jews who came from the mountainous regions of southern Morocco. A central feature of their religious life was devotion to *tzaddikim*—sainted rabbis whose graves were found throughout the region. Jews visited these graves, as individuals or on pilgrimage occasions, hoping that a *tzaddik* would act as an intercessor supporting their prayers for health, sustenance, or offspring. While hope for the intercession of a *tzaddik* is a known pattern in other versions of Judaism, such as Hasidism, the local saints of southern Morocco were foreign to the Israeli landscape and to the secular Zionist understanding of Judaism. Bilu describes how the dreams of one man succeeded in conceptually transplanting a Moroccan *tzaddik*, Rabbi David u-Moshe, from a shrine in Morocco to the Israeli town of Safed. Driven by deep personal needs, the man—Avraham Ben-Haim—was able to present his dreams as relevant to a wider community of Moroccan Jews. Their recognition of the messages in the dreams, and their regular visits to the site, have created a new, and now thoroughly established, pilgrimage shrine.

The Role of Dreams in Building
Rabbi David u-Moshe's House

Rabbi David u-Moshe's House, along with other pilgrimage centers, provides a cultural resource through which the group consciousness of traditional Moroccan Jews is heightened and their distinctive ethnic identity reconsolidated. As such, the *hillula* in Safed may be
conceived of as an ethnic renewal ceremony (Gluckman 1963; Weingrod
1990), which reflects the growing confidence of an émigré in being part
of the contemporary Israeli scene, while, at the same time, indicating
a strong sense of ethnic distinctiveness. Given this social significance,
the most striking feature of Rabbi David u-Moshe's House is that it was
erected through the spontaneous initiative of one person whose background and education clearly place him among the rank and file. In
building the site, Avraham was inspired by dream messages delivered to
him by Rabbi David u-Moshe. His success in reviving a pilgrimage tradition, in which thousands of people participate, should be attributed
primarily to the impact that these dreams had on his fellow Moroccans.
The oneiric encounters with Rabbi David u-Moshe, which continue up
to today, constitute for Avraham confirmational evidence that his liaison with the saint is permanent and inseparable. For him the dreams are
a constant reminder urging him to pursue his calling with the same dedication and stamina that were characteristic of his first steps on the site.
Before sketching the development of Rabbi David u-Moshe's House,
through Avraham's dreams, the cultural traditions from which these
dreams have emerged should be briefly reviewed.

The idea that dreams have mantic properties with direct consequences
to waking life is taken for granted in the Bible, in which the dreams of
people of prominence, like Jacob, Joseph, Pharaoh, and Nebuchadnez-
zar, are taken to be messages from God (Spero 1980). The Talmud, a
compilation of numerous rabbinical teachings, contains different, at
times opposing, views concerning dreams (Bakan 1958; Bilu 1979; Lorand 1957).[1] Though some of these conceptualizations insightfully anticipated modern psychological dream approaches (for example, "nothing is shown [in a dream], but the thoughts of one's heart"), the idea
that dreams are heavenly messages, "one-sixtieth of prophecy," represents a dominant approach there as well (Spero 1980). This approach

was maintained in sources as distinct as Maimonides and the Zohar, both of which contend that, since traditional means for prophecy are no longer available, dreams may be the contemporary vehicle for divine inspiration.

While Jewish Moroccan dream conceptions were undoubtedly influenced by these classical sources, they were also shaped by indigenous Moroccan culture, in which dreams are accorded an important role (Kilborne 1978; 1981; Westermarck 1926). This influence is particularly manifested in dreams associated with folk veneration of saints. In both Muslim and Jewish hagiolatries, a special genre of visitational dreams has prevailed focusing on the potentially rewarding encounter with the saint (Bilu and Abramovitch 1985; Crapanzano 1975). The fact that in both groups these dreams have often been associated with the saints' tombs make them quite akin to the widespread phenomenon of temple sleep or incubation (Dodds 1958; Edelstein and Edelstein 1945). This prevalent dream pattern is explicated as reflecting universal human needs to perceive healers in dreams (O'Nell 1976, p. 65). While Jewish Moroccan visitational dreams do not necessarily involve ailing patients with medically defined symptoms, they exist against a background of specific life predicaments of which the saint is expected to relieve the dreamer, his devotee (Bilu and Abramovitch 1985).

As visitational dreams, Avraham's oneiric encounters with Rabbi David u-Moshe seem to emanate from a solid, well-defined cultural tradition. In his case, however, the dreams served to create a uniquely enduring alliance with the saint that brought forth a dramatic transformation in his life and had a considerable impact on the Moroccan community at large.

Before the first revelation of Rabbi David u-Moshe in 1973, Avraham's life had consisted of two distinct periods, separated by the aliya to Israel in 1954. All his years in Morocco had been spent in the village of Imi-n-Tanout, southwest of Marrakesh. Avraham views those years with nostalgic affection, stressing the harmonious relations within the Jewish community and between Jews and Muslims as well as the spirituality and strict observance of the laws that marked the Jewish life style there. His linkage to the saints, which was established at an early age, was fed by two sources: first, like many other inhabitants of southern Morocco, his infantile recollections were vividly embedded with visits to the local saints of his village. Second, and more important, some of Avraham's own forefathers were considered tzaddikim by their fellow

Jews. The fact that those admired nobles and sages were all on his maternal, less cardinal, side may have created a motivational background conducive to Avraham's future initiative, for his claim to having a share in their *zekhut* (virtue, blessedness), heretofore far from guaranteed, now could be forcefully asserted. Avraham was particularly attached to the later exponent of this familial thread of piety, his maternal grandfather, Rabbi Shlomo, who was venerated by the Jews of Imi-n-Tanout in his lifetime. His death in the town of Essaouira (Mogador), where he had been receiving medical treatment, constituted a traumatic experience of loss and privation for Avraham. These feelings were exacerbated by the fact that the Jews of that coastal town, well aware of the late rabbi's virtue, hastened to bury him in their cemetery. It might be suggested that in building Rabbi David u-Moshe's House, Avraham has unconsciously compensated for the vacuum created by his grandfather's disappearance. The original situation, in which the family tzaddik was appropriated by others, to be buried afar, has been reversed by bringing a tzaddik from afar into the house.

Another familial tradition related to tzaddikim might have served as a model for Avraham's later project. According to this tradition, the tomb of a second sainted figure of his maternal ancestors, originally located at Marrakesh, miraculously reappeared in the cemetery of the Mount of Olives in Jerusalem.

Like all the Jewish boys in his native village, Avraham acquired his Jewish education in the community synagogue (*sla*), under the strict discipline of the local rabbi. He quit his studies in early adolescence and became a shoemaker, following his father. He pursued this occupation until his immigration to Israel at the age of twenty-four. At that time Avraham was already married and father to a six-month-old daughter.

Ever since his aliya, thirty years ago, Avraham has lived in Shikun Canaan in Safed. Since his parents and most of his siblings were settled in the same neighborhood, the extended family has managed to preserve a sense of union and togetherness supported by growing feelings of patriotic pride and rootedness in their place of living. Like many of his fellow newcomers, Avraham had to give up his former occupation and earn his living as a forest worker. Unlike most of them, however, he has stayed in this job until this day, clearly one of the lowest in prestige and salary on the vocational echelon. During the first harsh years after the aliya, the rapidly growing family faced considerable economic difficulties. Nevertheless, Avraham was more than content to live in Safed, a town imbued with a special mystical atmosphere and surrounded by many saints' tombs. Some of these tombs are located on the surrounding hillsides where Avraham spends most of his working time and it is possible that some of his inspiration was acquired there.

While the local tzaddikim constituted natural foci for resuming hagiolatric practices in the new country, Avraham was still attached to the saints of Imi-n-Tanout and, most of all, to his pious grandfather, Rabbi Shlomo. The painful separation from the latter was particularly felt during the first year after their aliya in which the economic situation of the family was quite shaky. It is not surprising, therefore, that during that year Avraham had a few dreams in which he was visited and encouraged by Rabbi Shlomo. The last of his dreams bears special significance in light of the ambiguity in saints' allegiances instigated by the transfer from Morocco to Israel. It was dreamed on a Saturday night, after Avraham had found a large sum of money that helped him celebrate the Sabbath in abundance.

On that night I see the tzaddik, Rabbi Shlomo, in a dream. He says to me: "Listen, look who is standing next to you." I turned my face and I saw Rabbi Shim'on Bar-Yohai. He [Rabbi Shlomo] said to me: "Here he is, [standing] next to you. If you need something, you just come to him. He will give you." Rabbi Shim'on took a loaf of bread, handed it to me, and said: "Go, make your Sabbath, from now on you won't be lacking anything."

The message of the dream is quite explicit: though in Morocco Rabbi Shlomo had been the patron of his grandson, in Israel he transferred him to the custody of Rabbi Shim'on, a most potent saint who resides in the vicinity of Safed. Thus the transition from Morocco to Israel was completed through a symbolic reorganization of saints' allegiances. Two points are worth mentioning in this regard. First, this dream marked the termination of Avraham's repeated oneiric encounters with Rabbi Shlomo. Second, when Avraham established a liaison with Rabbi David u-Moshe eighteen years later, Rabbi Shim'on was present in some of his dreams, just as Rabbi Shlomo had been before him.

Avraham's growing attachment to the local tzaddikim was expressed in the names he gave to his two oldest sons. (All in all, he has ten children, six of whom are boys.) His first Israeli-born son, whose birth date coincided with the dream episode discussed, was accordingly named Shim'on, while the second bears the name of Rabbi Meir. The burial sites of these two sages, located at Meron and Tiberias respectively, are by far the largest pilgrimage centers in Israel. Avraham's third son was given the name of his venerated grandfather, Shlomo.

The neighborhood synagogue at Shikun Canaan was another area in which Avraham's religious faith and dedication to the saints could be expressed. He was one of the founders of the synagogue and soon became its *gabbai,* an administrative role that constituted excellent preparation for the organizational task of running his later enterprise. In this job he participated in organizing the hillula of Rabbi Ya'akov Abu-Hatsera, the most popular tzaddik among the historical sainted figures of Moroccan Jewry, which, in the synagogue context, took the form of a communal meal (*se'uda*). In 1971 a dispute among the worshipers made it impossible to conduct the *se'uda* in the synagogue. Avraham, infuriated by the participants' lack of readiness to relinquish their quarrel for such sublime an end, publicly announced that he would arrange the meal for Rabbi Ya'akov at his place, using his own modest means.

This commitment, in which a personal initiative replaced an institutionalized pattern in maintaining hagiolatric practices, may be conceived as a significant anticipation of Avraham's later project. The model for admitting a saint into one's own house had thus been established on a modest ground. (The synagogue se'udah involved no more than a few dozen celebrants.) Unsurprisingly, it was supported by a dream encounter with the tzaddik involved:

I saw myself walking on a plateau [full] of sand, and it was terribly hot there. Then I was running together with all those people [of the synagogue]. I was so thirsty that I almost fainted. I began to tremble all over my body. Suddenly I saw a mountain on which a rabbi was seated holding a big book in his hand. All the grass around him was made of big snakes. He looked around and said: Woe to the one who enters this place, I'll send the snakes against him! I stood up and he said: "No, *you* can come; *you* shouldn't be afraid, come on, hold this stick!" All the snakes lowered their heads, and I entered. He filled a glass of water for me and I drank it. He said: "Do you know who I am?" I said: "No." [He said:] "I am Rabbi Ya'akov Abu-Hatsera." Then he said: "You should proceed [in your way]. You won't be lacking anything."

The plot of this dream, which depicts the dreamer's singular success in achieving contact with the tzaddik despite hindrances and predicaments, conveys the sense of Avraham's calling precipitated by his public commitment to Rabbi Ya'akov. The saint's grace is bestowed on him alone, while all other synagogue attendants fail to gain access to the tzaddik. Variations on this theme recur in his later dreams related to Rabbi David u-Moshe. The dream is replete with biblical associations. The metaphor of water relieving the thirsty supplicant brings to mind similar images depicting contact with the divine in Psalms (and blessing, uttered over water, has long been Abu-Hatsera's peculiar method of choice in healing), and the juxtaposition of the stick to the snakes in a competitive context seems to allude to the contest between Moses and Pharaoh's royal magicians. (If correctly deciphered, this association may indicate the dreamer's deep-seated messianic fervor.) It should be noted that the latter episode took place in Egypt, where Rabbi Ya'akov's burial site is located. The dream setting (sand, extreme heat) seems to be adapted to the desert ecology of that country as probably perceived by the dreamer.

Notwithstanding these biblical associations, a more recent, personally based episode seems to have participated in the construction of this dream. During the summertime Avraham and some of his fellow workers used to take refuge from the heat in an ancient burial cave near Safed, ascribed to two Talmudic sages, Abbaye and Rava. On Fridays they stored, in the chilly cave, bottles of wine that they used to celebrate the approaching Sabbath. On one Friday afternoon a worker, who had been sent to bring the wine, returned in panic after he had seen a snake at the entrance. Other companions tried to force their way in, but they were also deterred by the reptile. Avraham alone was able to enter the cave and to retrieve the wine safely. Since he had met no snake on his way he interpreted the episode as a divine message indicating his virtue over his companions'. The impact of this occurrence seems to have been reflected in the dream of Rabbi Ya'akov. The transfer might also have been facilitated by the fact that the two groups, Avraham's co-workers and his fellow attendants, greatly overlap. It should be noted that the dream ends with the same reassuring message that sealed the oneiric encounter with Rabbi Shim'on: in both cases nurturance is guaranteed to the loyal supplicant.

These two dreams were selected from a larger collection of visitational dreams, all of which belong, insofar as Rabbi David u-Moshe is concerned, to the prerevelation period. Hence the idea that the latter tzaddik's apparition was an unexpected act of sudden inspiration cannot be maintained. More correctly, it appears as the product of a persistent process of active search in the course of which a veteran member of the cult of the saints gradually shifts saint allegiances until he finds his own patron tzaddik. Rabbi Shlomo, a natural object of veneration, is rightly his own, but his reputation among the Moroccan émigrés is meager. Rabbi Shim'on is the most reputed saint in Israel, a core symbol of mysticism and piety, but his tradition is well established and cannot be appropriated by any single devotee, dutiful and resourceful as he may be. This also holds true for Rabbi Ya'akov, whose living descendants' claim as his legitimate heirs cannot easily be challenged. Rabbi David u-Moshe, a tzaddik whom Avraham claims not to have known in Morocco, seemed to be a cultural figure ready to be enshrined. Well known and highly venerated by many southern Moroccan Jews, the hagiolatric practices related to him lacked focus and coherence, since his sanctuary had been left far behind.

In explicating the timing of Rabbi David u-Moshe's apparition, Avraham's stage in his life cycle seems significant. As he approached midlife, the growth of his family has been attenuated. His last son was born a few months after the visitation of Rabbi David u-Moshe in 1973. He was given, of course, one of the tzaddik's names, Moshe. The appearance of the saint thus marked the termination of the fertile phase of family expansion followed by a shift toward spiritual concerns, more appropriate to midlife.

In 1972, Avraham's dearest brother and neighbor was killed in a ridiculously minor car accident in which neither the car nor the other passengers was hurt. Avraham, basically optimistic and complacent, became despondent and melancholic and could not find consolation. To his ninth child, who was born a few months later, he gave the name of his beloved brother. The loss created in Avraham a state of emotional turmoil that constituted a fertile matrix for the appearance of the tzaddik. As will be shown, it was Rabbi David u-Moshe, in one of his first oneiric apparitions, who put an end to Avraham's prolonged distress.

The event that immediately precipitated Rabbi David u-Moshe's first visitation was Avraham's firm intention to move from his apartment to a bigger, more comfortable place in another neighborhood. The change was prevented at the last moment by the saint's announcement that he desires the old apartment as his permanent abode. As a result, Avraham and his family were tied to their original place of residence by inextricable bonds. It should be noted that the same sequence of events—an intention to leave followed by a renewed commitment to one's place of residence—has underlain the erection of other sacred sites in Israel. It also has found varied expressions in other dreams that will be discussed.

The revelation of Rabbi David u-Moshe in 1973 marked a dramatic transformation in Avraham's life. From then on the saint's oneiric messages became his sole guidelines for action. One of these first messages was to write down his dreams and to distribute them in all the Moroccan communities in Israel. In complying with the tzaddik's command, Avraham dramatically and sweepingly transformed his private vision into a public affair, shared and supported by many. The announcement to the public includes Avraham's first initiation dreams. The ornate style of rendering, which stands in sharp contrast to Avraham's plain oral recounting of his dreams, betrays the fact that he was helped by the local rabbi in formulating the announcement. Nevertheless, he insisted that the written report constitutes a veracious representation of the saint's messages. In fact, when the scribe dared to deviate somewhat from the original version, an acute attack of dizziness, allegedly brought on by the tzaddik, forced him to reword the text as presented to him by Avraham.

Announcement to the Public

I, Avraham Ben-Hayim, who live in Canaan, Building 172, in Safed, the Holy City, have been privileged by the Lord to see wonders. And as I was ordered, I make known to you a message from our master the tzaddik, Rabbi David u-Moshe, may the memory of the tzaddik be for a blessing, who has revealed himself to me many times.

In my first dream I looked, and lo! There stood before me a man dressed in white, and the radiance of his face was like an angel's. He approached me, seized my hand, and led me to high hills. And among their huge boulders, I saw a white stretch of land. When we came to this clearing, he sat on the ground and said to me: "See, only ten people celebrate and mark my hillula day. And I ask you: Why have those who left Morocco forsaken me and deserted me? Where are all the thousands—my followers and believers?" I replied to him: "Do you really want them to return to Morocco from Israel to perform the hillula?" The man took me again by the hand, turned me around, and asked: "What place is this?" I answered him: "This is my house." The tzaddik continued: "In this place I want you to observe my hillula day, from year to year." I asked him: "What does my lord want?" And he answered me: "I am the man who revealed himself to those who loved me in Morocco. I am Rabbi David u-Moshe!!! I am he, the man who makes

supplication and prays before God everyday to preserve the soldiers of Israel, on the borders of the land! If so, why have they deserted me, those
who left Morocco? Now here I am in the Holy Land, and my request is that
they renew the marking of my hillula."

Two days later, he returned and revealed himself to me in a dream, at a
time when I was tossing in my bed between sleep and wakefulness. He
woke me up and said to me: "My son, you made a mistake when you told
people you saw me in a dream. You should have said to them that you saw
me eye to eye. But never mind, I forgive you for this. And now hear my
words: I left Morocco and came here, because this place is holy, and I chose
you to be my servant in this holy work. And now, you will do this:

1. Establish a place for yourself where candles will be burned in my
   memory and whoever comes to pray and to make supplication for his
   soul will light me a candle!
2. Beside the place of the candles, set a collection box, and each will do-
   nate according to his desire and his means!
3. Whoever approaches the place of the candles will do so with awe,
   love, and wholeheartedly!
4. He who enters this place must be clean, in his body and his deeds!
5. It is forbidden to deal in and sell these candles or these memorial
   cups. Whoever wishes will light a candle, on condition that he be
   clean, as stated above!
6. The place will be open to the public night and day!
7. In the feast of my hillula, there will be no distinction between big and
   small or between rich and poor, but all will be equal.
8. My hillula will be held on the eve of the new moon of Heshvan. If the
   new moon of Heshvan falls on Friday, the hillula will take place on
   the preceding Thursday!
9. Warn your wife and the members of your household, not to allow entry to a man or a woman who is unclean!
10. With the contributions that will accumulate in the collection box,
    enlarge the place, so that it will be able to contain the thousands of
    people who will come here to celebrate and to pray!

After three days the tzaddik again revealed himself to me in a dream in
the night, and this time he was accompanied by two men. He turned to me
and asked: "Do you recognize these?" I answered: "One I saw with you in
the second dream, and the second one I recognize from a different dream."
The tzaddik continued: "Do you know who they are?" I answered him:
"The first is Elijah the Prophet, remembered for the good, and the second
is Rabbi Ya'akov Abu-Hatsera, may the memory of the tzaddik be for a
blessing." The tzaddik nodded to signal agreement, and he concluded his
words as follows: that I have to be strict and to let into this place only people
who are clean in body and soul.

As the tzaddik has requested, we shall hold the hillula. God willing, on the night of the new moon of Heshvan, this year and every year, at my house as mentioned above.

May the Lord help us for the sake of His honor and His great name.

Come one and all, and may the blessing be with us and with you!!!

In the first dream the tzaddik's transition from Morocco to Israel and his selection of Avraham's house as his new sanctuary are straightforwardly portrayed. The dreamer's underlying wish seems to have been externalized and displaced onto the saint since it is he, rather than the dreamer, who initiated his move to Safed. The latter is described as a passive object on whom the tzaddik's grace impinges. The written version of the dream somewhat blurs the fact that Avraham did not identify the saint on his first apparition. While this ignorance is typical of visitational dreams in general (see Bilu and Abramovitch 1985), in this case it was congruent with Avraham's own claim not to have known the saint before the revelation. Long after the tzaddik's first visitation, however, Avraham retrieved a long-forgotten childhood memory that may have contributed to his selection. The fact that Avraham altogether forgot that episode, which concerned gathering contributions for the saint's box, may have found expression in the tzaddik's allegations in their first oneiric meeting: "Why have those who left Morocco forsaken me and deserted me?" Avraham's covert sense of guilt, indicated by the deserted saint's reproach, may have reflected a collective mood of many former devotees who had also been dissociated from their once-cherished saint on immigrating to Israel. Unlike them, the saint appears attuned to the prevailing sentiments in contemporary Israel and prays for the soldiers on the borders.

The second dream in the announcement, in which the saint paradoxically denies the oneiric nature of his first apparition (thus enhancing its credibility), includes ten precepts (echoing the ten commandments) that establish the rules of conduct in the reconstituted site of the tzaddik. Though most of these requirements reflect the traditional pattern of saint's veneration, they also convey Avraham's vision and confidence in the prospects of the place as a major pilgrimage center.

In the third dream, the tzaddik is accompanied by Elijah the Prophet and Rabbi Ya'akov Abu-Hatsera, two eminent figures whose appearance grants more credence to the messages in the former dreams. Although Avraham's initiative is oriented toward one particular tzaddik, his project is supported by other saints as well. As will be shown, some of these saints claimed their share in the new site.

The second announcement to the public (which is too lengthy to present here) reflects Avraham's growing assertiveness and sense of confidence in his calling following the recurrent visits of the saint and the positive response of the community. It includes one detailed dream account in which the encounter with Rabbi David u-Moshe is created along lines inversely related to the first version. The dreamer, determined and tenacious, heads for the tzaddik's place in Morocco. After overcoming many obstacles on the way, he reaches the cave in which Rabbi David u-Moshe is studying Torah with other sages. He takes the saint on his shoulder and brings him to his home in Safed. The former pattern of an active, initiating saint vis-à-vis a passive adherent is thus reversed. The second announcement ends with the same injunctions as the first one, but their tone is more commanding and assertive. In addition, the tzaddik explicitly condemns any attempt to celebrate his hillula outside his chosen abode in Shikun Canaan, which he designates as his permanent home.

The third announcement, which was published around 1975, departs sharply in content and style from the two earlier publications. Designated "a call for the purity of the family," it is essentially a moral comment in which different misfortunes and adversities, from car accidents to terrorist attacks, are attributed to negligence in maintaining purity laws related to the ritual bath. While this information was disclosed to Avraham through his dream encounters with the tzaddik, no mention is made of the new site, the legitimacy of which seems to have been already secured. This was the last announcement Avraham dispatched to the public. The sweepingly growing recognition of his place throughout Moroccan communities in Israel has made the dissemination of further announcements superfluous.

Before publicizing his newly erected site as a healing shrine, Avraham had to come to terms with a personal predicament that haunted him for a long time, namely, his brother's untimely, futile death. As noted, this event might have urged him to seek the protection of an omnipotent patron in the first place. As might be expected, the tzaddik soon intervened to terminate his devotee's prolonged distress. In one of his first oneiric apparitions he took Avraham to a magnificent garden and picked one of the most beautiful roses that grew there, explaining that in the same way God selects the best people to reside with him. Under his explicit demand Avraham stopped his mourning and complaints. The significance of the saint as an indispensable resource at times of personal crisis was thus well established.

Following the apparition of Rabbi David u-Moshe, Avraham's life
has been drastically reconstituted. As the saint's emissary he has dedicated all his free time and energy to the shrine he has founded, fluctu-
ating between inspiring moments of spiritual exaltation invoked by his
intimate contacts with the holy and long hours of routine work in maintaining the site to serve the perennial flow of supplicants and to prepare
for the next hillula. In one of his first postrevelation dreams this drastic
transformation was expressed through the theme of death and rebirth,
a common metaphor for articulating abrupt and profound changes
in life:

I am asleep and suddenly I see that someone is coming. A man, he brought
a kind of notebook. He said to me, "Do you know from whence I bring
this?" I said, "From whence?" He said, "From a celestial court. I have
brought it." I said, "How come? Is this a law court?" "Yes, this is a kind of
law court." I said, "What is it for?" He said, "Do you know, up to this
hour—this is your life. That's it. Finished." I see myself as if I am dead. I
hear people talking. This man, with his lies, talks of the tzaddik. Everyone
says something. All this in a dream. While I am like this, all of a sudden I
see that someone arrives. He passed his hand over me and said, "Get up!"
He said, "Do you know who I am?" I said, "Yes." He said, "I am Elijah the
Prophet." I said, "What's here?" He said, "True, your life was finished but
do you see this one with the fringed garment praying for your sake?" I said,
"I see two." He said, "Who are they?" I said, "Rabbi Ya'akov Abu-Hatsera
and Rabbi David u-Moshe." He said, "I see only one! Do you know what
he says?" "What says Rabbi David u-Moshe?" I said, "What does he say?"
"Listen well. He says that your years will be renewed, since no one has been
born yet who does what you do and takes care of what you take care of." I
asked him, "And what will be the end of the matter?" He said to me, "Do
you know how much [time] is left until the hillula?" I said, "No." He said,
"There remains seventy-six days, by calculation. Take out six days, there
will remain seventy [days] exactly." He said, "After this hillula, in another
seventy days, you will have about seventy years. Now you are here. You must
hold seventy hillulot." I said to him, "How have I merited this?" "You have
merited it, because [in] everything you do for the tzaddik, you do not con-
sult with anybody." And then he turned around and addressed Rabbi David
u-Moshe and said "No! I have added two more years to you. Seventy-two.
And after seventy-two years, the Lord will have mercy." He added: "Do you
see all these people who are talking? Their time has yet to come. But slowly,
slowly!" And he pulled out a sort of paper from his pocket and spread it
out like a map. He said, "Do you see this plan and these buildings? You will
yet make them from this collection box. All this will be executed. Only patience. As for the people who are holding hillulot [elsewhere], I will bring
them here. Till they assemble here." And then he was gone.

Avraham's premature death would have put an end to his initiative and therefore altogether discredited it, as indicated in the dream by the denigrating response of the people around his dead body. To forestall this, the same triad of saints that appeared in the first announcement (Rabbi David u-Moshe, Elijah the Prophet, and Rabbi Ya'akov Abu-Hatsera) grant Avraham seventy-two more years of life. Since during his rebirth Avraham was in his forties, this increment would draw him near the ripe old age of 120, the ideal life span according to Jewish tradition, usually reserved for the righteous. The quota of years added to Avraham's life follows a peculiar sequence of permutations, which seems to be based on mystical traditions. According to a midrash, Adam yielded seventy years from his life span to King David.[2] According to the kabbalistic doctrine, seventy-two is a number impregnated with holiness, since it contains one of God's most enigmatic and potent appellations.

The temporal contingency between this dream and the preceding one does not seem haphazard, since both of them concern death. It might be conjectured that Avraham, taken aback by his brother's untimely end, feared a similar fate. The brothers, apart from being inseparably attached to each other, were close in age, and their life courses were quite similar. Avraham was spared his brother's destiny, however, because of the protective cover of the saint, which his brother had lacked.

After Avraham's rebirth, each of his site-related activities has been initiated and monitored by the tzaddik, as clearly indicated in the epilogue of the dream. Rabbi David u-Moshe appears as the architect of his own shrine. He also takes it upon himself to castigate Avraham's opponents and to bring his devotees to his place. The fact that these adherents were described as holding hillulot elsewhere is significant, since in order to turn his newly erected site into a widely attended pilgrimage center, Avraham had to abrogate those domestic hillulot symbolizing the decentralized nature of hagiolatry in the early postimmigration era. Indeed, the centripetal emphasis has become a recurrent theme in the saint's oneiric instructions to Avraham. When he himself lit a candle for the tzaddik in his brother-in-law's apartment in Tiberias, he was immediately informed by Rabbi David u-Moshe of the inappropriateness and futility of his act: "I have put out the candle . . . [since] I do not want the candle here! Only in the place where I dwell." The saint also appeared determined in regard to collection boxes: "Whoever comes [asking] for a collection box, do not give it to him! Whoever wants some-thing, let him come and put it here in the box." On another nightly visit he reprimanded Avraham for allowing a supplicant to take a portion of the sacrificial meal back to his home. When Avraham questioned this prohibition, the saint explained that "if one takes [the portion] and gives it to other people, they *won't come: but if they all come here, they'll eat and be satisfied*" (emphasis added).

Following the charismatic phase of the early postrevelation era, in which Rabbi David u-Moshe's House emerged as the saint's chosen abode, there came a long period of strenuous efforts aimed at develop-ing the site, securing the economic basis of the hillula, and crystallizing its patterns. In pursuing these goals, Avraham could not rely on his own resources alone but had to gain the cooperation of many artisans and the acquiescence of various civil servants. Since the latter were quite often hostile to his demands, the saint's support became all the more important during that period of institutionalization. Two episodes clearly demonstrate the indispensable role played by the tzaddik during that time:

The tzaddik came and said to me: "Listen, if you have money you can build. Build, by force. If they want to take you to court, go to court. If they say to you: Destroy this place, you say to them: I built, you destroy, and in that hour they'll see who is sitting in this place."

A contractor came and I asked him to finish a room or two for me. He didn't want to. He couldn't care less. I sought out the tzaddik and said to him: "You dwell here now: Go to the contractor and talk to him." He went. For two days he [the contractor] and his wife could not sleep. On Friday he came to me and said: "In the name of the Lord, ask the tzaddik to let me be." He [the tzaddik] came to him [the contractor] in a dream . . . He said to him: "Either you finish the place or I'll finish you." He came and asked him forgiveness.

The first dream deals with the most pressing problem that Avra-ham has had to face up to now, the granting of permits from various municipal and governmental agencies for enlarging the site and install-ing facilities (such as bathrooms, an abattoir). While in this dream the tzaddik merely encourages Avraham to pursue his goal despite the officials' opposition, in the second episode his intervention is more strongly felt as he forces a recalcitrant contractor to keep a commitment heretofore abrogated. What is witnessed here for the first time is an oneiric apparition of Rabbi David u-Moshe involving people other than

Avraham. Such dream messages have allegedly compelled many of Avraham's antagonists, from a jealous old neighbor to the mayor of Safed, to acquiesce to many of Avraham's initiatives that they had formerly resisted.

Notes

I wish to express my appreciation to I. Ben Ami for permission to quote excerpts from his article (1981) about the dreams.

1. See Babylonian Talmud, *Berakhot* 55a–57b.
2. See the Zohar on Genesis 5:1, English translation by H. Sperling, M. Simon, and P. Levertoff (London: Soncino, 1933).

References

Bakan, D. 1958. *Sigmund Freud and the Jewish Mystical Tradition.* Princeton, NJ: D. Van Nostrand.

Ben Ami, I. 1981. "The Folk-Veneration of Saints among Moroccan Jews; Traditions: Continuity and Change. The Case of the Holy Man, Rabbi David u-Moshe." In *Studies in Judaism and Islam.* S. Morag, I. Ben Ami, and N. Stillman, eds. Jerusalem: Magnes Press, 283–345.

Bilu, Y. 1979. "Sigmund Freud and Rabbi Yehudah: On a Jewish Mystical Tradition of 'Psychoanalytic' Dream Interpretation." *The Journal of Psychological Anthropology* 2:443–63.

Bilu, Y. and H. Abramovitch. 1985. "In Search of the Saddiq: Visitational Dreams among Moroccan Jews in Israel." *Psychiatry* 48:83–92.

Crapanzano, V. 1975. "Saints, Jnun and Dreams: An Essay in Moroccan Ethnopsychiatry." *Psychiatry* 38:145–59.

Dodds, E. R. 1958. *The Greeks and the Irrational.* Berkeley and Los Angeles: University of California Press.

Edelstein, E., and L. Edelstein. 1945. *Ascelapius: A Collection and Interpretation of the Testimonies.* Baltimore, MD: Johns Hopkins University Press.

Gluckman, M. 1963. *Order and Rebellion in Tribal Africa.* London: Cohen and West.

Kilborne, B. 1978. *Interpretations du Rêve au Maroc.* Claix: La Pensée Sauvage.

———. 1981. "Moroccan Dream Interpretation and Culturally Constituted Defense Mechanisms." *Ethos* 9:294–312.

Lorand, S. 1957. "Dream Interpretation in the Talmud." *International Journal of Psychoanalysis* 38:92–97.

O'Nell, C. W. 1976. *Dreams, Culture, and the Individual.* New York: Chandler and Sharp.

Spero, M. H. 1980. *Judaism and Psychology.* New York: Yeshiva University Press.

Weingrod, A. 1990. *The Saint of Beersheva.* Albany: State University of New York Press.

Westermarck, E. 1926. *Ritual and Belief in Morocco.* London: Macmillian.

ושננתם לבניך ...והגית בו יומם ולילה...

Figure 14. Men study Talmud with women in the background. Conducting Torah study in same-gender groups is the norm in Orthodox life. (Photo by Daniel Gilburd. Courtesy Novelty Ltd.)

CHAPTER 14

Religion, Study, and Contemporary Politics

Tamar El-Or

One of the major changes in Jewish religious life in this century has been the extension of Torah literacy and education to include women. This is not a single trend, however, and its implications vary according to the group within which it has taken place. In the United States, the term "religion" typically connotes "spirituality," while when an Israeli Jew hears the word "religion," the sphere of "politics" immediately comes to mind. Tamar El-Or depicts the study of Torah in one specific setting in contemporary Israel, a class of women in a university identified with Religious Zionism. The setting is dynamic, because everything is in flux. The women are encouraged to ask questions, but authority remains with the male rabbi-teacher. At the time of El-Or's field research, this community felt threatened by the peace process, which was giving up land to Palestinian Arabs, a development that made some Religious Zionists wonder about the nature of the Israeli state. The teacher raises these questions by reference to famous rabbis cited in the Talmud. In contrast to the situation described in chapter 8, in which rabbinic insights are viewed as having to be adjusted to fit contemporary life, this teacher assumes that the wisdom of the ancient rabbis is greater than that of any contemporary political leader. The situation observed by El-Or is further complicated, because everyone in the classroom knows that her political and religious sympathies lie in a different direction. Her ethnography of Torah study taps into tensions in the country that are simultaneously intellectual, gender based, religious, and political and that can have life-and-death consequences.

Rabbi Akiva and Rabbi Ben-Zakkai in an Israeli Classroom

ETHNOGRAPHY FROM A WOMEN'S COLLEGE FOR JEWISH STUDIES AT BAR-ILAN UNIVERSITY

In traditional Jewish communities, schooling for women was sporadic. It was only in postemancipation Europe that the idea of universal education for girls took root. Eventually, the notion developed that women should receive some systematic exposure to religious texts as well. This idea spread and took various forms in different sectors of the Jewish world in the twentieth century (Weissman 1976, 1993; El-Or 1994; Granite 1995). While Torah literacy enabled women to share more fully the cultural world of Jewish men, the way it developed in each setting reflected the values and sociopolitical contexts in which the study of texts emerged.

The different shapes that Torah study may take, and the specific meanings it can absorb in particular settings, may be seen in an ethnography of several lessons given at the *Midrasha Le-Banot* (Women's College) at Bar-Ilan University in Israel (henceforth Bar-Ilan). Bar-Ilan is a Religious-Zionist institution located in the center of Israel. It represents an ideology which claims that it is possible to combine modern Jewish nationalism (Zionism) with orthodoxy.[1] The University thus offers a standard university curriculum with compulsory Jewish studies. It accepts students regardless of nationality (Palestinian or Jewish), degree of religiosity, or gender.[2] At the same time, Orthodox Jewish faculty is preferred.

The women's *Midrasha* was established on the campus in 1976 next to a men's *Yeshiva*. These two institutions are open only to religious Jewish students, and many of them opt to take their compulsory Jewish studies courses there, rather than within the standard Bar-Ilan curriculum. The existence of that option for enrollment in Jewish studies courses creates a dividing line that separates the general student body from those who are Religious-Zionist students, and a further division based on gender exists in the latter category. The university's declared policy of "creating a meeting point" between nonreligious and religious Jews is thus subverted by the existence of this option.

Between 1992 and 1995, I conducted fieldwork at the *Midrasha*, participated in several courses, and held long interviews with more than

forty students. Researching the *Midrasha* was my next step after studying patterns of literacy among ultraorthodox women (El-Or 1994), who
have minimal intellectual contacts with other cultural worlds. Though
students at Bar-Ilan accepted in principle the importance of a general
education, the *Midrasha* and *Yeshiva* turned into "homes" on campus for religious students attending school for the first time in a co-
educational system, and with nonreligious peers. Twenty-one-year-old
Ora said:

After the weekend, when I have a big pack full of things I need for the week,
I go first to the *Midrasha* and leave it there before continuing on to my
classes. The *Midrasha* is my home on campus. I sometimes go there to re-
lax, to meet girlfriends, to be among my own. This is the first time I am
studying with nonreligious people, and with males, and it's not that simple.
I prefer the cafeteria there, and I use the synagogue. The secretaries know
me. It's kind of home.

Ora is an undergraduate student majoring in chemistry and Jewish philosophy. She takes courses at the *Midrasha* beyond the required ones,
as do many of her female friends. They are part of a new generation of
Religious-Zionist women who seek more Jewish education.

The opportunities for Jewish higher education for religious Zionist
women are growing steadily; twenty years ago there was none. This ethnography focuses on the example of women identified with Religious
Zionism that originated in Eastern Europe and that has become a powerful force in Israeli society. This historical origin also contains the roots
of the political movements related to the *Midrasha*. As we shall see,
other histories—ultraorthodox, secular Zionist, and Palestinian—are
relevant to the ethnography and were explicitly or implicitly "present"
in one way or another during the observations and interviews I carried
out there.

The Religious-Zionist community operates a separate public education system under State supervision. It offers a standard curriculum
along with its own style of Jewish studies. Graduates follow routine
careers of their own choosing, unlike ultraorthodox Jews, who keep to
circumscribed occupations. The ultraorthodox rejection of secular life,
and its preference for a "society of men scholars" (Friedman 1987),
strongly influence the Religious-Zionist community. In a multicultural
society in which they enjoy the benefits of a modern state, the ultraorthodox chose to reject modernism and Zionism. This creates a dilemma for Religious Zionists who are committed to becoming a vital

part of modern society while remaining Orthodox. They are forced to ask: Who follows the correct Jewish path? Who is a better Jew?

The Six-Day War (1967), when Israel conquered territories inhabited by Palestinians, provided new ways of answering this cultural question. The Religious-Zionist community began to emphasize its nationalistic side and became the leader of the "Greater Israel" ideology. Some of its members led the settlement movements in the occupied territories under the approving eye of several governments and for a while were at the forefront of Israeli Jewish society. They presented themselves as the new Zionist pioneers, armed with the Bible and a messianic theology (Aran 1991). The urge for Jewish studies was both an inner imperative and an outer need vis-à-vis competing Jewish literacies—readings of Jewish texts and Jewish history—both secular and ultraorthodox.

During the period of this study (1992 to 1995), the Labor-led government under Prime Minister Yitzhak Rabin made serious steps toward accommodation with the Palestinians. This process entailed returning land to Palestinian control and placed the followers of the "Greater Israel" ideology under serious political threat. In the eyes of many Israelis, they came to represent the "enemies of peace," the crazy fundamentalists, the "Arab killers." Being excluded from the political and ideological center by the Labor government, in coalition with the Israeli left, created stress and uncertainty. One response was to seek refuge and safety in the study of texts, where they reconfirmed their threatened identity, a development that affected both men and women.

As stated, the phenomenon of women studying Jewish books, more than their mothers had, began before this ideological threat emerged. A rather recent development was the exposure to texts such as the Talmud, which previously were only open to males. As with study among males, topics in the Talmud are easily linked to contemporary concerns (Heilman 1983). I met these women studying Judaism, and reflecting on themselves, in a fairly new educational institution while they were experiencing chaotic political upheaval. Being permitted, as a cultural outsider, to study with them meant that I was privy to discussions of their most cherished values. The texture of their studies under the tutelage of a (male) rabbi, and the discussions arising from them carrying political overtones, are illustrated in my field notes.

This series of ethnographic notes, to which I have given the title, "The Extended Case of Rabbi Akiva and Rabbi Ben Zakkai," reflects class discussion, led by a rabbi-teacher, on January 2, 1994. They contain verbatim statements of the participants, plus my own notes at the time describing the setting and class interaction. In the version that follows, additional explanations in italics have been added to clarify the content of the discussion and indicate the broader cultural and political issues to which these discussions point.

THE EXTENDED CASE OF
RABBI AKIVA AND RABBI BEN ZAKKAI

It is the second week of a full strike in all Israeli universities, called by the faculty. Bar-Ilan is also on strike, but classes continue as usual in the *Midrasha*. Sanctions never apply to Torah studies. The front page of the *Midrasha* newsletter announced in large typeface: "Notice! Classes at the *Midrasha* meet even when the University is on strike." The men's *Yeshiva* is not on strike either. Most of the women would normally be on campus for regular university studies, but today all of them have made a special point of attending class; very few are absent. They come from far and near as well as from the occupied territories. Before the class began the rabbi approached me and said:

You remember our original agreement, right? You've come to study and nothing else.

On hearing the rabbi's question, I have that familiar feeling, the fear of lying, the anxiety over losing my material. What do I care, he can't take away what I've already got, there's nothing he can do, anyway, he knows I'm doing research, he gave me permission to be here. At the same time there is the desire to continue to be accepted, to cooperate, not to be cut off. I responded:

Of course I remember; how could I forget? In fact I thought about dropping by to talk to you about it, because, you know, it's not exactly . . . I know I said I'm studying and studying means I'm studying Torah and also a little about how the women study and all that.

The rabbi explained the background to his question:

I just don't want to end up looking like that *rebbetsin* from the *Gur Hasidim* in your book.

Using the Yiddish term *rebbetsin*—rabbi's wife—derisively, he referred to the Hebrew version of my book about the Gur Hasidim (El-Or 1994), which he had read.[3]

The class is about to begin, and all the women are looking at us. It is embarrassing. We exchange a few words about a woman he knows who is a student of mine, and he begins the class:

So, you all remember what we read last week in the Babylonian Talmud, Tractate Berachot, page 28b. There we met Rabbi Yohanan ben Zakkai on his deathbed, tearfully parting from his beloved students. We tried to understand from the written text what he fears. A righteous man like Rabbi Yohanan Ben-Zakkai, what does he have to fear from the heavenly court? After we have read together some selections from the Bible and other parts of the Gemara, I want to show you a Gemara I'm sure you're all familiar with, the Gemara in which Rabbi Akiva mocks Rabbi Yohanan Ben-Zakkai and calls him a fool—a fool for having chosen Yavne and its scholars instead of Jerusalem and its sovereignty during the Great Rebellion against the Romans.

Rabbi Yohanan Ben-Zakkai was a first-century sage who lived at the time the Romans destroyed the Jerusalem Temple (70 C.E.), after the Jews had revolted. Ben-Zakkai advocated accommodation to the Romans rather than total confrontation with them and sought permission to continue the study and teaching of Torah in a town called Yavne, fifty kilometers west of Jerusalem. Following the destruction of Jerusalem and the Temple, and between the two revolts against the Romans (70–135 C.E.), Yavne became the spiritual center of the Jewish people and the major seat of rabbinic learning. Rabbi Akiva was a second-century sage who supported a revolt against the Romans, led by Bar-Kokhba, in 132–35 C.E. After setting up the tension between the positions of Ben-Zakkai and Akiva, the Rabbi continued:

And you must also be familiar with Yehoshafat Harkabi's book, which presents Rabbi Akiva as an extreme nationalist who did not correctly read the military and political map and who led Israel to destruction by supporting Bar-Kokhba. I ask you, my dear girls, what's being said here? Rabbi Akiva didn't read Harkabi's book? Ah, that's funny, good, so he didn't read the book, but do you think then that he didn't know what Harkabi realizes today? I imagine Rabbi Akiva was aware of the Romans' might and understood what risks he was taking. What brought Rabbi Akiva to criticize his predecessor Rabbi Yohanan Ben-Zakkai, seventy years after Rabbi Yohanan Ben-Zakkai chose the Torah and not national sovereignty?

Yehoshafat Harkabi, then a retired general and historian (he died in 1996), published a book in 1983 entitled The Bar Kokhba Syndrome *about Bar-Kokhba's revolt against the Romans. It portrayed the rebellion as an act of zealots that in the long run resulted in the exile of Jews from the land of Israel. Prodding the students for an answer the rabbi, turned to them patronizingly, using a Yiddish term:*

Nu, meidelech [So, little girls], what do you think?[4]

One of the girls, Efrat, responded:

Rabbi Akiva represents the Israeli Jew, the Jew who doesn't compromise his honor, who doesn't surrender. Like the Jews who fought in the Warsaw Ghetto and didn't go like lambs to the slaughter. Rabbi Yohanan ben Zakkai represents the Jew in exile who takes into account that there are women and children here: "Let's get what we can." There were people like that in the Holocaust, too, and we know what their accounting led to in the end.

Yael continued, also explaining the difference between the two positions:

Today there are also those who use force and those who follow the spiritual Torah path. Rabbi Akiva simply wanted to show that the Jews had power, to give the people the message that there is hope and that miracles can happen, and that you should do what you have to do without making compromises.

Rachel then explicitly justified each position:

Yohanan ben Zakkai was prepared to give up the external trappings of sovereignty for wisdom and knowledge and the Torah, and Rabbi Akiva simply didn't believe that you could live only under the crown of the Torah without the crown of kingship and priesthood.[5] They're two different opinions, two different views of the world. You can't say that one is right and one is wrong.

Efrat further reflected:

It's really amazing if you think about it in the context of our own times.

The Rabbi rejoined:

I don't really want to talk about the context of our times, but since you've already mentioned it, on the eve of the declaration of independence of the State of Israel in 1948, there was heated debate about whether to declare its independence. Ben-Gurion decided to make the declaration against the judgment of many who were afraid of how the Arabs would react. Do we know whether his decision was the right one? We don't know, because not enough time has passed. I only want to talk about the moment of doubt, that every leader has to go to his grave with his doubts. That is the reason that Rabbi Yohanan ben Zakkai cries in front of his students: he still is not sure he acted properly. Take Menahem Begin, he punished himself while he was still alive. He put himself under house arrest because he understood in retrospect that his decision about the Lebanon War [in 1982] had been in error. It's a matter of the moral greatness of the leader. I don't want to continue with analogies to today, only to tell you that a leader as great as Yohanan ben Zakkai lived with his doubts, and that says something about the measure and the depth of the man. Because today it seems to me that our leaders never agonize over anything.

David Ben-Gurion was the first prime minister of the State of Israel, and Menahem Begin was the first prime minister, elected in 1977, who represented the major nationalist party, the Likud. The latter resigned from his position in 1983, confining himself mainly to his own home for the rest of his life. The rabbi, calling this self-imposed "house arrest," accorded moral stature to the decision and contrasted him with the current political leaders. One student, Shulamit, questioned the contrast:

Maybe that's tactical; maybe they agonize but make a show of being certain.

The Rabbi replied:

I hope you're right. I have a feeling that our leaders today are not on the same moral plane. But let's return to the matter at hand. Who was right in retrospect, Rabbi Akiva or Rabbi Yohanan Ben-Zakkai? We have the historical perspective to judge them.

The women know history proved Rabbi Akiva wrong; the Bar-Kokhba revolt led to the destruction of the center part of the country, to many deaths, and to the exile of the Jewish people. They also know that the Torah enabled the Jewish people to survive in exile for close to 2,000 years without national sovereignty, but they still do not want to say anything critical about Rabbi Akiva. Even I, although not part of their subculture, was taught in the secular Zionist school system to revere Rabbi Akiva. He was presented as a great scholar who would not give up his right to study. I knew him as a humanist and a hero. When we were children, the Bar-Kokhba revolt was depicted as a heroic chapter in Jewish history, an example to be emulated by the Zionist revival in Israel.

The rabbi again pressed for an answer:

Nu, girls? You don't want to say anything bad about Rabbi Akiva; you don't want to say that he made a mistake? You're allowed to, you know. After all, on the face of it Yohanan ben Zakkai was right. I know, in Ulpena they don't tell you that great rabbis can make mistakes, right?[6]

Leah ventured a response:

Maybe, but it could be that according to Rabbi Akiva's way the exile would have lasted less time.

The Rabbi continued:

Okay, but you're forgetting an important historical point. Rabbi

Akiva was, in his time, already confronting Christianity, which offered a universal religion with no connection to national identity. The concept of the chosen people was under threat. Anyone could join the new religion, regardless of nationality. That is what concerned Rabbi Akiva. In his eyes, Yohanan ben Zakkai's proposal for a spirituality not dependent on national affiliation put what is unique to Judaism at risk. And that idea continues to exist today. If you cross the bridge here by the university into B'nei Braq [an ultraorthodox town], you will hear the same opinions, this very day: spiritual Judaism without any connection to nationalism. Even though Rabbi Akiva failed militarily he did not fail historically. Why? He brought the aspiration for national existence, the hope for national rebirth, into Jewish discourse. There is a need for opposing forces of impetus and restraint. That's the way critical thinking grows; that's how development takes place. Like the tension between the Hasidim and the Lithuanians, that in the end has a positive effect. I don't want to think what the fate of the Jewish people would have been had it not embodied both these forces, spirituality and nationalism.[7]

When he finished making his case, Efrat raised her hand and said:

Rabbi, I know you already said that you don't like to talk about contemporary issues, but with the situation the way it is, it really is hard not to apply it to today.

The Rabbi responded in a manner that made reference to my presence:

Apply it to today? Do you want me to talk politics? Oh, all right, we'll close all the windows. Tamar! Stop writing.

All eyes are turned toward me. They laugh and someone says, "She's probably got a tape recorder." The rabbi continued:

Look, in my opinion, everything that's happening now is really an expression of the deep and fundamental cultural war under way in Israeli society, for which the debate over the territories is just a cover. I'm in favor of putting all the cards on the table. We must decide what kind of Jewish state we want here when it comes down to it. There are several models: Rabbi Shach's, Shulamit Aloni's, ours, Rabin's, many kinds. A decision has to be made. I'm not afraid of a fight. It doesn't have to be a fight with rifles. It is a very deep struggle, and it has to be fought.

The Rabbi, "putting his cards on the table," pointed to the range of cultural and political positions and leaders who attempt to shape Israeli society: Rabbi Eliezer Shach, the leader of the world of "Lithuanian," Yeshiva-

oriented, Judaism within the ultraorthodox world; Member of Parliament Shulamit Aloni, for many years the leader of the Citizen's Rights Movement in Israel, who symbolized the "antireligious left" in the eyes of many ultraorthodox; and Yitzhak Rabin, elected Prime Minister in 1992, who brought about the historical agreement between Israel and the Palestinians.[8] One of the students, Ora, wondered about the definiteness of the Rabbi's position:

Maybe the time is not ripe for decisions. Like we don't have a constitution because it's not possible. If there was a decision there would be two nations here, there would be a split.

The Rabbi answered clearly:

I prefer a split.

Ora pressed him further:

And if there is a decision you don't like, a democratic decision on a model that you don't accept, would you accept it? And if there won't be any difference between Jewish and Arab citizens? If there is full equality of rights, or a binational state?

The Rabbi stated unequivocally:

If the state is not Jewish, I won't be part of it.

Following this, there was silence in the classroom.

After the class I walk with the rabbi to his office. Some of the students want to talk to him, but he puts them off for a few moments. He leaves the door open, and we sit down across from each other. I propose an alternative reading to his interpretation of the story about Yohanan ben Zakkai and Akiva. I continue with the same doubt that Ora raised about how deciding not to decide can be a solution: a mutual recognition of distinctions, separation of religion and state. He listens with interest and appears to be thinking about it seriously. I share with him the shock I felt at what he said about not being part of a binational state and preferring a split. He then explained:

I simply don't think that Rabin today has the same morality as Yohanan ben Zakkai had. Even though he made a similar momentous decision, I'm not sure he isn't sleeping nights—I'm not sure he has the same degree of spiritual greatness, that drunken peasant.

I responded with my view:

I agree that he does not have moral greatness, and I don't see him as a great spiritual leader. He's carrying out a policy that others formulated, and he can lead. I don't believe he's sensitive or moral, but I believe in the road he's taking.

The rabbi then made a suggestion:

Perhaps we have to give it a chance, to try it. Why don't you raise your hand in class and say what you just said. It's very important for me.

His suggestion was unexpected, and I demurred:

I don't feel comfortable talking. It's not my place. I'm not part of all this.

Nevertheless, he persisted:

Please, I want you to offer your interpretation of the story, what you told me here. I'd like you to say it in class, including your political interpretation.

I never presented my political interpretations in front of that class, or anywhere else, although as the remark about the tape recorder shows, most of the students could guess where I stand. At that time, a year before the assassination of Prime Minister Rabin, I intended to interpret the dialogues in the class as metaphoric of the current position of Religious Zionism. The rabbi, a main participant in those dialogues, expressed the ambivalent stand of his community. On the one hand, he was very clear about his preference for "Israel as a Jewish State" as opposed to Israel as "a state of all its citizens," both Jewish and non-Jewish. He even declared that he was prepared for a national split, a statement that seemed to take the students by surprise.

On the other hand, he showed a certain cautiousness with regard to these views. His characterization of Rabin as a drunken peasant took place only in his office. It was also in that private discussion that he indicated he was keen to stay within the "new Israeli collective" and sought an opening through which he could slide back into it. It seemed to me at the time that the second tendency was stronger, even as the aching ambivalence remained. While making this assessment, I could not foresee the extreme steps that one person in his religious community would take in order to "correct" this ambivalence, by violent action toward the "accused person" who had been singled out by the rabbi himself.

Notes

1. Religious Zionists are Orthodox Jews who joined the Zionist movement. Their religious political ideology was molded mainly by Rabbi Kalisher (1795–1874), Rabbi Alkalai (1798–1878), and Rabbi Kook (1865–1935) and stands in contradistinction to ultraorthodoxy, which rejects the values of modernity.

2. Bar-Ilan University has 21,000 students. Seventeen thousand attend the main campus in Ramat-Gan, and the rest study in four satellite campuses, including one in Ariel in the West Bank. Forty percent of the students are religious, the rest are not; 62 percent are women, 38 percent men; and 2.5 percent are Palestinian citizens of Israel.

3. The Hasidim derive from a religious movement in Eastern Europe, spreading from southeastern Poland and the Ukraine, in the second half of the eighteenth century. They were vigorously opposed by the *Mitnagdim*, who were centered in Lithuania. Within the Hasidic movement, the Gur Hasidim are one of the largest and most influential groups today.

4. *Nu*, originally a Yiddish and now also a Hebrew term, can be roughly glossed: "Okay, so what do you have to say?"

5. One expression of traditional Jewish "political theory" is that leadership is divided among those wearing three crowns: that of the monarchy, that of the priesthood, and that of (knowledge of) the Torah.

6. A boarding high school for Religious-Zionists girls. Today there are nine throughout the country that enroll more than two thousand students. They are part of the separate public education system under State supervision mentioned above but represent a more strict education than standard high schools for Religious-Zionist girls.

7. On the *Mitnagdim*, see note 3.

8. In the Labor-led government elected in 1992, Aloni was also at first appointed to be Minister of Education and Culture. Rabin had earlier served as prime minister from 1974 to 1977. He was assassinated during his second term, in November 1995, by a young man who was a student at the Bar-Ilan Yeshiva.

References

Aran, Gideon. 1991. "Jewish Zionist Fundamentalism: The Bloc of the Faithful in Israel." In *Fundamentalisms Observed*, E. R. Marty and R. S. Appleby, eds., pp. 265–345. Chicago: University of Chicago Press.

El-Or, Tamar. 1994. *Educated and Ignorant: Ultraorthodox Jewish Women and Their World*. Boulder and London: Lynne Rienner Publishers.

———. 1998. *Next Passover: Women and Literacy in the Religious Zionist Community* (in Hebrew). Tel Aviv: Am Oved, forthcoming from Wayne State University Press (in English).

Friedman, Menachem. 1987. "Life Tradition and Book Tradition in the Development of Ultraorthodox Judaism." In *Judaism Viewed from Within and Without*, H. E. Goldberg, ed. Albany: State University of New York Press.

Granite, Lauren, B. 1995. *Tradition as a Modality of Religious Change: Talmud Study in the Lives of Orthodox Jewish Women*. Ph.D. diss., Drew University.

Harkabi, Yehoshafat. 1983. *The Bar-Kokhba Syndrome: Risk and Realism in International Politics*. Chappaqua, NY: Rossel Books.

Heilman, Samuel. 1983. *The People of the Book: Drama, Fellowship and Religion.* Chicago: University of Chicago Press.

Weissman, Deborah. 1976. "Bais Yaakov: A Historical Model for Jewish Feminists." In *The Jewish Woman,* E. Kolton, ed., pp. 139–149. New York: Schocken Books.

———. 1993. *The Education of Religious Girls in Jerusalem during the Period of British Rule.* Ph.D. diss., Hebrew University (in Hebrew).

Figure 15. Ethiopian Jewish man bent over a book. He is wearing a white robe and turban, customary for the *qessotch* (priests) and holy men of the Ethiopian Jewish community. (Date and source unknown. Courtesy Judah L. Magnes Museum.)

CHAPTER 15

Ethiopian Jewry and
New Self-Concepts

Hagar Salamon

Although Jews in Israel and Jews in America often experience and
shape Judaism in different ways, some issues arise that connect them.
One such issue is the Jews of Ethiopia who became known to the European Jewish world in the middle of the nineteenth century. With the
encouragement of American Jewish organizations, they reached Israel
en masse in the 1980s and early 1990s. These Jews differed widely from
other Jewish groups because their religious tradition was not affected
by rabbinic Judaism and because their skin pigmentation is "black,"
making them different in appearance from the majority of contemporary Jews of European provenance. Since they became known to the
wider Jewish world, and particularly since their arrival in large numbers in Israel, the Jews of Ethiopia have stimulated many questions
about Jewish identity, both with respect to them and to Jews all over
the world. In the selection that follows, Hagar Salamon probes these
questions, showing how they entail components of religion, race, and
the relationships between Israeli and Diaspora Judaism.

Judaism between Race and Religion:
The Case of the Ethiopian Jews

The establishment of the State of Israel brought together
Jews from many lands who differ widely from one another in stature and
skin color.[1] Jewish identity, which in the various Diaspora communities

was defined primarily vis-à-vis a non-Jewish other, assumed new dimensions with the ingathering of the exiles when, for the first time, Jews coming to the Promised Land found themselves living side by side with Jews so utterly different from them, both physically and culturally.

While actually wide in variety, Jewish ethnic diversity in Israel is officially simplified into an East/West dichotomy.[2] Jews originating from Asia and Africa are lumped into the single category of Sephardim or "Oriental" (in Hebrew "mizrahim"), while European and American Jews fall under the collective term "Ashkenazim." Within these two sweeping categories—"Ashkenazim" and "Oriental" are countless popular subdistinctions and accompanying stereotypes. Throughout the history of the State of Israel, relations between "Oriental" and "Ashkenazic" Jews have been charged with tension, based on strong sentiments regarding the privileged position of Ashkenazic Jews in Israeli society. A dynamic of paternalism and power relations, ubiquitous in encounters between East and West, rears its head across the public sphere in education, economics, and politics—and emerges at many levels of social relations and cultural expression.

Interethnic diversity and Jewish "otherness" was a confounding phenomenon for Israeli Jews and encouraged the search for an "other" located outside the group boundary. While Jewish-Israeli identity has taken shape, *inter alia,* vis-à-vis various Jewish "others," the diametrically opposed Arab "other" thus conveniently deflected tension from troubling interethnic relations.

The question of boundaries between the Jewish majority and the Arab other, which overshadows and blunts the effects of inter-Jewish difference, penetrates the inter-Jewish discourse in many and diverse ways. Harvey Goldberg (1985) makes the lucid observation that this pattern is exemplified by the way in which stereotypic characteristics associated with Jewish ethnic groups are symbolically related to the distinction between Jew and Arab. Because of similarities, both cultural and physical, between "Oriental" Jews and Arabs, these groups are perceived as somehow akin to each other in the Israeli consciousness, and so Arab stereotypes are applied to "Oriental" Jews. But to equate the groups absolutely would erode the boundaries between them and, as Goldberg suggests, would be tantamount to the realization of a lurking and ever-present fear: the "Arabization" of Israel. The Arab stereotype, a synthesis of perceptions and associations, was therefore fragmented, such that each "Oriental" Jewish subgroup was assigned a different stereotypical characteristic—the Moroccans were perceived, particularly in the 1960s and 1970s, as "aggressive," the Yemenites as "authentic," the Kurds as "primitive" and so forth.[3]

The arrival of sixty thousand Ethiopian Jews to Israel during the last two decades has offered a new frame of reference for defining Jewish-Israeli identity—a Jewish "other." Since the qualities that determine interethnic boundaries are dynamic, and largely a factor of historiocultural conditions, the social divisions in Israel, up to the arrival of Ethiopian Jewry, were constantly shifting across Jewish ethnic lines, with a decided Arab other from which Jewish society distinguishes itself. Intergroup tensions, throughout the years in Israel's immigrant society, centered, aside from ethnicity, on class, and newcomer-versus-veteran-citizen status—but only with the arrival of the Jews of Ethiopia did long-submerged tensions between race and religion in Judaism well to the surface. Hitherto dormant race issues have become the new focus of the interethnic discourse, presenting new material for considering Judaism on the axis of race and religion.

Ethiopian Jews are the only group perceived as both Jewish and black, Jewish and racially other and have thus attracted far more attention than other groups of a similar size in the Jewish state. The very existence of this community presents paradoxes to Jewish identity, and thus Ethiopian Jews serve as a prism through which symbolic dimensions of Jewishness are refracted in many directions.

BACKGROUND

Originally, the Beta Israel (Falasha), lived in northwestern Ethiopia in approximately five hundred small villages scattered across a vast territory, dispersed throughout a predominantly Christian society.[4] Though no difference in physical appearance distinguished these Jews from their neighbors in this African country, as skilled—albeit low status—craftspeople, they were an occupational as well as a religious minority. Moreover, they clearly saw themselves as a distinct group, maintaining a faith that the majority of Ethiopians had forsaken for the younger and now dominant creed of Christianity. Strongly identifying themselves with the Torah (*Orit*, the Old Testament written in *Geʿez*), which was the central focus of their beliefs, they meticulously observed its laws and dreamed of the coming of the Messiah and their return to the legendary Jerusalem.[5]

The modern identification of the Beta Israel as part of the Jewish world was a consequence of the missionary activities of the Protestant

"London Society for Promoting Christianity amongst the Jews of Ethiopia," beginning in 1858.[6] This, more than anything else, marks the point at which the Ethiopians came to the attention of world Jewry, first in Europe and later in the United States. Until world Jewry "discovered" them, the Beta Israel had shaped and expressed their identity within the context of the wider stream of Ethiopian history. Missionary activity made them aware of a more universal form of Jewish identity. The new awareness of the larger Jewish world outside Ethiopia was a dramatic turning point in their history.

A number of prominent Jewish leaders, attracted by the exotic nature of Jewish life in the "land of Kush," responded to the missionary threat and began to lobby for aid to be sent to the Beta Israel, then known as the Falasha.[7] Attempts were made to bring them closer to other Jewish communities by publicizing their story, finding similarities between their rituals and beliefs and those of normative Judaism, and even reforming religious practices to bring them closer to those of other Jews (by introducing, for example, the lighting of Sabbath candles, the symbol of the Star of David, and the idea of abolishing animal sacrifices). Such efforts continued into the present era, when the Jewish Agency and other organizations worked to strengthen the ties of the Beta Israel to world Jewry and Israel.

Jerusalem, which had been primarily a symbol of a lost era for these Jews, became a reality with the founding of the State of Israel in 1948. The aspiration to reach "Zion" provided yet another motive for struggle and for survival. The new state quickly enacted the Law of Return, ensuring open immigration for all Jews and affirming the position of the Jewish state as sanctuary and homeland. Initially, however, the Beta Israel, despite their self-definition and their struggles in Ethiopia as Jews, were not recognized as Jews under this law. In addition to questions about their Jewishness, political, social, and medical considerations were deterrents to the Ethiopians' aliyah to Israel during the early years of mass immigration to the country.

Only in 1973 was there a religious ruling recognizing the Beta Israel as Jews. Drawing on rabbinic opinion from more than four hundred years earlier, Ovadia Yosef, the incumbent Sephardic Chief Rabbi of Israel, declared that the Ethiopian community was descended from the lost tribe of Dan.[8] Significantly, this proclamation linked the Beta Israel to the Jewish people in a way that did not challenge the otherwise underlying presumption that common descent is the key to Jewishness.

Despite the chief rabbi's ruling, followed by an interministerial committee, which in 1975 officially recognized the Falashas as Jews entitled to automatic citizenship under the Law of Return, the Beta Israel remained a source of contention in Jewish discourse. Even after their immigration began in 1977, bitter disputes about their identity continued. If questions raised in Israeli Jewish society based on the relationship between identity and the criterion of origin had been avoided in the past, Ethiopian Jews now made evasion impossible. The chief rabbi's decision made reference to *pzurot Israel* (the dispersed ones of Israel) and *shivtei Israel* (the tribes of Israel), thus invoking the legend about the dispersion of the "Ten Lost Tribes" to all corners of the earth. The ruling paradoxically invoked the myth of shared Jewish origins to substantiate group membership for a population so visibly distinct and illuminated the difficulty inherent in a post-Holocaust Jewish identity based on ethnic and racial distinctions.

The chief rabbi's recognition also enabled Jews in Israel and the Diaspora to lobby for their cause. As the Jews of Ethiopia began to appear on the agenda of a growing number of Jewish organizations, Israel came under increasing pressure to agitate for their exodus.[9] Beginning in 1977, successive Israeli governments turned their attention to this group. By the middle of 1997 virtually all its members had immigrated. This period saw drastic changes in internal Ethiopian politics and in Ethiopia's relations to the West. Sensitivity and flexibility were required to negotiate the myriad political complexities.

Beginning in 1980, Beta Israel, first in the northern parts of Ethiopia and later from all the regions where the Jews lived, crossed the country's border into the Sudan. There they waited in refugee camps for months and sometimes years to be taken in groups to Israel. The first massive wave of immigration was in 1984, when Israel, in the dramatic campaign that became known as Operation Moses, flew almost seven thousand people to the Jewish state over the course of two months. By the time the campaign ended in early 1985, the total number of Ethiopians in Israel had reached over 14,000.

The effects of the trek to the Sudan and the sojourn in the Sudanese refugee camps were devastating. There was hardly an individual who did not lose family members along the way, while others were left behind in Ethiopia (Kaplan and Rosen 1994: 62–66). Family reunification thus became the most urgent concern of the Ethiopian community in Israel. Owing to political events and other considerations, only 2,500 additional immigrants were able to make their way to Israel between 1985 and the end of 1989. Some arrived directly from the Ethiopian capital, Addis Ababa; others came in small groups through the Sudan.

In 1990, encouraged by representatives of the American Association for Ethiopian Jews, the community in Ethiopia began to migrate to Addis Ababa. The numbers of those waiting in the capital for exit visas reached twenty thousand by the summer of 1990. It was a time of great political turmoil in Ethiopia, but the pressure on Israel to help the waiting Jews was so great that a massive campaign was launched. Code named Operation Solomon, the campaign reunited most of the Ethiopian Jews in Israel with their families. Over the course of thirty-six hours in May 1991, more than 14,000 individuals were airlifted to Israel. Several thousand more have come since 1991 (Kaplan and Rosen 1994: 66). Today virtually all Ethiopian Jewry lives in the Jewish state.

Many in Israel saw the ingathering of this ancient Diaspora community as a deeply moving affirmation of the state's basic raison d'être. An editorial in the *London Times* praised the Israelis' daring, comparing them to Moses and Aaron in their efforts to rescue the "lost tribe" (Rapoport 1986: 179). Images of the Exodus from Egypt are also laden with meaning for the Ethiopians, and the parallels between their journey and that of the ancient Israelites are sources of pride for the Ethiopian community.

The Beta Israel, once a marginal group in Christian Ethiopia, has become a highly visible community whose presence carries a great deal of symbolic value in Israel. Their long journey, full of vicissitudes, has been accompanied by many struggles and bitter disputes. They continue to be the focus of debate, with some Israelis identifying with their struggles and championing their cause and others still questioning their "authenticity" as Jews. Beyond the Beta Israel's "exotic" characteristics as an isolated Jewish group in the heart of Africa, as a community both Jewish and black—coreligionists to their fellow Israelis but of a different race—they challenge prevailing understandings of Judaism.

RELIGION

Since the founding of the State of Israel, responsibility for Jewish religious affairs has been vested in the chief rabbinate. This body alone has been given the authority to render operative and binding rulings on many questions of Jewish religious status that penetrate all realms of life, from the Law of Return through family law. The ruling by Chief Rabbi Ovadia Yosef recognizing the Beta Israel as authentic Jews therefore did not merely open the doors to immigration. It also gave the chief rabbinate religious jurisdiction over the immigrants, planting the seed for future jurisdictional struggles. And indeed, despite having affirmed the Ethiopians' communal status as Jews, the rabbinate expressed reservations about the personal status of individuals. The Ethiopians' ignorance of postbiblical rabbinic literature and law *(hala-kha)* gave rise to concerns that centuries of divorces and conversions performed by the Ethiopian Jewish priests *(qessotch)* might be invalid. According to the rabbinate, this called into question the religious status of hundreds of Ethiopians, with *mamzerut,* illegitimacy stemming from nonhalakhic divorce, being a particularly grave concern.[10] In an attempt to rectify this situation, the rabbinate, throughout the 1970s and early 1980s, required of the Ethiopian immigrants a modified conversion ceremony consisting of ritual immersion, acceptance of rabbinic law, and a symbolic recircumcision for men.

Ethiopian immigrants vehemently rejected the rabbinate's claims regarding their personal status. A series of demonstrations (widely covered by the Israeli media) by members of the community and their supporters gradually led to de facto removal of the rabbinate's restrictions and requirements—without the rabbinate officially changing its stance. First, the conversion requirement was modified to apply only to those seeking a marriage license. Eventually, the compromise adopted was to teach the priests the strictures of *halakha,* so that in serving their community they could operate according to the understandings of rabbinic Judaism.

Many Israelis viewed the chief rabbinate's demands that the Beta Israel undergo conversion as fundamentalist religious harassment of a "quiet" and "naive" population. The Beta Israel's lack of familiarity with *halakha*—the reason for the rabbinate's special requirements—is depicted, in this viewpoint, as emblematic of a pure, unspoiled ancient Judaism and contrasted to a rabbinical establishment that imposes fixed religious precepts and overlooks diversity.

The Jewish world at large, caught up in a struggle with the Orthodox rabbinate, latched onto the Ethiopian cause where the relationship between religion and descent was concerned. Rallying to the support of the Ethiopian community, they pointed to the many Jews who, unlike the Beta Israel, do not observe basic religious commandments found in the Torah but are accepted as Jews by the rabbinate because their descent is unquestioned.

RACE

Hidden behind the often-asked question of "are the Falasha *real* Jews?" is a silently gnawing preoccupation with race. Of all characteristics symbolizing identity, physiological features—and in particular skin color—are the most prominent and immutable, and so the Ethiopian Jews' skin color is central to the ongoing discourse relating to this group. The convergence of underlying tensions between race and religion in Judaism, and the widely held religious belief of a common origin for all Jews, struck a discord and sparked emotionally charged fundamental questions of Jewish identity.

One of the first public reactions to Operation Moses referring to racial issues came from Africa: an editor in the Kenyan capital of Nairobi suggested that the airlift might put to rest the old "Zionism is Racism" canard. On the other hand, Mengistu Haile Maryam, the Ethiopian ruler at the time, railed that the Zionists had "kidnapped" thousands of black Africans in order "to complete their ethnic collection." William Safire of the *New York Times* countered, "for the first time in history, thousands of black people are being brought into a country not in chains but as citizens" (Rapoport 1986:176). As these voices contended, Ethiopian immigrants found themselves singled out as "blacks" for the first time in their history.

The Beta Israel are the focus of attempts by Jews outside Israel, particularly those in the United States, to disprove allegations that Judaism is racist. Amid tension between Jews and blacks in the United States, the Ethiopian Jews are touted as proof that in Judaism race is not a condition of group membership. Additionally, the "rescue" of the Beta Israel and their settlement in the Promised Land were experienced by many American Jews as a corrective to the traumas of the Holocaust and guilt they felt about their inability to rescue Jews trapped in Europe.[11] For a number of American Jewish organizations and U.S. government officials who played a vital role in the rescue of these Jews, activism was perceived as a way of making amends for the past, in particular for their role in preventing immigration by European Jews fleeing Hitler in the years before World War II (Gruber 1987: 148).

Both airlifts, Operation Moses and Operation Solomon—launched by the Jewish state in cooperation with U.S. Jewry and the American government to save a small, beleaguered minority group—became a source of pride for the Jewish world. These secret operations were compared with other missions such as the Entebbe rescue, in which Jewish captives were freed by Israeli soldiers in the very heart of Uganda. Through operations Moses and Solomon, a forgotten Jewish tribe otherwise destined to disappear was brought home.

Before Operation Moses, the issue of race had rarely if ever been explicitly discussed in Israel. Indeed, given the heightened sensitivity of the connection between Judaism and race in the wake of the Holocaust, to even suggest a link between Jewishness and racial categories was taboo. Although groups of differing complexion, on a continuum from light to dark, live together in Israel, it is only the Jews of Ethiopia who are seen unequivocally as "black." Previously, the category of otherness that "black" connotes to Israelis was reserved primarily for Arabs, with whom the dividing lines are not racial.

A latent awareness of the issue of race was evident in the public debate over the group's absorption into Israeli society. The hope that the Ethiopian immigrants would not become second-class citizens was voiced repeatedly. Care and sensitivity were called for to avoid a situation in which these immigrants would be ultimately employed in unskilled labor, known as *avoda aravit* (lit. Arab labor), since it is mainly performed by Arabs, and also referred to as *avoda sheḥora* (lit. black labor). Such concerns regarding other immigrant groups like the Russian Jews who came to Israel in the same years as the Ethiopian Jews were never voiced.

An attempt to obscure the impression of "otherness," particularly in the early stages of the Ethiopians' acculturation, was made by placing the Beta Israel's color on a continuum with that of earlier Jewish immigrant groups, in particular the Jews of Yemen and India. For example, popular jokes linked the Ethiopian and Yemenite Jews, and the immigrants themselves continually sought physiological likeness to these and other dark-skinned Jewish groups in Israel.

A notion expressed by the Beta Israel that was documented in Ethiopia before their immigration held that they originally had been white but had become black because of the climate in North Africa. After immigration, the skin of the "real" Jews among them was sure to revert to white. Over time, however, this belief was transformed, to "color doesn't come out in the wash."

The issue of color and race carries multiple levels of association and meaning for the Ethiopians themselves, stemming not only from their experience in Israel but also from categories deeply embedded in Ethiopian culture. Although the immigrants seldom mention it, they participated in Ethiopia in a system that assigned different categories and statuses on the basis of color. The Beta Israel perceived themselves, along with their Christian neighbors, as "red." "Black" referred only to members of low-status groups, among them, slaves. These deeply rooted perceptions, so basic to Ethiopian culture, were a powerful factor as the Beta Israel community came to terms with its situation in Israel.

The warm and affectionate reception that greeted the Ethiopian immigrants on the level of media coverage, government slogans, and other popular expressions, and far exceeded the welcome enjoyed by any of the other immigrant groups to Israel, was a facet of the smothering paternalism that greeted their arrival. Their blackness was interwoven with romantic notions that the Jews of Ethiopia came "straight from the time of the Bible to the twentieth century." They were commonly depicted as "unspoiled, quiet and polite." [12]

Given these widespread perceptions, many observers in Israel and abroad could only explain the raised voices and even outbreaks of violence at some demonstrations staged by Ethiopian Israelis in terms of spoiled innocence. Occasional reminders that violent struggle, internal and against outside forces, had been a continuous part of Ethiopian experience in Israel and Ethiopia, were generally ignored; the image of the "noble savage" continued to dominate.

Race issues continued to brew on many levels, but it was only the occasion of a major crisis, the Ethiopian blood scandal, that brought them to the surface.

THE BLOOD SCANDAL

At the beginning of 1996, a prominent Israeli newspaper revealed that officials of the country's blood bank had for years been routinely disposing of blood donated by Ethiopians. Such had been the secret practice since research linked the HIV virus to Africa. In fact, among the group that awaited visas in Addis Ababa, the high incidence of AIDS and of individuals testing HIV positive created a tangible concern for the general population's safety. [13] The blood was disposed of immediately, without being checked, and certainly without notifying the donors. [14]

The blood scandal proved to be the catalyst for Ethiopian expressions of frustration over a wide range of issues. [15] It marked, moreover, a point of no return in the discourse on race and racism in Israel. The fact that the incident focused on a physical matter as permanent and unchangeable as blood—the same hue no matter what color the skin—strengthened growing feelings that racism had for many years quietly existed behind a "color-blind" veneer.

The incident opened an era of explicit discussion on racial relations. Using the terms "race" and "racism" in relation to internal Jewish affairs had previously been off-limits in a society that reserved them exclusively for relations between Jews and non-Jews. Direct discussion of racial boundaries led to new questions in additional arenas, both within Jewish society in Israel (for example, Oriental Jews versus Ashkenazic Jews) and in reference to non-Jewish groups in the country—principally Palestinian Arabs, Druze, and Bedouins. In the wake of the demonstrations over the blood scandal, a young leader of Ethiopian origin was for the first time included by the Labor party as a candidate for the Knesset, the Israeli parliament. His election campaign was financed in part by an Israeli Muslim Bedouin, who in a public interview explained his support with the words: "We blacks must help each other."[16] This expression reflects a prevailing sentiment of various Jewish ethnic groups in Israel. A saying commonly heard in the context of the multiethnic experience in Jewish Israel is: "There (in my country of origin) I was a Jew; here I am Moroccan, [or Kurdish, or Russian]." Increasingly, Ethiopian Jews feel that: "There I was a Jew; here I am Black (*kushi*)."[17] This experience creates new borders that simultaneously connect and separate different groups and subgroups in varied and dynamic manners.

"Blackness" as a prominent identity symbol overtaking religion, reflects a process that plays an increasingly pivotal role among the youth of Ethiopian origin in Israel. They strongly identify themselves with black musicians, mostly from the United States. Posters of Michael Jackson, or more recently, Bob Marley, on backgrounds of green, red, and yellow, symbolizing for them the Ethiopian flag, are displayed in their rooms. Occasionally Rastafarian hairstyles, "boom boxes," and other symbols of identification with American blacks are seen as well. Observed on a recent New Year's Eve at one of the "Soweto" clubs springing up around Tel Aviv's central bus station were not only foreign laborers from Ghana and Nigeria and black American marines temporarily stationed in Israel but also young Ethiopian Israelis. Outward manifestations of black identity may be concentrated among younger Ethiopians, but there are signs that it is penetrating other parts of this population as well.

Though a sense of separation on the basis of color may be growing stronger in Israel, other responses are also in evidence. Bumper stickers distributed in the past few months bear the slogan: *Am ehad, harbeh tzvaim* ("One people, many colors"). A deeper reading suggests that through these stickers an attempt is being made to move from the categorical distinction of white versus black to a much wider range of colors that encompasses all Jewish ethnic groups in Israel. The use of the word *Am* (people) builds a Jewish connection that blurs the religious common base, reaching instead in the direction of a common fate and shared experience.

Conclusions

Although the precise religious status of Beta Israel was the subject of debate and controversy even before their arrival in Israel, the topic of racial identity and even more generally the connection between Judaism and race, emerged only relatively late, and explosively, as topics of explicit public discussion. In discussing a process that is comparatively recent in its origins and in a continuous state of flux, any conclusions are by their very nature highly dynamic.

As we have seen, the Ethiopian Jews have served as a catalyst for the exploration of a variety of topics hitherto dormant in Jewish consciousness. Their presence as a group with different skin color and a "deviant" form of Judaism challenges simplistic assumptions about the physical and spiritual unity of the Jewish people. The often-competing attempts of different Israeli and Jewish groups to include them in their definitions of Jewishness and peoplehood bring into high relief questions of power and authority regarding national and religious boundaries and identity.

The arrival of Ethiopian Jewry to Israel under the Law of Return expands traditional views of Judaism to include a conception of Judaism as a multiethnic culture. As Beta Israel's experience unfolds, and their encounter with world Jewry plays out, the ever-shifting kaleidoscope of Jewish identity takes on new color and form. The ethnographic boundaries of Judaism are expanding, opening the way for the very components of the discourse—religion, race, and origin—to enter and exit the arena, perhaps even to be replaced by factors yet unknown. Given the centrality of identity issues in contemporary Judaism and the din of voices competing over the question of "who is a Jew?" it is highly likely that the search for definition of self and other will continue to occupy and preoccupy Israelis and the Jewish world for many years to come.

Notes

1. The most well-known discussion of this question to date, preceding the immigration of the Jews of Ethiopia to Israel, is found in R. Patai's *The Myth of the Jewish Race* (1975).

2. Official government documents citing demographic data consistently divide the Israeli population into two categories: Asia/Africa and Europe/America.

3. Despite the fact that the terms "Jew" and "Arab" are presented as opposites in the Israeli context, the relations between the groups, both actual and conceptual, are anything but clear and absolute from a Jewish standpoint. The Arab "other" is thus conceived of compositely and complexly as "aggressive" and "primitive" and at the same time "indigenous" and "authentic."

4. In most publications they were usually referred to as "Falasha." They themselves employ the name "Beta Israel" (the House of Israel) when referring to their Ethiopian past and Ethiopian Jews when referring to their new status in Israel.

5. *Ge'ez* is ancient Ethiopic, Ethiopia's Semitic liturgical tongue used by Jews and Christians alike. The Torah-centered, prerabbinic religious observance of the Beta Israel is a function of their existence as a Jewish community separated from other Jewish populations.

6. For more information on the activities of this mission and its influence on the Falasha, see Kaplan 1992: 116–42; Quirin 1992: 179–91.

7. *Kush* is the biblical term identified by commentary as ancient Ethiopia. See also note 17.

8. In particular, the opinion of the Radbaz, acronym for Rabbi David Ibn Abi Zimra of Egypt. See also Rapoport 1981: 1–14, 201–3; Waldman 1989: 74–76; Kaplan and Rosen 1994: 62.

9. See, for example, Kaplan and Rosen 1994: 60–69.

10. The status of *mamzer* is a result of forbidden marriage (not premarital relations) and is applied to the offspring, who are proscribed from marrying other Jews.

11. In discussions of the Beta Israel, echoes of the Holocaust arise in myriad forms. See, for example, Messing 1982: 11–53.

12. Similar expressions echo in Israeli memory about the Jews of Yemen and the Jews of India. See, for example, Goldberg, 1985.

13. *Ha-ve'ada leberur parashat terumot hadam shel olei Etiopia* (The investigative committee of the "blood donations affair" of Ethiopian immigrants), Jerusalem, July 1996.

14. Following publicity of the affair, the Ministry of Health issued a series of confused explanations, portraying its actions in terms of the general public's safety and explaining that dispensation of the blood had been concealed from the public out of the fear of stigmatizing the Ethiopian Jewish community. Despite the Ministry's gestures, within a few days unprecedented expressions of frustration were sounded among the Ethiopian immigrants. Bitterness and anguish ignited in a violent demonstration by thousands of Ethiopian Jews and their sympathizers, who viewed rejection of the blood donations as the culmination of snowballing race issues. See also Seeman 1997.

15. On blood as a key symbol for the Beta Israel while being in Ethiopia, see Salamon 1993.

16. The Bedouins serve in the Israel Defense Force, fighting alongside Jews against Arab members of their own faith.

17. *Kushi* in its modern colloquial sense defies straightforward translation. While on a popular level, *Kushi* is akin to the American word "nigger," it has an additional meaning as deriving from the Biblical *Kush* (see note 7). Early in the development of written Hebrew, it was extended to include all black Africa and black people generally.

References

Goldberg, H. "Historical and Cultural Dimensions of Ethnic Phenomena in Israel." In *Studies in Israeli Ethnicity*, A. Weingrod, ed. New York: Gordon and Breach, 1985, pp. 179–200.

Gruber, R. *Rescue: The Exodus of the Ethiopian Jews*. New York: Atheneum, 1987.

Kaplan, S. *The Beta Israel (Falasha) in Ethiopia: From Earliest Times to the Twentieth Century*. New York: New York University Press, 1992.

Kaplan, S., and Rosen, C. "Ethiopian Jews in Israel." In *American Jewish Yearbook 1994*, vol. 94, D. Singer and R. Seldin, eds. New York: American Jewish Committee, 1994, pp. 59–109.

Messing, S. *The Story of the Falasha: "Black Jews of Ethiopia."* Brooklyn: Balshon, 1982.

Patai, R. *The Myth of the Jewish Race*. New York: Scribner, 1975.

Quirin, J. *The Evolution of the Ethiopian Jews: A History of the Beta Israel (Falasha) to 1920*. Philadelphia: University of Pennsylvania Press, 1992.

Rapoport, L. *The Lost Jews: Last of the Ethiopian Falasha*, New York: Stein and Day, 1981.

———. *Redemption Song: The Story of Operation Moses*. New York: Harcourt Brace Jovanovich, 1986.

Salamon, H. "Blood between the Beta Israel and Their Christian Neighbors in Ethiopia: Key Symbols in an Inter-group Context." *Jerusalem Studies in Jewish Folklore* (in Hebrew), 1993, pp. 117–134.

Seeman, D. "One People One Blood: Religious Conversion, Public Health, and Immigration as Social Experience for Ethiopian-Israelis." Ph.D. diss., Harvard University, 1997.

Waldman, M. *Beyond the Rivers of Ethiopia: The Jews of Ethiopia and the Jewish People* (in Hebrew). Tel Aviv, Israel: Ministry of Defense, 1989.

Glossary

Boldfaced items also appear as entries.

A brief note on the transcription of Hebrew words: In modern times, Hebrew is pronounced in two major ways, known conventionally as the Ashkenazic and Sephardic pronunciations. While Ashkenazic Jews constitute the larger percentage of the world Jewish population, a version of the Sephardic pronunciation has become standard in Israeli speech and thus has had a major impact on the way Hebrew is now taught and pronounced in Diaspora communities. In addition (and partially deriving from the above differences and trends), various conventions for transcribing the letters of the Hebrew alphabet into English exist. The same Hebrew letter might be represented as Ch, as Ḥ, or simply as H as in the name of the holiday Hanukka. In this book, and in the glossary that follows, I have attempted to standardize spellings in accordance with contemporary Israeli speech and by using a minimalist system of transcription (for example, by dropping a final h, which is not pronounced: Hanukka rather than Hanukkah, for example). In some instances, however, it has been necessary to retain the initial transcription of the authors, and in such cases alternate spellings are included in parentheses. When the difference of an author's spelling is in the addition of a final h, or in the use (or non-use) of marks such as a hyphen, this has not been indicated in the glossary. Also note that this book uses an apostrophe to represent the Hebrew letter *alef* and a single quote to represent the letter *'ayin,* even though there is no distinction in the pronunciation of the two characters among many Hebrew speakers today.

Aggada:	A part of rabbinic literature including stories, ethical and moral teachings, and theological speculations and does not concern **halakha** (rabbinic law).
Aliya:	Immigration to the Land of Israel.
Ashkenaz:	A place/people in the Bible (Genesis 10), which me-

dieval Jews applied to the Rhineland when communities developed there. The Yiddish language, and Ashkenazic laws and customs, were later carried eastward so that Eastern European Jews also belong to the Ashkenazic tradition. People who lived in the area or who originated from it are known as Ashkenazim.

Bar and Bat Mitzvah: Religious majority. Reached at the age of thirteen by boys and twelve by girls. Since the late Middle Ages, boys reaching bar mitzvah recite blessings at a public reading of the **Torah**. Various forms of marking bat mitzvah have emerged since the nineteenth century.

Davening: Praying. From the **Yiddish** word "daven," with an English suffix.

El Mole Rahamim: A prayer, in **Ashkenazic** tradition, asking for God's mercy on those who have died.

Gemara: The part of the **Talmud** composed of discussions, interpretations, and disputes relating to the laws of the **Mishna** and also containing **aggada**. Two versions of the Gemara developed, one redacted in Palestine in 400 C.E. and the other in Babylonia (Iraq) in about 500 C.E.

Haftara: A portion from a Prophetic book of the Bible read publicly in the synagogue on Sabbaths, festivals, and fast days, following the reading from the **Torah**-scroll.

Halakha: The traditions, from the time of the **Talmud** and onward, which deal with ritual, ethical, civil, and criminal law.

Hametz: Leaven. Food containing hametz may not be eaten on **Passover**.

Hanukka: An eight-day holiday beginning on the twenty-fifth day of the month of Kislev (in December), commemorating the victory of the Jews over the Syrian Greeks and the restoration of the Temple service under the leadership of the Maccabees in 164 B.C.E.

Haredim: Ultraorthodox Jews characterized by their critique of modern society and a tendency to observe rabbinic law in strictest fashion. They also reject **Zionism** and the claim that the State of Israel represents the fulfillment of Jewish aspirations for religious and national redemption.

Hasid (pl. Hasidim; Hasidism, a religious movement): A pious person. Hasidism was a popular movement in the eighteenth century, first spreading in regions of southeast Poland and Ukraine. It stressed worshiping

God through personal piety and ecstasy. Hasidic communities were formed around a charismatic rabbinic leader, often called a **tzaddik**, who came to be known by the name of his town in Eastern Europe (for example, Gur, Lubavitch). Often portrayed as being in tension with the learned leadership cultivated in **yeshivot**, Hasidism and its rabbinic opponents joined forces in the nineteenth century within the streams of orthodoxy and **ultraorthodoxy**.

Havura (pl. *havurot*): A group of people coming together for purposes of prayer or study, based on shared religious viewpoints and sociality.

Hillula (pl. *hillulot*): A feast day and celebration marking the anniversary of the death of a venerated rabbi.

Kabbala: Traditions of mysticism that developed in Spain and Provence in the twelfth century. Sometimes, the term "kabbala" is used to refer to Jewish mysticism in all periods.

Kaddish: A prayer sanctifying God, which is associated with mourning and remembering the dead.

Ketubba: Rabbinic marriage contract.

Kibbutznik: Member of a kibbutz, or collective Israeli settlement.

Kippa: A ritual skullcap. Also called a "yarmulke."

Kosher: The term, meaning "fitting," or "permitted according to law," is used most commonly with regard to food.

Matza (pl. matzot; also matzoh, pl. matzohs): Unleavened bread eaten at **Passover** because of the rule forbidding **hametz** during that festival.

Mezuza (pl. mezuzot): A ritual case, containing short sections of the **Torah** written on parchment, that is attached to the doorpost in Jewish homes.

Mikve: A ritual bath. Its most essential contemporary use is for purification after menstruation so that sexual intercourse may be resumed.

Minyan: A quorum of ten Jews, which is the minimum number required to conduct public prayers.

Mishna: The earliest codification of rabbinic law, which took its final form about 200 C.E.

Passover: The week-long festival taking place on the fifteenth of the month of Nisan (in the spring) that commemorates the exodus of the Israelites from Egypt.

Purim: The holiday commemorating the events recorded in the biblical book of Esther, in which the Jews of the

Persian Empire were saved from a plot designed to destroy them.

Rabbi Shim'on Bar Yohai: A second-century mishnaic sage who, in fleeing from the Romans, is said to have lived many years in a cave in the Galilee. The mystical Zohar book, which scholars see as written in the thirteenth century, was attributed to him. The putative date of his death, the eighteenth of the month of Iyyar, or Lag Ba'omer (thirty-three days after **Passover**), has become a minor festival.

Rosh Ha-Shanah: New Year holiday, coming at the beginning of the month of Tishri (in the fall).

Seder: The domestic celebration taking place on the first night of **Passover** in Israel and on the first two nights in the Diaspora. It consists of reading and discussing a narration of the exodus from Egypt, the performance of related rituals, and the singing of psalms and hymns, all of which bracket a festive meal.

Sepharad: A biblical place name (Obadiah 1), applied to the Iberian peninsula in medieval times. After expulsions from Spain and Portugal at the end of the fifteenth century, Spanish Jews (Sephardim) spread to Mediterranean lands, to Northwest Europe, and to the New World. Later, Jews who had been forced to convert to Catholicism but maintained their Judaism secretly (Marranos), rejoined the ranks of Spanish communities. Today, Sephardic may refer to Jews who speak a Judeo-Spanish language ("Judezmo," "Ladino") or to those descended from the émigrés from the Iberian peninsula. More broadly, the term refers to Jews who came under the influence of these émigrés and who accepted Sephardic law, liturgy, and customs.

Shabbat: The Sabbath.

Shavuot: The Feast of Weeks. One of the pilgrimage festivals prescribed by the Bible to take place fifty days after the first day of **Passover**. Tradition designates it as the day on which the Torah was given on Mt. Sinai.

Shoah: Hebrew term for the Holocaust.

Shofar: A ram's horn. Used in antiquity during the anointing of kings or the proclamation of the jubilee year, sounding the shofar is now an integral part of the **Rosh Ha-Shanah** service and concludes the prayers of **Yom Kippur**.

Shtetl: (Yiddish: small town): A town, usually with a market, in the countryside in Eastern Europe.

Shul: Synagogue (in Yiddish).

Sukkot: The pilgrimage festival of Tabernacles (booths), on the fifteenth of Tishri, in the fall, which continues for seven days. As in the case of other festivals, an extra day is celebrated in the Diaspora. The last day is called Hoshana Rabba and entails a procession with willow branches and the other arboreal ritual items mandated on the holiday. The day immediately following Sukkot is an independent festival known as Shmini Atzeret. Together they form an eight-day holiday series (nine days in the Diaspora). The last day, known as Simḥat Torah, marks the turning point in the annual cycle of ritual **Torah** reading.

Talit (also *talis*): A shawl, with four ritual fringes, used during prayer, mainly during the morning service.

Talmud: The term is most commonly used comprehensively to include both the **Mishna** and the **Gemara**, which developed in the postmishnaic period but also can refer to the later work alone.

Teshuva: The process of becoming more religiously observant (literally, return).

Tish‘a Be-Av: A fast day, the ninth of the Hebrew summer month of Av, which commemorates the destruction of the First Temple by the Babylonians and the Second Temple by the Romans.

Torah: The term has many referents. 1) The physical Torah-scroll, which must be handwritten on parchment and is prepared by a scribe. 2) The contents of the Torah in the form of a book, the ḥumash, which may be glossed "the five books [of Moses]," corresponding to "the Pentateuch" in Greek-derived English. 3) The whole tradition of Jewish sacred literature, including the *ḥumash* and other sections of the Hebrew Bible (the Prophets and the Holy Writings), along with the works of rabbinic culture like the **Talmud** and the subsequent discussions and codifications of talmudic literature produced from ancient times to the present.

Tu Bi-Shvat: The fifteenth day of the month of Shvat (about February). In the **Mishna**, this date is recognized as the New Year with regard to trees, and the **kabbalists** of sixteenth-century Safed created rituals appropriate to it. The holiday also achieved prominence in **Zionist** tradition because of its association with the land.

Tzaddik (pl. tzaddikim): Literally: righteous person. Among North African Jews, a sainted rabbi believed to have the power of curing and miracle working while alive and after death. Graves of tzaddikim often became pilgrimage sites (see **Hillula**). In **Hasidic** tradition, a tzaddik is the charismatic center of the community.

Ultraorthodoxy:

See **Haredim**.

Yeshiva (pl. yeshivot):

An academy of higher Torah study. Mostly known for the study of **Talmud**, some emphasize other styles and branches of learning as well. Traditionally, only men study in a yeshiva.

Yiddish:

The Jewish language (called Judeo-German by linguists), which took form about the tenth century and characterized **Ashkenazic** Jewry.

Yom Kippur:

The Day of Atonement, on the tenth of the month of Tishri (in the fall).

Zionism:

A movement, first developing in nineteenth-century Europe, which stressed the national existence of the Jews. It claimed that, as a nation, Jews had the right to return to their own land to freely realize their collective life.

Sources of the Selections

Chapter 1. Ghitta Sternberg, "The Ethos of an Eastern European Community." This chapter is taken from *Stefanesti: Portrait of a Romanian Shtetl* (Oxford: Pergamon Press, 1984), pp. 203–14. Reprinted with the permission of Esther Sternberg and Aline Sternberg Petzold.

Chapter 2. Irene Awret, "Preparing for Passover in North Africa." This chapter is taken from *Days of Honey: The Tunisian Boyhood of Rafael Uzan* (New York: Schocken), pp. 49–59. © 1984 by Irene Awret. Reprinted by permission of Schocken Books, distributed by Pantheon Books, a division of Random House, Inc.

Chapter 3. Susan Starr Sered, "Religious Roles of Elderly Women." This chapter is taken from *Women as Ritual Experts: The Religious Lives of Elderly Jewish Women in Jerusalem* (New York: Oxford University Press), pp. 65–66, 79–86. © 1992 by Susan Starr Sered. Reprinted by permission of Oxford University Press, Inc.

Chapter 4. Frida Kerner Furman, "Synagogue Life among American Reform Jews." This chapter is taken from *Beyond Yiddishkeit: The Struggle for Jewish Identity in a Reform Synagogue* (Albany: State University of New York Press, 1987), pp. 51–60. Reprinted with the permission of Frida Kerner Furman.

Chapter 5. Samuel C. Heilman, "Orthodoxy in an American Synagogue." This chapter is taken from *Synagogue Life: A Study in Symbolic*

Interaction (Chicago: University of Chicago Press, 1976), pp. 12–24. Reprinted with the permission of the University of Chicago Press and of the author.

Chapter 6. Chava Weissler, "Worship in the Havura Movement." This chapter is taken from "Making Davening Meaningful: Worship in the Havurah Movement," *YIVO Annual* 19 (Evanston: Northwestern University Press and the YIVO Institute for Jewish Research, 1990), pp. 255–67. Reprinted with the permission of Northwestern University Press and the YIVO Institute for Jewish Research, and with the permission of the author.

Chapter 7. Lynn Davidman, "Turning to Orthodox Judaism." This chapter is taken from "Teachings on Jewish Religious Observance," in *Tradition in a Rootless World: Women Turn to Orthodox Judaism* (Berkeley: University of California Press), pp. 144–53. © 1991 The Regents of the University of California. Reprinted with the permission of the University of California Press.

Chapter 8. Einat Ramon, "Tradition and Innovation in the Marriage Ceremony." This chapter is adapted by the author from "A Wedding in Israel as an Act of Tikkun Olam," in Debra Orenstein, ed., *Lifecycles, Vol. 1: Jewish Women on Life Passages and Personal Milestones* (Woodstock, VT: Jewish Lights Publishing), pp. 161–72. © 1994 Debra Ornstein. Permission granted by Jewish Lights Publishing, P.O. Box 237, Woodstock, VT 05091.

Chapter 9. Fran Markowitz, "A Bat Mitzvah among Russian Jews in America." This chapter is taken from "Rituals as Keys to Soviet Immigrants' Jewish Identity," in Jack Kugelmass, ed., *Between Two Worlds: Ethnographic Essays on American Jewry* (Ithaca: Cornell University Press, 1988), pp. 128–40. © 1988 by Cornell University. Used by permission of the publisher.

Chapter 10. Claudio G. Segrè, "Books as a Path to Jewish Identity." This chapter is taken from *Atoms, Bombs, and Eskimo Kisses: A Memoir of Father and Son* (New York: Viking, 1995), pp. 114–27. Reprinted with the permission of Elisabeth Segrè.

Chapter 11. Ismar Schorsch and Jackie Feldman, "Memory and the Holocaust: Two Perspectives." Ismar Schorsch, "The Sword and the Book," appears here in English for the first time. It was published in German in *LBI Information* no. 5/6 (Frankfurt/Main: Leo Baeck Institute, 1995). Published courtesy of the author. Jackie Feldman, "'Roots in Destruction': The Jewish Past as Portrayed in Israeli Youth Voyages to Poland," was written for this book.

Chapter 12. Danielle Storper Perez and Harvey E. Goldberg, "Meanings of the Western Wall." This chapter is taken from "The Kotel: Toward an Ethnographic Portrait," *Religion* 24 (1994): 317–28. Reprinted with permission of the journal and of the authors.

Chapter 13. Yoram Bilu, "A Moroccan Jewish Shrine in Israel." This chapter was taken from Harvey E. Goldberg, ed., *Judaism Viewed from Within and Without* (Albany: State University of New York Press), pp. 292–306. Reprinted by permission of the State University of New York Press. © 1987, State University of New York. All rights reserved.

Chapter 14. Tamar El-Or, "Religion, Study, and Contemporary Politics." This chapter is adapted by the author from "Multi-Literacies and Democracy: Religious Zionist Women Reading Actuality in Antiquities," *Jewish Social Studies* 4 (1988): 133–55. Reprinted with permission of Indiana University Press.

Chapter 15. Hagar Salamon, "Ethiopian Jewry and New Self-Concepts," was written for this book.

Contributors

IRENE AWRET is an artist and writer who lived in Safed, Israel, and now resides in the United States. The subject of her book, *Rafael Uzan,* still lives in Safed.

YORAM BILU is a Professor in the Departments of Sociology and Anthropology and of Psychology at the Hebrew University of Jerusalem. He is author of *Without Bounds: The Life and Death of Rabbi Ya'aqov Wazana* (Detroit: Wayne State University Press, 2000).

LYNN DAVIDMAN, a sociologist, is an Associate Professor of Judaic Studies and American Civilization at Brown University. Her book *Tradition in a Rootless World* (Berkeley: University of California Press, 1991) won the 1992 National Jewish Book Award in the category of Contemporary Jewish Life.

TAMAR EL-OR is a Senior Lecturer in the Department of Sociology and Anthropology at the Hebrew University of Jerusalem. She is the author of *Educated and Ignorant: Ultraorthodox Women and Their World* (Boulder, CO: Lynne Rienner, 1994).

JACKIE FELDMAN is a Lecturer in Anthropology at the Jordan Valley College and in the Department of Land of Israel Studies at Beit Berl Teachers' College. He has recently published "National Identity and Ritual Construction of Israeli Youth Pilgrimages," *Neue Sammlung* 40, no. 4 (October–December 2000): 499–517.

FRIDA KERNER FURMAN is Professor and Chair of the Department of Religious Studies at DePaul University. Her last book, *Facing the Mirror: Older Women and Beauty Shop Culture* (New York: Routledge, 1997), is a study of the social and moral life of older Jewish women and received the 1997 Elli Kongas-Maranda Prize of the American Folklore Society/ Women's Section.

HARVEY E. GOLDBERG is a Professor in the Department of Sociology and Anthropology at the Hebrew University of Jerusalem. He is the author of *Jewish Life in Muslim Libya: Rivals and Relatives* (Chicago: University of Chicago Press, 1990).

SAMUEL C. HEILMAN is Harold M. Proshansky Professor of Jewish Studies and Sociology at the City University of New York. His most recent book is *When a Jew Dies: The Ethnography of a Bereaved Son* (Berkeley: University of California Press, 2001).

FRAN MARKOWITZ is an Associate Professor of Anthropology in the Department of Behavioral Sciences at Ben-Gurion University in Beersheva, Israel. Her most recent book is *Coming of Age in Post-Soviet Russia* (Urbana: University of Illinois Press, 2000).

EINAT RAMON is a Lecturer at the Kibbutzim College of Education in Tel Aviv and a Fellow at the Shalom Hartman Institute in Jerusalem. Her dissertation at Stanford University, "God the Mother: A Critique of Domination in the Religious Zionist Work of A. D. Gordon," is forthcoming in Hebrew.

HAGAR SALAMON is a Senior Lecturer in the Department of Jewish and Comparative Folklore at the Hebrew University of Jerusalem. She is the author of *The Hyena People: Ethiopian Jews in Christian Ethiopia* (Berkeley: University of California Press, 1999).

ISMAR SCHORSCH is a historian and chancellor of the Jewish Theological Seminary of America. He is the author of *From Text to Context: The Turn to History in Modern Judaism* (Hanover, NH: Brandeis University Press, 1994).

CLAUDIO SEGRÈ (1937–1995) was born in Italy and grew up in the United States. He was a historian and writer who taught at the University of Texas, Austin, focusing on modern Europe and fascism. He authored *Italo Balbo: A Fascist Life* (Berkeley: University of California Press, 1987).

SUSAN STARR SERED is Director of Harvard University's Center for the Study of World Religions research initiative in "Religion, Health and Healing." Her most recent book is *What Makes Women Sick?: Maternity, Modesty and Militarism in Israeli Society* (Hanover, NH: University Press of New England, 2000).

GHITTA STERNBERG (1921–1997) was born in Romania and moved to Canada in 1938. Her book *Stefanesti: Portrait of a Romanian Shtetl* (Oxford: Pergamon Press, 1984) began as a translation of her mother's diary and was supplemented by her own memories, her anthropological training, and interviews with surviving townspeople living in Netanya (Israel), Montreal, and New York.

DANIELLE STORPER PEREZ is a researcher in anthropology and sociology living in Jerusalem, who retired from the Centre National de la Recherche Scientifique. Her most recent book is *L'intelligentsia russe en Israël: Rassurante étrangeté* (Paris: CNRS éditions, 1998).

CHAVA WEISSLER is Philip and Muriel Berman Professor of Jewish Civilization in the Department of Religion Studies, Lehigh University, Bethlehem, Pennsylvania. Her study of the religious lives of early modern Jewish women, *Voices of the Matriarchs* (Boston: Beacon Press, 1998), won the Koret Award in Jewish History in 1999.

Index

Text: 10/13 Galliard
Display: Galliard
Composition: G & S Typesetters, Inc.
Printing and Binding: Thomson-Shore, Inc.